SOLDIER OF CONSCIENCE

All royalties from the sales of this book will go to good causes around the world, including Scoliosis Support & Research

www.ssr.org.uk

SOLDIER OF CONSCIENCE

FROM FIGHTING THE IRA TO BATTLING PTSD

WAYNE INGRAM M.B.E

Pen & Sword
MILITARY

AN IMPRINT OF PEN & SWORD BOOKS LTD.
YORKSHIRE - PHILADELPHIA

First published in Great Britain in 2025 by
PEN AND SWORD MILITARY
An imprint of
Pen & Sword Books Limited
Yorkshire – Philadelphia

Copyright © Wayne Ingram M.B.E, 2025

ISBN 978 1 03612 937 8

The right of Wayne Ingram M.B.E to be identified as Author of this work has been asserted by him in accordance with the Copyright, Designs and Patents Act 1988.

A CIP catalogue record for this book is available from the British Library.

All rights reserved. No part of this book may be reproduced, transmitted, downloaded, decompiled or reverse engineered in any form or by any means, electronic or mechanical including photocopying, recording or by any information storage and retrieval system, without permission from the Publisher in writing. NO AI TRAINING: Without in any way limiting the Author's and Publisher's exclusive rights under copyright, any use of this publication to "train" generative artificial intelligence (AI) technologies to generate text is expressly prohibited. The Author and Publisher reserve all rights to license uses of this work for generative AI training and development of machine learning language models.

Typeset in Times New Roman 11.5/15.5 by
SJmagic DESIGN SERVICES, India.
Printed and bound in the UK by CPI Group (UK) Ltd.

The Publisher's authorised representative in the EU for product safety is Authorised Rep Compliance Ltd., Ground Floor, 71 Lower Baggot Street, Dublin D02 P593, Ireland.
www.arccompliance.com

For a complete list of Pen & Sword titles please contact
PEN & SWORD BOOKS LIMITED
George House, Units 12 & 13, Beevor Street, Off Pontefract Road, Barnsley, South Yorkshire, S71 1HN, England
E-mail: enquiries@pen-and-sword.co.uk
Website: www.pen-and-sword.co.uk

or

PEN AND SWORD BOOKS
1950 Lawrence Rd, Havertown, PA 19083, USA
E-mail: uspen-and-sword@casematepublishers.com
Website: www.penandswordbooks.com

Contents

Foreword		vii
By way of explanation…		x
Chapter 1	1969–1986: Childhood – when kids could be kids!	1
Chapter 2	1987: "You'll never make anything of yourself…"	14
Chapter 3	1990–91: South Armagh	24
Chapter 4	1993–94: Belfast	34
Chapter 5	1994–95: Run Aground	50
Chapter 6	1997: Mass Graves	61
Chapter 7	1997–2003: Stefan	79
Chapter 8	2003: Amnesty	90
Chapter 9	2003: David Dunaway	97
Chapter 10	2003: The Operation	105
Chapter 11	2003: Post-Op	124
Chapter 12	2004: The Final Cut	128
Chapter 13	2004: Broken	134
Chapter 14	2005–2010: The Beginning	136
Chapter 15	2010: Back Home	155
Chapter 16	2010: Preparation	161

Chapter 17	2010: Remote Healing	165
Chapter 18	2010: Essential Travel	173
Chapter 19	2010: First Impressions	180
Chapter 20	2010: Incarcerated	187
Chapter 21	2011: Destiny	204
Chapter 22	2012: God's Will	212
Chapter 23	2012–2013: The Orphanage	219
Chapter 24	2014: The Next Operation	229
Chapter 25	2014: A New Directive	239
Chapter 26	2014–2015: The Life Raft Challenge	244
Chapter 27	2015: The Challenge	251
Chapter 28	2015–2016: The Final Operation	273
Chapter 29	2016–18: Consequences	286
Chapter 30	2017–2019: Time Management	289
Chapter 31	2019–20: Scoliosis – and that bloody virus!	298
Chapter 32	2021: Mental Health	306
Chapter 33	2022: The Walk	311
Chapter 34	1993–2023: Mental Injury	317
Chapter 35	2021: Respect, Reparation, and Recognition	330
Chapter 36	2021: Postscript	332
Dedication	2023: Not the end. Nowhere Near, in fact…	333
Bonus Page	2024: Afterthoughts	337

Foreword

Wayne Ingram has lived a full and eventful life. From soldiering in Northern Ireland and Bosnia, to providing close protection as a paramedic in Iraq, and heading up health and safety at an industrial gold mine in West Africa. When not overseas, he has worked diligently as a paramedic and part-time firefighter. Wayne has always thrown himself into his work with gusto, professionalism and a large slice of humour.

Great wonder, then, that he also manages to find the time for all his charitable work. But this he does with the same enthusiasm and passion he has shown in all his endeavours.

From a very young age, Wayne had wanted to be a soldier, his dream becoming a reality when, in December 1986, at the age of 18, he enlisted into the Royal Armoured Corps. At the time, the Troubles in Northern Ireland were at a high, so he was soon patrolling the streets of Belfast and 'bandit country' in South Armagh. It was whilst on the streets of Belfast in 1993, that an event was to happen that would have a profound effect upon him. Witnessing a friend getting severely wounded by an IRA improvised grenade, the trauma of the event would only become apparent to him years later. At the time, like many others, he put it to the back of his mind and, as the saying goes, he soldiered on.

It was his second tour in Bosnia in 2003 that would put him on a path that would change the course of his life, and that of others. It was there that he came into contact with the family of a four-year old boy, Stefan

Savic. Stefan had a severe facial deformity and, being a father himself, it touched Wayne deeply. He felt compelled to help Stefan and his family in any way that he could, immediately mobilising those around him to help raise funds so the little boy could have life-changing corrective surgery in London.

This started a thirteen year journey to get Stefan the help he needed, to enable him to live a normal life. This included garnering the services of a renowned Harley Street surgeon, Dr David Dunaway, who, like Wayne, was touched by Stefan's plight and so offered his services for free. Raising funds, sorting out accommodation and providing all the support the family needed, Wayne's efforts directly led to Stefan being able to live his life like any other child and teenager.

But then Wayne was always more than a soldier. After his heartbreaking medical discharge from the Army, due to a recurring ankle injury, he dusted himself down and put his skills into working for the emergency services, becoming a paramedic and retained firefighter. In between, his career took him to countries which would not be at the top of most lists of places to visit.

Wayne has had his own demons to contend with, all of which he talks openly of in the pages of this book. Recognising his own PTSD, caused by years in war zones and as a paramedic, including the harrowing scenes he witnessed in Bosnia, he sought and got the help he needed.

This book, written to raise funds for Scoliosis Support & Research, a charity close to his heart, is, like Wayne, much more than the story of an ex-squaddie. What comes through is his compassion, empathy and his sheer bloodymindedness to get things done, no matter how difficult and no matter how many barriers are put in front of him. The comments from friends and colleagues at the end of each chapter are testament to his character and altruistic nature.

Like Wayne, the book is laced with compassion, empathy, a lot of soul-searching and a very large dollop of humour, all of which combine to make a most enjoyable read. Not wishing to give away any spoilers – but how many people do you know who would contemplate walking seventy miles, from Portland to Southampton – backwards (yes, backwards!) – or spend a full week on a raft in Portland harbour with only a day's rations and water? All to raise money to help others less fortunate than himself.

Not many I'm guessing.

But Wayne Ingram, MBE, would!

And for that, and many more reasons, I salute you, my friend.

By way of explanation...

First of all, I must begin this book – account – whatever, with some provisos. I am not a literary genius, nor am I an academic with words. I left school at the age of 15 with very little in the way of educational qualifications, so please take this into account as you read, and please – NO red pen!

In addition, I've learned that military personnel – be they serving or veterans – have a seriously different sense of humour than our civilian friends. Along with the numerous tragic incidents throughout my life there have been just as many humorous ones, so I've included both in this book for balance as you join me on my journey.

I'm just a man who has lived an interesting life, making multiple choices and errors of judgement along the way. Some of my mistakes were unforgiveable, but many of my choices turned out well and benefited others. I'm a firm believer that this is just part of what makes us human. I've seen many good and terrible things in life, including many which I would not wish upon anyone. I've learned that behind every door, and every life, is a story – one that is rarely obvious to others. I believe that each of us has a personal and intrinsically-felt destiny, or life opportunity, that is unique to ourselves – and that if we watch for the clues, take the chances when they come, and keep on correcting our course as we follow our life path, then we can fulfil it. It won't be easy, of course – nothing this important ever is – but it will clearly define who we are, as the best we can be, before it's our turn to move on.

By way of explanation...

We were born on time and, one day, on another time and date, we shall die. In between, the seconds will pass, one by one, until our sands run out and the clock stops. But although our place in history is set, and will never come again, we have the freedom to change a multitude of outcomes, make the world a better place for others, and enjoy the process along the way!

After five days on the open sea, alone in a tethered life raft – hungry, thirsty, and devastatingly lonely – you can't help but think of all the life choices you've ever made that have brought you to this point...

This is my story, about how I came to meet an inspirational young person named Stefan and how he changed my life for the better. So, if you're looking for covert government conspiracies, machine gun firefights, and running through enemy territory with a grenade gripped in my teeth, this is not the book you're looking for... I am no hero – except maybe in my children's eyes, as I constantly attempt to be a good example to them.

I've tried to capture the human element of being a soldier, how effective the British Army is with hearts and minds and, most of all, that if you try hard enough, then anything can be achieved. Yes, absolutely anything – if you're prepared to pay the price.

So please don't tell my granddaughters, Evie and Ella, that the missing nail on my big toe was due to an ingrowing toenail. They think it was bitten off by a shark!

Chapter 1

1969–1986
Childhood – when kids could be kids!

I was raised in South London by caring, loving parents, Glenn and Brenda. In her early years, my mum was a 'lollipop lady' for the council and a cleaner in our local bingo hall, though later on she worked in the City for the government. My old man was a firefighter in the London Fire Brigade. Money was tight, which is why they both had second jobs to make ends meet. When he wasn't putting out fires, my dad worked as a doorman at the ironically-named Flickers, a local night club in Tooting Bec. He'd also drive delivery lorries around the capital, and I still remember the excitement of accompanying him – the adventure of climbing Everest each time I ascended the step into the footwell, scaling my way up to the bouncy front passenger seat, and feeling the sense of total invincibility at the peak, high above all the other traffic, and breathing in the heady smells of diesel fuel, exhaust, and the many different cargos from inside the cab.

Then, along with Tony and Karen, my younger brother and sister, we'd accompany Mum to the local bingo hall on Brighton Road, playing with the other children as their mothers cleaned up the place ready for the next evening's gathering of elderly ladies eager for excitement. It used to be a cinema, so it was a fantastic place to run up and down the multiple stairways, exploring, hunting one another down, and telling ghost stories in the hushed darkness of the balcony.

Although I was born in New Addington, Croydon, we soon moved into a small cottage behind Purley fire station, and life as a child was brilliant in the mid-70's. During school holidays and weekends, we'd meet shortly after eight in the morning on bikes with no brakes and not a single helmet between us. We'd constantly be modifying our own bikes, with scant regard as to how safely an over/undersized wheel, or a different type of handlebar scavenged from the scrapped bikes we'd find, behaved in practice. The important thing was how cool they looked, and these unorthodox one-wheel drive vehicles would regularly take us on exciting adventures and manoeuvres, returning back to base only when we got hungry or to patch a bloodied knee.

There were times when we didn't come in all day, because sustenance was always available at someone else's house. Mum didn't have a clue where we were from hour to hour, and the only way to make contact was from a public phone box – but we always came home safe. Of course, this would be unthinkable nowadays, but they certainly weren't uncaring parents. It was just how things were back then.

To make a phone call we either needed coins, or asked the operator to reverse the charge – which not only went onto the home phone bill, but incurred additional costs too. Add to that the number of calls we made to each other from home, and it wasn't surprising that my dad eventually fitted a small, silver drum lock to the dial. Being kids, it didn't take us long to learn how to bypass it, by simply lifting the receiver and tapping one of the black switch hooks underneath to dial the number instead. So if you wanted to dial '725' you'd first tap the button seven times – pause – then twice – pause – then five times, and more often than not the old pulse-dial telephone system would put you through. Unfortunately for Dad he didn't know this trick and could never fathom how the bills were so unaccountably high each month!

Back then, the words 'health' and 'safety' were rarely used in the same sentence. I remember playing Cowboys 'n' Indians in the woods at the top of our road. Each of our small groups spent hours whittling their chosen length of wood to form a bow, before sourcing a stock of straight-ish shafts from a branch of the same wood – and a lot of time and effort went into picking the right ones! To finish off, we'd use string or fishing line to ensure the bow was arched with as much tension as possible. Fully armed, the battle would start, with one group approaching from each end of the wood to wage war in the centre, pulling back the string as far as it would go before loosing our arrows. If I saw my own children doing this today my heart would stop... but in those days we were invincible! A hit counted as a kill, and makeshift arrows flew from one child to another from every direction as each attempted to win the war, with no consideration whatsoever given to potential eye damage.

Then there was the communal campfire in the same woods. Our parents didn't bat an eyelid when we went out with potatoes in our pockets, to cook on the end of a stick over the flames. Sometimes they'd turn out well, but even though most were burnt black on the outside and raw in the middle, each was consumed as if it was a Michelin-star meal.

Other times we'd make our way to local Reedham railway station, on Old Lodge Lane. I don't know if it's still there, but there used to be waste ground at the front of the station, and on this were the huge concrete blocks that had been planted there (we were told) to prevent incoming German tanks from progressing if they invaded during the war. Though now overgrown with weeds, we were still able to jump from one to the other as we became battle-hardened troops traversing enemy territory. Our time there always ended with a game of 'Dare', which was probably the most stunningly stupid thing we ever did as kids. But when you're young you don't do risk assessments, and if you're scared you don't say anything, because the risk of being ridiculed is even greater. The game involved one person, or several at once, making their way to the railway bridge, climbing the iron supports directly underneath it, and shimmying along the girders supporting the road above until we were directly over the railway line itself. Then we'd wait until we could hear the London to Brighton train approaching, because this was the cue to getting into position atop a horizontal girder, hand and knees braced on each side, and wait for the powerful updraft to hit as the train thundered beneath us at 90mph. I still remember being shit-scared the first time I did this, as the steaming, deafening behemoth passed below me, but as time wore on we ended up relaxing and even enjoying the wind as it bore us upwards.

As I write this now the incredible stupidity, the recklessness, and the risks associated with our actions were absolutely unbelievable. But you don't think of this when you're a child. You only think of the fun, and how cool it makes you look in front of your mates.

I spent a lot of time with a friend named Andrew Brown, who would go on to join the Royal Green Jackets. We both knew we wanted to join the Army, and would do anything we thought could give us a head up as a soldier. When we learned that our basic training would include boxing, we each got ourselves a pair of boxing gloves in advance and stood in the front garden of his house beating the crap out of each other, believing it would somehow toughen us up. Especially as Andy's father was the local vicar, who said that this was character-building, and the way boys should be.

Another thing we did to prepare us for army life was hunting each other with air rifles. Armed with one of these, and a pocketful of pellets each, we'd jump on the bus and head to our favourite battleground in the large woods near Old Coulsdon. Andy started at one end and I at the other, each of us hunting down our quarry to pre-empt the skills we'd later learn in the military – and we had no qualms about slowly pulling the trigger once the other was in our sights. This carried on until a truce was called, and we'd compare the bruises our pellets had left on each other's skin. Thinking back now, on how a couple of teenagers could get on a bus with air rifles over their shoulders, without causing a single eyebrow to raise or head to turn. How the world has changed!

My air rifle did get me in trouble one day. Both my parents were at work and I was in the garden watching Karen and Tony play in my go-kart. They'd intertwined their legs together, and this gave me a brilliant idea. I made my way to the house and, pausing only to collect my trusty rifle, stealthily made my way up the stairs to our bathroom, in which the window opened from the bottom upwards. I raised this quietly, and then carefully acquired my target. Because they were my family, instead of using lead pellets I deployed bitten-off chunks of school eraser, and

I cried with laughter as each rubbery round hit their bare legs, and revelled in their horror as their locked lower limbs prevented them from escaping my line of fire...

"Just what the hell do you think you're doing, young man???"

I froze, caught in the very act. Retribution had suddenly arrived in the form of my father standing in the bathroom entrance, and who had actually added several more expletives to the above sentence. The game was up. I'd been captured by the enemy after it had returned home early due to sickness and my punishment was to bend out over the window ledge as he shot the remaining bits of rubber into my arse cheeks from the corridor. Yes, I know I fully deserved it, but ever since that day I've always made sure to have a spotter with me!

It seems sad to me that children today don't seem to have the adventures that we had. Other than those boys and girls whose parents have enrolled them into the Scouts or Guides, very few seem inclined to go into a wood, build their own camps and dens, and cook spuds on an open fire. Have we, as adults, forgotten what children enjoy most? I recently heard that the reason more children need spectacles nowadays is because they rarely go into the open countryside, their eyes don't develop long-distance ranging, and their focal distance stops at the walls of their room.

My eagerness to join the Army almost cost me my career before it had even started. I was at home, bored with babysitting Karen and Tony, so I went outside from where I could view the local firefighters practicing on their tower – and this gave me an idea. Though we were at least a hundred miles from the sea in any direction, we had a rubber dinghy in the garden to play in, and the long, detachable paddle handles which accompanied it were hollow. I ran to the local corner shop and brought a packet of rockets (Error of Judgement #1) – the ones that lasted about two seconds and made a high screeching sound – and once again, no questions were asked of a child my age. I already had the rocket launcher, and now I had the ammo, so now it was time to target the enemy – all those unsuspecting firemen on a hook ladder forty feet off the ground. (Error of Judgement #2)

This is where my plan literally backfired. Loading the rocket into the end of the tube, and hoisting it onto my shoulder as I'd seen in the movies, I got Karen to light the fuse as I took aim along the rear of the barrel (Error of Judgement #3). However, I had not checked for obstructions nor cleanliness (Error of Judgement #4). Unbeknown to me, they'd used the paddle earlier to launch tennis balls, and one end had got into the mud. So, with the rocket's escape route well and truly obstructed by mud, my right eye took the full force of the blast. Long story short, my aunt had to dash round to look after my brother and sister, my uncle had to drive me to Mayday Hospital and Mum had to finish work early. Thankfully, Karen escaped injury, but I got a clout round the ear, I looked like a pirate for several days afterwards, and the firemen were totally oblivious of their lucky escape that day.

To this day I don't think we were naughty, bad, or uncontrollable. We were just children, and kids at that time lived differently from those of today. However, that said, we always had respect for our parents and other adults, and anyone in a uniform was like a god to us. The words 'please' and 'thank you' regularly leapt off our lips, and our parents knew that whenever they took us out in public, we would always behave impeccably.

The only thing I'd ever wanted, since the age of five, was to join the Army, and nothing was going to get in my way. For me, primary school was just a hindrance, and if I'd been given the chance at a young age between school and the military, I'd have happily packed my kit bag and left home. Sadly, I never used school to its best advantage, and always thought the days long and boring, because they never taught me the stuff I really wanted to learn. Instead, especially in my later years, I'd usually end up in trouble and join the school's punishment program. A popular reprimand was litter duty, where you'd have to walk around the school grounds during lunchtime, picking up rubbish and dropping it into a black bag. Then you'd deliver the bag to whichever teacher was presiding over this particular detention group. One was Mrs West who, after giving us our bags, instructed us to return to her with our individual accomplishments just before the lesson started. Stomping around the

1969–1986: Childhood – when kids could be kids!

field, and feeling that the world was against me, changed in the blink of an eye when I noticed that the school caretaker kept chickens at the top of his garden, which could be entered easily from the school field. More importantly, the chickens were tame, and as I entered the garden they all came clucking over to me, bobbing their heads in collective accompaniment. For several moments my good angel on one shoulder was urging me not to do it, while the smirking devil on the other made it very clear how funny it could be. Without thinking further, I picked up the nearest chicken and transferred it carefully into the black bag where, to its credit, it remained profoundly docile and trusting on my return journey to the school. This now heavy and bulky bag was then presented proudly to Mrs West who, on opening it, let out a chilling, impulsive shriek as the chicken, its head still bobbing, jumped out of the bag at her. Unbelievably, it was only at this point that I realised I'd made a huge mistake, as the whole class erupted, creating the loudest noise I'd ever heard in my life. Mrs West was screaming, most of the girls were screaming with her, and every boy in the room was laughing – which of course summoned the most proximate male teacher, Mr. Baker, from the history lesson next door. After silencing the class, and ensuring Mrs West was okay, he promptly dragged me out into the corridor, lifted me onto my tiptoes by my sideburns, and made me swear to God that I would never, ever do anything like this again. Later in life I'd have stubbornly given him my name, rank, and number – the big three – but as a 10-year-old child I just started crying and did exactly as I was told. At the end of the day, my sideburns still burning, I met Mum at her usual lollipop spot. She knew that something wasn't right and insisted on knowing what was wrong until I finally told her everything that had happened – except the bit about the chicken. We went straight home and she informed my Dad, who was off work at the time, and he listened very carefully indeed, his face reddening, his muscles tightening the more he heard. His dad and uncles had always taught him that family came first, and no one should ever hurt or harm them, so I was bundled into the car and driven to my school. We arrived just as Mr Baker was leaving his office, and that was when Dad marched right up to him, grabbed both of his sideburns, lifted him up from the floor, and told him to pray to God that he didn't bloody well beat the crap out of him there and then! But it didn't end there, because as news of the chicken's involvement gradually came to light, my father's attitude changed. He wasn't going to let Mr Baker off the hook for physically assaulting his child, but boy, was I going to pay for it once we got home. Mr Baker never forgot the experience either and would often ask me afterwards how my dad was, and if he fancied going for a drink with him, to make amends.

Another incident involved detention after school, where we'd sit in the art studio on the second floor writing out lines. I don't know if schools still have them, but paints then were mixed from large tins of different powder colours. Alone in the room, having completed my task with time to spare, I started looking around, and noticed that the red paint tin had its lid off. This clearly needed investigation, so I had no choice. The window was open, too, so I took a scoop and threw a small amount outside to study the effect. The resultant red cloudburst looked amazing, so I had to find out what a whole scoop could do. Once again, the combatants on my shoulders were in full battle, with one incredulously asking, "What on earth are you thinking?" and the other, "What's the point of detention if you're not going to learn something? Go for it!" The powdery cloud from the first scoop looked awesome, quickly dispersing through the air and turning the entire view through the window a devilish red. Then the other colours followed – Green! Blue! Yellow! And they looked absolutely incredible too until, scoop by scoop, I'd used up the whole term's supply. Next morning the entire detention class was lined up in front of the headmaster, who demanded to know who had desecrated the pathway with a kaleidoscopic conflagration of colours. I hadn't thought to look, but what went up must have come down, and the psychedelic pastiche on the ground beneath the art room window would have delighted anyone raised in the sixties. To my credit, I did the right thing and confessed, had to clean it up over my lunchtime, and was given a week of extra detention.

One thing I did achieve during my final year was a starring role in the school's production of 'Oliver Twist'. Following my interview,

1969–1986: Childhood – when kids could be kids!

singing 'I'm Forever Blowing Bubbles', I was given the part of the Artful Dodger, a role of which I could be truly proud. I put everything into learning my lines and gave my best in every performance. The key role of Fagin was played by fellow pupil Matt Bardock, who went on to a successful career in TV, with roles in Dr Who, The Bill, Midsomer Murders, and playing paramedic Jeff Collier in the long-running 'Casualty' series. My own claim to fame was when I brought Oliver to Fagin's den, to find that Matt wasn't there yet. Quickly improvising, I announced that he must be at the Nags Head and promptly instructed one of his pickpockets to go and get him before he drank too much! The Croydon Advertiser gave us a fantastic writeup, stating that both Matt and I could have West End careers if we so chose! Ah well, I'd have only ended up marrying Minnie Driver or Sandra Bullock, instead of Cara, the absolutely stunning bedrock of a life partner I have now. But I'm happy to say that Matt and I have remained close friends since and he continues to entertain us on our TV screens.

As I said, all I ever wanted to do was join the Army. I lived my young life with my goal already secured, so for me it was already a huge adventure. But once I entered secondary school, it became an even bigger problem.

Purley Boys School had its own history long before I crossed its threshold. At the time of writing this, a snippet from Wikipedia states that *"Purley High School had a reputation for strictness and for the frequent use of corporal punishment, with records showing a peak in canings of 43.7 per 100 pupils in the year 1977/78"*. I must admit that on my first day I was apprehensive, as rumours of the Head walking around spontaneously caning people left, right and centre was on every boy's tongue, well before we'd even started a lesson. To add prowess to injury, he'd been in the post for almost twenty years, and had had plenty of practice. Mr Derek Akers was always dressed immaculately in his black gown and square black academic cap, and carried a frighteningly springy cane. At first, I saw him as the enemy, though I quickly found him to be a firm but fair teacher and quite an amazing gentleman who only wanted the best for his charges. One morning, as I arrived at the school gates,

Soldier of Conscience: From Fighting the IRA to Battling PTSD

Mr Akers asked me there and then what I wanted to do when I left school. Quick as a flash, I answered proudly, "The Army, sir". His reply to this was just as instantaneous, "No, you should join the Navy, young man!" From what followed it quickly became clear that, according to him, any career in the military should be within the Senior Service. However, my mind was already set and, unwavering, I stuck to my guns. After several minutes trying to change my mind, he realised he was wasting his time, and ended with "Oh, go away, boy…" I didn't know it at the time, but he had served an exemplary career as a naval officer and, according to rumours, had actually fought at sea during WWII!

One morning I and several others were caught sliding on ice in the playground by a school prefect, who ordered us to stop. However, to buck authority after he'd left, we continued. But it wasn't long before he returned, with the added warning that if he caught us again, he'd send us for the cane. So, we tested this precept, he followed through on his promise and we were collectively sent to the head of 4th Form. He was a great guy whose partner, another brilliant man, was also my house tutor. Forming an orderly queue outside his door, we entered one at a time to have two strokes across our backsides which, to be honest, wasn't too bad. I was the last in line and my mate in front of me was the son of a fireman my dad served with. He entered to see two teachers standing in the room, one holding the cane and the other as a witness. They were rumoured to be gay and in a relationship together, and I could hear what was being said from outside the door. The one with the cane said, "Right, this is going to hurt you more than it is me. Bend over!" And my mate replied, "Well, to be honest, sir… I'd rather have the cane, please…". My explosive outburst from the other side of the door, and the fact that I couldn't breathe for laughing, led us to the head's office. All I could think of, waiting nervously outside his office, was if I should tell him that I'd changed my mind, and it was a sailor's life for me...

Four professionally-administered strokes each later, and with bums like baboons, we'd both learned our lesson – or so I thought!

Later that day I was going home on the bus – an old red London double-decker like in the TV programme 'On the Buses' – with an open

1969–1986: Childhood – when kids could be kids!

rear entry for getting on and off, and once you'd got on you could go straight upstairs. For some reason I'd got into an argument with another pupil named Andrew Boyle (not his real name) and, just as he was getting off, he called my mother an insulting name. But the bus was stuck in a long queue of traffic, so I jumped off, ran after him, threw him against a shop window, gave him a quick right hook to the chin, and was back in my seat as the bus pulled away. Feeling pleased with myself that justice had been duly served and well-deserved, I was incapable of considering the repercussions that could possibly follow my impulsive actions. Until the following morning, when I arrived at school and was immediately summoned to Mr Akers' office, inside which were Andrew and his mum, who was holding up Exhibit A – his ripped school shirt. I put on my best puppy dog eyes of innocence until both of them pointed at me and said, "That's him!" I was still protesting my blamelessness as the first of four strokes further deepened the bruises from the previous day. But as I left, fuming with the injustice, Mr Akers explained to me that he didn't mind boys being boys, but when it involves parents then he has to be seen to act. So, not a good start to the week – eight strokes of the cane by Tuesday morning, and an entire backside of black stripes that would make a zebra proud.

Another fond memory is sex education lessons. A class of 15-year-old boys, full of pubescent testosterone, sitting innocently behind our wooden desks – the ones which opened at the top and had circular holes in the right-hand corner for an inkwell – nervously awaiting whichever teacher had drawn the short straw to take the lesson. To our surprise this time, in walked Mr Akers, who stopped in front of the class and just glared at us, as if peering into our very souls and thoughts. A riveting silence held the room as he continued to stare. Then, when we felt we could take no more of the suspense, he opened with "Masturbation!" Another breathless pause, as every child in the room waited for what was to follow. Then, just as candidly, he let loose with, "It stops you revising, and it puts spots on your forehead!" And as he turned and left the room, closing the door behind him as the lesson ended, twenty-plus teenage boys, in unison, raised their hands up to their foreheads!

At the end of each day Mr Akers would always stand at the bus stop outside school, proud as punch of us all, to see his boys on first. It was on my last day at school that year, as I walked past him, that he took hold of my shirt to stop me, and said, "Ingram, I strongly recommend that you do not return to school after the holidays, because you'll never make anything of yourself". This was Friday afternoon, and he was unaware that I'd had enough of school, and had already arranged to start work, the following Monday morning, at the Houses of Parliament. Today, I like to think that I'd make him proud. Rest in peace, Mr A. You were a gentleman, I will always remember you as an example, and I am genuinely sorry that I caused you so much grief!

"Hi mate

I do remember getting caned there on more than one occasion. You didn't have to do a lot to get beaten with a big stick in that school…

I guess it was Roy W who said that he'd rather have the cane. I already had my whacks before you, but I do remember it being talked about afterwards! We had some great times. Great memories and friends – but I wouldn't want to go back there…

Do you remember that time Akers was taking a Year 4 class, and he got a kid to bang on the glass to try and get our attention because we were messing about on our way to woodwork? Stupid idiot broke the glass, so he sent someone over to get us out of woodwork.

In front of the whole class, he grabbed us by the ears, dragged us up to the window, and told us it was our fault – and we'd have to pay for it ourselves and fix it after school on the last day of term!

Took us bloody ages, and it was nearly dark when we got out of there…"

Anthony McCormack

1969–1986: Childhood – when kids could be kids!

"My first memory of Wayne was him singing a spirited version of 'Mirror in the Bathroom' by The Beat, in Mr Edam's class around 1980. We were 10 years old and had been asked to 'perform something'.

Wayne's singing was, I remember, particularly committed. He was always fairly 'full on' in everything he did at school – whether it was playing 'The Artful Dodger' in our production of Oliver, or getting himself into trouble for over-boisterous behaviour in the classroom. Over-boisterous, but never malicious, and whenever I think of Wayne at that time, it always makes me smile. He was great fun!

It is of no surprise to me that Wayne has gone on to forge such an incredible life. With boundless reserves of energy, combined with his inquisitive nature, he has (against our head teacher's questionable remark) achieved truly remarkable things

I am immensely proud to have him as a friend. He is one of life's true rough diamonds…"

Matt Bardock

Chapter 2

1987

"You'll never make anything of yourself..."

It was true. I'd actually managed to secure a job at the Houses of Parliament. Well, when I say 'I', I mean my parents did, through a couple who lived at the top of the road. Roy was a black-cab driver, and Dot worked for a temporary recruiting agency. My job entailed correcting the copies of Hansard each morning and taking them to their respective departments. Hansard is a booklet of the speeches due in parliament that day, but sometimes a speech had to be removed and it was our job to do this. We'd guillotine the redundant speech out, stick the remaining booklet onto waxed paper, and then photocopy it to make a new master from which hundreds more would be created. Once boxed up, it became the solemn responsibility of a cocky 15-year-old with a trolley to deliver one to 10 Downing Street and the others to the House of Commons canteen, the Lords restaurant, and various other places around the building. However, my favourite memories weren't from meeting all the famous public names of those days, but from joining the chief librarian each day, after he'd made us both a cup of tea, who regaled me with tales of his life as an army officer. This continued for several months until they offered me a full-time position but, adamant as I was about joining the military, I turned it down. My friends said I was daft – I was a 16-year-old boy earning over £1,000 a month! – and even now, as I write, it seems a crazy decision, but money isn't everything. Far from it. As I reflect on everything I've been through since then, the suffering I've seen and experienced and the differences I hope I've made, I know that I wouldn't – couldn't – have chosen a different career path.

Bored, I left the job shortly afterwards but, not wishing to be out of work, I was helped by my Dad to find another temporary job in the recruitment department of London Fire Brigade. I was already well into my own recruitment process for the British Army, and each day during my lunch period I'd run the streets of Lambeth trying to get as fit as I possibly could in preparation. Again, I was invited to stay on until I was old enough to join the Brigade properly at 18, but my mind was firmly set. Don't get me wrong here – there's nothing wrong with the Fire Service, and it would have been an amazing career. I still have absolute respect for my Dad and what he and the rest of his 'family' did every day, going into blazing buildings armed with nothing but their black tunic, yellow leggings, and personally-issued axe secured to their belt. I also spent a lot of time at Purley fire station, making cups of tea for the crew on White Watch, in return for letting me play snooker in their attic room. But I'd known my destiny from a young age and finally, on 8th December 1986, I arrived at Cambrai Barracks in Catterick, North Yorkshire to join Intake 86/18 of the British Army's Royal Armoured Corps. This turned out to be a very short introduction to military service, because after just two weeks we were sent home on Christmas leave. But during those fourteen wonderful days I'd already decided that this was the life for me and had even made some friends, including Tony Dixey. He and I kept in contact over the holiday period and even returned to camp together a few days early. We were both hooked on this life and would remain friends right throughout our basic and second phase training – but as often happens, we went our totally separate ways once we'd been designated to different regiments.

You may have read in books, and especially the press, about bullying during basic training. I can only vouch for what I saw and experienced and can truthfully say that I never once witnessed this, to myself or anyone else. Basic training is meant to be hard; it's designed to transform young civilians into soldiers and exemplary citizens – and if it was easy, then everyone would pass, albeit at a very low level. One example was the dreaded 'river run' on the North Yorkshire moors. We'd run several miles from camp, in near-freezing conditions, to the bank of a small stream about five feet wide and up to three feet deep in some parts. We were all lined up on the bank at a deep stretch, and Corporal Lythgoe shouted "Right, when I say jump, you fuckers will all jump… Ready? JUMP!" As one we all jumped into the freezing cold river, ready to prove our worth as soldiers, and stood to attention as icy water quickly filled our boots and worked its way up our combat trousers. "What the fucking hell are you idiots doing?" he demanded, "I said 'Jump' – Up! Not into the fucking water! What's the bloody point of that?" But his logical remonstration ended with a smile, and it was clear that we weren't the first to have blindly followed orders without thinking. Ten press-ups in the stream for punishment started the river run from here, followed by five miles of splashing, tripping, and slipping on wet rocks on our way back to camp. Along the route were several low tunnels which were only passable on your hands and knees, and sometimes, for realism, they'd let off CS gas canisters in there beforehand. For the record, an encounter with CS gas (or its crystals, which are the base for police spray or Mace), is not like you ever see in the movies. There, the hero gets sprayed directly in the eyes, screams for a moment, shakes his head, then brushes it away before getting back into the fight. In reality, you'd be in absolute hell. You can't do anything, your eyes screaming with the blazing pain. Your tears make it worse, because the stuff reacts to moisture, and the more you instinctively try to brush it away, the deeper down it goes into your eye sockets.

The final section of the tunnel disappeared into a black underground puddle, so you had to fully submerge yourself head-first into the U-bend and trust that your mate who'd gone before you would grab your wrists and pull you the rest of the way through. Then together, this sodden mass of mud and men would continue running back to camp, in full view of the other recruits, to form up outside the barracks, where we were instructed to re-form in fifteen minutes for the next session. Were we being bullied? Not to me, we weren't. Were we being trained? Too right we were – to our limits – so that we'd learn to go further beyond them each time.

Thinking back, it's odd the things you remember and what slips your memory. For the life of me I can't recall how we ever managed to get, and keep, our uniforms clean and presentable for the countless parades we had to attend. But I clearly remember parading outside in 'mess tin order' – when our entire squad stood stark naked with only our mess tins veiling our John Thomases.

During basic training each troop of (usually) ten soldiers lived in the same room, each with his own locker, bed, and grey footlocker – and everything in each locker had a designated place. Each morning you'd strip your bed down and make a bed block – the blankets and sheets forming a 'sandwich filling', which was wrapped in the orange/brown bed cover. You'd put this at the top of your bed in place of the pillow, with your mirror-finish bulled boots, clean mess tins, and other bits of kit laid out below it, and a specifically marked-out length of wood assigned to each room ensured that each block was the correct size and shape. Laying out each bed and locker this way enabled inspection to be carried out efficiently each morning, and the inspecting officer was guaranteed to throw at least two (and sometimes all) of the blocks onto the floor if they didn't meet expectations. Then as soon as he left, there was a mad scramble to find your own kit from amongst everyone else's scattered around the floor. But gradually, day by day, I was reshaped from a cocky, mischievous, 17-year-old boy into a strong, fit young man who could follow instructions, perform basic first aid, use a map to get from one place to another under cover of darkness, and strip down and reassemble a multitude of weapons – from a submachine gun (SMG) to the 120mm main gun of a Chieftain battle tank – also in the dark. Though the only war we were involved in at the time was in Northern Ireland, we still prepared for being sent there, or if the Russians invaded!

In March 1987, and still not 18, I was badged 2RTR (Second Royal Tank Regiment) and sent to Fallingbostel in Germany to join the rest of my regiment stationed there. For a teenager this was a real eye opener, as my only previous experience outside the UK was a family holiday in Spain. Germany was split West and East, the Berlin wall was still there, and wages were paid in deutschmarks (DM), each consisting of 100 pfennigs, with 3DM to the British pound. A beer cost just 75 pfennigs and each squadron had its own bar in the cellar. I also learned that in the 'red light' district of Hamburg, a lady of the night would cost you 50DM. Amazing memories were created in these bars, and you'd often hear the clattering of young soldiers walking around with Grolsch bottle caps attached to their civvy shoes. My lungs took a hell of a pounding as I didn't smoke, but in those days people smoked everywhere. The cellar ceilings were no higher than eight feet, so by the end of the evening you were breathing a constant white fug which hung around everyone's heads, while The Clash and The Jam blared out from most of the rooms. Fortunately I loved both and, from my point of view at the time, Germany was heaven for me.

On arriving at the squadron I was immediately placed in the NIGS room, which I was told stood for 'New in Germany', and was a rite of passage where every new soldier started. It was a large room, consisting of four spaces, each with two lockers, a bed, and a blanket draped between the spaces to act as a doorway. This would be my accommodation for the next nine months. It turned out to often be the only place where people would chat to you freely, because as a NIG no one would talk to you for the first six months unless you were on exercises, ranges, or deployed. Some might consider this cruel, but every soldier before us had been through the same ritual, so it was simply accepted as par for the course of becoming accepted. One vital test to be passed was to find a flag from a local motor company and hang it from your wall or pin it to the ceiling. All the local car companies had multiple flags hanging from poles outside their establishments, so your job was to find one that had 'fallen down' and decorate your space with it. But there are always more ways than one, and I simply did a deal with a guy who was being posted back to the UK. On my first weekend I was invited to join several older members of the squadron for a schutzenfest in Walsrode, a village some 20km from Fallingbostel. This was my first introduction to German beer, and the famous Stein I'd heard so much about. Everything was going really well, and I was perfectly drunk when the fight started. A group of local guys had decided to take on one of our corporals and, before I knew it, tables were being overturned and punches thrown. I looked at another NIG who'd arrived in the country a day after me, psychically asking one another if we should join in, but just as we stood up a man-mountain named Trigger Roy looked at us both sternly, and said "Not now, boys...", before passing us two fresh Steins and wading into the fracas to break it up. So we sat getting to know each other, becoming more and more intoxicated, and the fight ended just as we'd finished our glasses.

Several black eyes were on display at Monday morning's parade, and as the squadron sergeant major (SSM) asked each soldier, as he walked along the line, how they'd got their bruises, he always received the same reply – that they'd slipped on the stairs. With a knowing look he turned to the squadron quartermaster sergeant (SQMS) and said, "Q, our stairs seem to be getting a little dangerous. Take a look at them, would you?" To which the SQMS gave the regulation-issue, "Sah!"

Life as a trooper in 2RTR was good, but I soon realised that unless I was on a firing range, firing a tank cannon, it could get quite boring. Exercises were usually conducted on the training ground in Soltau, where we'd be in a wood for days on end under camouflage netting. There'd be the occasional battle in which we'd participate, then we'd return to the woods for several more days sitting it out. This was all part of our training, however, and I eventually learned to understand the term "Hurry up and wait...".

During my first exercise I learned two valuable life lessons as a soldier living out of his tank. The first was how to operate the boiling vessel (BV), a glorified kettle that all crews used in their respective vehicles. It plugged into the system via a standard military 10-pin connector and, as long as the engine was running, the water would boil. Tin cans of composite (compo) rations could be put inside to heat up, so you could have a hot meal when you stopped, and with the boiling water you could make a brew as well. Well, that was the idea, and it would have worked perfectly had I not misinterpreted my troop sergeant's instructions to fill the BV with food before we left camp. I dutifully opened each can and emptied them all into the BV, and later that day received a clout round the ear when we couldn't have a brew!

The second error was in learning to preload the BV with water and tins at the end of the day, in case you didn't have time next morning. This way you could always guarantee a hot breakfast when you stopped. But I hadn't read the labels properly, and our beans and sausages turned out to be pilchards in tomato sauce, which tasted vile when warmed up and make for a sickly breakfast. We were famished and ate them anyway, but I certainly wasn't the most popular rookie that day.

Something I'd never expected to learn on my first exercise was how my daily constitution would be affected. The exercise was for three weeks, but by the end of the second week I desperately needed to pass the heavy-duty compo rations I'd been eating during this time. After a discreet question to my troop sergeant, he advised me to go outside and conduct a 'shovel recce'. The blank look on my face told him that I hadn't a clue what he was talking about, so he calmly instructed me to go into the woods with a shovel and a toilet roll, find a tree with a low branch at right angles to the trunk to hold the roll, dig a hole near the branch, lower my coveralls to my ankles, do my business then use the tactically-positioned roll, shovel the lot into the hole, cover it with soil, then pull up my coveralls and return, mission accomplished. In other words – Easy peesy. So I found the right kind of tree, dug a hole, dropped my coveralls, squatted over the hole, and dropped my payload which, though desperate to escape after two weeks of solitary confinement, now felt like a very intimate part of me. After using the strategically-placed toilet roll, I shovelled everything into the hole, ensured there was no trace of my passing, and pulled up my coveralls. Perfect, I thought. I felt as one with the earth, and a true soldier. Until I pulled my lapels together and felt something warm and organic slither across my neck. I froze instantly. *Snakes are coldblooded* though fear quickly turned to panic as the smell made me realise what had actually happened. My close friend had come out far longer than I'd expected, and only half had landed on the ground. The other half had dropped inside my tunic, and in

1987: "You'll never make anything of yourself..."

my haste to get dressed I hadn't noticed! This clinging, now-unwanted companion, having unstuck itself from my neck, was now slithering down my back, trying to make its way back to base. To an onlooker, the way I was undressing, wriggling, and jumping around, trying to shake the bloody thing off, must have looked like I was having a nerve agent attack. I wasn't popular that day, either, once I'd got back inside the confined space of the tank. I am proud to say, however, that since then my aim has been honed to perfection, and I always check the hole in the ground for precision bombing.

You see a lot of odd things in the Army – some of them unforgettable, some of them inexplicable. Even when we were operating fully-tactical, how on earth did Wolfgang find each and every squadron from his mobile catering van? Did he have his own 353 radio? Did he have someone on the inside? And how the hell did he drive across tank-tracked and boggy terrain that would regularly claim our four-wheel drive Land Rovers? Whatever his secret, he never failed, and would regularly and reliably arrive at each secret location and sound his signature tune, whereby our soldiers would crawl out of their camouflaged hides in droves to buy his freshly-cooked, non-army issue bratwurst sausages, frikandellen, chicken breast chips, and bags of mayonnaise. Yep, the Russians certainly missed a trick here!

I really enjoyed the fitness training in the regiment, especially rugby, and being part of the regimental team was another opportunity to drop myself in serious trouble. I must have been very easily led in those days – yes, most definitely. One Saturday night we were in the club bar. Several members were absent because the warrant officers and sergeants' mess were holding their summer ball, so they had to perform waiter duties. Had they been here, we might not have succumbed to the temptation. We'd already consumed copious amounts of Grolsch, and maybe our judgements were a little clouded, but me and Taner Goksoylar (affectionately known as Ali) were talked into staging – to put it delicately – a strategic disruption event. We stripped naked, put on our boots and balaclavas and, on the word 'Go!' burst out of the building to streak around the parade ground. It was absolutely vital, we were instructed, to circumnavigate the sergeants' mess house en route. Only after the event did we hear from one of the squad members, who was standing next to the Regimental Sergeant Major (RSM) at the time, how well this precision operation had been planned. The RSM had just got up to speak, opening with the standard, "Colonel, ladies, and gentlemen…" when he stopped suddenly in surprise, his face reddening. Arm fully outstretched, pointing towards the window, he exploded with "…Catch those perverts!!!" Repercussions were inevitable. The next morning an impromptu regimental parade was held in the gym, where the RSM informed us that he had been informed who it was, and advised us to come forward. But instead we kept quiet, waited, and endured long, sleepless nights while I anguished over whether or not I should present myself to his office and get it over with. But in the end, my natural cowardice won out over his bluff, and the incident eventually passed unsolved.

Several months later, after we'd won a final, the RSM attended the club bar to congratulate us. The team got on really well with him– which is why, when he returned to his table from the bar, he found two balaclavas strategically positioned there for his eyes only. Without flinching, he turned to us with a smile, stared us straight in the eyes and, in a low voice, said "I knew it was a couple of you bastards…".

> "The best memory I have with us two was doing that French commando course. But more importantly, do you remember the piss-up in the Squadron Bar soon after we got back to Fallingbostel, with the Kent police rugby team?
>
> Long story short: Things were getting really out of hand from them – it was the cellar bar – so you popped up to our room and grabbed one of the blue hand grenades we'd been issued on the commando course – that when it exploded, covered the blast radius in white powder.
>
> So, after getting our guys out of the bar, you lobbed it in amongst them and closed the bar door. Priceless! They got covered in talc, and also ringing ears…"
>
> Craig (Arny) Arnold – 2RTR

1987: "You'll never make anything of yourself..."

Points to note: Arny and I spent two years sharing the same 2-man room, both as Lance Corporals, from 1988-1990. The episode he describes above followed the 'murder' of our rugby club mascot – an inflatable life-size doll – who was fatally stabbed in the back by a member of the opposing team, and which required the appropriate retribution...

Wayne

"You can add that it should not have been too difficult to find out who it was, as I had two eyes tattooed on my arse and a flying donkey on my right arm. And you were at least six inches taller than me! Also, we ran around the Sergeants' mess twice, leaping up by the window doing star jumps – just to make sure we weren't missed!"

Taner Goksoylar (Ali)

Blimey! The scary thing about writing this is that my mind had blocked out us doing those star jumps...

Wayne

Chapter 3

1990–91

South Armagh

Believe it or not, after two years in Germany I was bored, and needed more action. I'd already received my first promotion to lance corporal, so when I heard they were looking for volunteers to join 3RTR in Northern Ireland, I got my name in quickly and joined Y Squadron under the careful support of an amazing sergeant named Andy Fisher, whose reputation, I soon learned, was nothing short of legendary here. Our squadron shared the grounds of a Royal Ulster Constabulary (RUC) station in Middletown, South Armagh.

To visualise the scene, imagine spending six months living in a large farmhouse surrounded by 12-foot-high grey metal walls. Atop the house was a brick-built sanger – a temporary fortified position – which allowed you to overview the small border town. At the entrance to the farm, across from a small concreted-over garden, was another sanger which adjoined a large metal gate. If, by now, you're imagining a small fortress, you'd be spot on. From inside, you could not only control who or what entered your space, but also the traffic lights outside. To the rear of the house, where the garden used to be, was our accommodation – complete with a mortar-hardened roof – where we slept. To the rear of this was the small RUC station with yet another sanger at the rear, overlooking the Irish border. The whole area was about 250m square which, by the end of our six months, felt like a high security prison. Our squadron was split between here and Keady, while another squadron and RHQ were billeted at Aughnacloy and Armagh City.

1990–91: South Armagh

This was my first introduction to a war zone, and I must say that I loved the environment – a typical rural tour of duty with most patrols made by helicopter, or drop-offs in vans modified to look like anything that wasn't a military vehicle. Some even had their rear windows fitted with a frame of drink cans, to look like it was full of them. Our time on tour was split between QRF (Quick Reaction Force) duties, responding to any incident or emergency, patrolling the border, and guarding the camp – mainly around the front, rear and top sangers. The rear and top gave perfect views over Middletown and the Irish border, while the front controlled the traffic to and from the south. A computer allowed us to input the registration plate of any vehicle stopped at the traffic lights – for as long as we needed – and if it informed us that a car was suspect, belonged to a person of interest, or believed used by a terrorist outfit, then we'd take action. We'd detain the vehicle while we contacted the Int cell for advice, or what they wanted us to do with it – and this could go several ways. We could simply log its traffic, two of us might go and chat with the occupants, or we could ask them to drive to the search centre for a thorough stripdown. One time we flagged a car and were instructed to have a chat with the driver. I noticed something wrong straight away – he was very nervous indeed – and if I'd been a dog my hackles would have been up. I informed Int, and the guys and the RUC forced him to drive into the search centre where he was questioned further, and his vehicle searched. Inside the doors, behind the fabric panels, were several thousands of pounds in cash. The RUC believed it was gun money, but in the end they couldn't prove anything illegal in relation to the money, the vehicle, or the driver, so they had to let him go – but we hoped it would send a warning to the IRA that we were serious, and they'd have to be a lot smarter next time.

This was Northern Ireland in July 1990, and the first six months saw us involved with several IED (improvised explosive device)-related incidents. In my first two weeks a nun was murdered, along with three uniformed RUC police officers, when an IRA team detonated a home-made bomb concealed in a culvert under the road. They knew the route the armoured car would take and had planned accordingly. But what they hadn't considered was vehicles travelling from the opposite direction, and at the exact moment that Sister Catherine's Mini Metro aligned with the patrol car over the culvert, a button was pushed from a safe location, and the devastating explosion killed all four instantly.

This was a wakeup call for us all, as it demonstrated that the IRA had no qualms whatsoever when it came to killing innocent civilians – a nun, for Christ's sake! – to achieve their goal. Later that day the IRA released a statement claiming full responsibility for the attack, but stating that the death of Sister Catherine Dunne had 'not been caused by accidental or terrorist detonation of an explosive device, but by a fluke set of unforeseen circumstances'.

It would be impossible to overstate our anger and contempt when we heard this statement of utter, gutless cowardice. Was it a fluke that the IRA had taken over a nearby bungalow, holding the father, mother, and their young children hostage at gunpoint? Was it an accident that the IRA had run a concealed command wire from their home to the road, where 1000lb of explosives lay prepared but hidden from view? Was it an inadvertent lapse of judgement when someone not only connected power and a switch to that cable, but triggered it to see what would happen just as an armoured patrol car drove over it? And was it so unimaginable that other vehicles might have wanted to use the road at that time?

The explosion left a crater 20 feet deep and 30 feet wide in the road. The armoured car was hurled over a tall hedge into a field to land on its roof. Three policemen in their thirties were killed. A 27-year-old Catholic nun was murdered – her convent was just 100m away from us – and her passenger was left with life-threatening injuries.

One of our corporals got in trouble at the time, when a guy named Desmond 'Dessie' Grew – the leader of the South Armagh provisional IRA and one of our 'most wanted' – was brought into our search centre, and the squadron OC (officer commanding) asked every soldier to come through the site so we'd recognise him in future. At one point Dessie turned to our Int corporal and said, "Youse guys have had it quiet, like…"

"Nothing we can't handle…" replied the corporal, curtly.

"Well," said Dessie, "Want me to bring the boys down to liven it up a bit?"

To which the Int corporal made the grievous error of responding "Do what you want, mate... We can handle it!"

The OC pulled him up heavily on that one – not just for allowing himself to be goaded, but for effectively giving the IRA permission to play their live action wargames with our soldiers.

Dessie got himself killed a few weeks later when, along with Martin McCaughey, he was retrieving weapons from an IRA arms cache – which just happened to be under covert surveillance by the SAS.

I wish I could say that I knew Sister Catherine, or any of the nuns at her convent, but the truth was that they shunned and avoided us. Whether they abhorred the idea of men with guns, or sided with their own countrymen, or were afraid of how supporting either side might affect them in the long term – I never found out. We were there purely to keep the peace and prevent people getting hurt. But everyone knew what the IRA was capable of – they'd made that very clear indeed – and no one had the slightest doubt that, had Dessie recovered those weapons in the dead of night, they'd have been used pretty damn soon afterwards.

We received intel that a lorry, packed with IRA gunmen in the back, was going to attack our base – by ramming the gate and launching a full-scale assault on our small camp. And when the reports came in as quickly and regularly as these were, we knew it was going to be soon. In the interim, all we could do was wait, our collective adrenal glands pumping, for the impending battle.

The IRA had already practiced this technique, a few months before our deployment. On 13 Dec 1989 a lorry full of IRA activists, armed with automatic rifles, grenades, nail bombs, heavy machine guns, rocket-propelled grenades, and even a fucking flame thrower(!), callously and mercilessly attacked eight soldiers from the Kings Own Scottish Borderers regiment (KOSB), who were manning a similar checkpoint to ours at Derryard, north of Rosslea in County Fermanagh. Their goal was to attack and totally destroy the entire vehicle checkpoint, as they knew it was only lightly manned. The IRA's intel was unquestionable, as they knew every detail of the base, including the exact number of troops who'd be there. But though they thought their plan foolproof, the Jocks had other ideas and, even after Private Houston was mown down the moment he approached the vehicle, and Lance-Corporal Patterson killed in the ensuing battle, the remainder still managed to force the fight back to the IRA, who fled the scene and drove all the way back to the border, where the truck was later found abandoned with a 460lb bomb, clearly intended for the base, still on board.

The IRA later admitted that their attack had not gone as planned, and this was due to the indomitable bravery shown by the KOSB. Survivors Corporal Robert Duncan and Lance-Corporal Ian Harvey were both awarded the Distinguished Conduct Medal, whilst Lance-Corporal Patterson received a posthumous mention in dispatches for his actions under intense fire.

RIP Private James Houston (age 22)
RIP Lance-Corporal Michael Patterson (age 21)

My four man team, commonly known as a bric, was manning the QRF from our room, just inside the main gate, which gave entry to our base. We were wearing more and heavier kit than normal, ready to meet the truck head on, while a VHS movie, which we'd watched many times before, was playing on the TV. Then it happened – a long burst of 7.62mm machine gun fire from the general-purpose machine gun (GPMG) in the top sanger. In a flash we were off – out through the gates, spreading out in formation ready to hit the incoming truck from all sides – into a completely empty street. All tensed up with nowhere to go, still scanning everywhere around us and feeling like unwitting actors in a 'Carry On' film, we made our way back through the gates with all the dignity we could muster to find out what had just happened.

One of our troopers, named Coco, was stationed in the top sanger – the one overlooking the village – and being bored he'd decided to carry out a stoppage drill on the machine gun. This would have been okay using the silver training rounds designed for such a purpose, but not the best of ideas with live ammo. Coco wasn't the brightest bulb on the tree, and tried to talk his way out of it, to the extent of blaming a workman with a pneumatic drill a full mile away. We heard later that the burst he'd fired had bisected a cow in an adjacent field, so not only was he fined a month's wages, but he also had to fork out for the farmer's loss.

Later during our tour, while on patrol, we witnessed an old lady dump a hessian bag into a stream, before walking away as if nothing had happened. When we went to investigate, we saw several kittens splashing about in the water so, being the hardened soldiers that we were, we waded quickly into the stream to retrieve them. Sadly, they were all incredibly young, and we only managed to save one from the litter. But even this one was touch and go, as it still needed milk, so we took it in turns to feed him with a syringe and rubber teat. Gradually, over the coming weeks, we could see he was growing, and was now able to drink milk unaided from a bowl, but he still needed caring for. By now it had got used to us and had become the troop mascot, and all was going well until I left him in Coco's care while we went out on patrol. On our return we couldn't see it anywhere, and Coco was unusually silent, so the conversation quickly turned to, "Coco, where's the kitten, mate?" To which Coco replied with "Umm... Erm... Well, I didn't mean it..."

"What didn't you mean, Coco?" I asked, now very concerned.

"Well I was tired. And I was keeping him warm..."

It took far longer than it should to learn that Coco had decided to keep the kitten in his bed while he went for lunch. Then, on returning to his room for a kip, he'd flopped straight onto the bed, having totally forgotten about the little furry ball curled up cosily under the covers.

I was lying on my own bed one afternoon when all hell broke loose. Our Sergeant Major stormed into the room and told us we were being 'crashed out' to reinforce a QRF that had been flown out to the Tassagh Road area, as another culvert bomb had just blown up an RUC armoured Ford Escort, and the guys were still inside. Two Lynx helicopters had left Aldergrove airport inbound to us, so we had to move quickly. Within minutes we were airborne. Most of our patrols were carried out via helicopter in this part of the world, due to the increased threat of bombs near (or beneath) the road. Unfortunately, this made the Lynx a perfect target for heavy machine gun fire while on the ground between landing and taking off again, and several attempts had already been made against other military aircraft, especially around Crossmaglen.

The Lynx needed to fly in fast, then drop quickly out of the sky onto the grass landing field, with the door gunner sweeping arcs with his GPMG. We'd then pile on as quickly and safely as we could, before aiming our muzzles downwards as the heli strained to either climb as high and fast as it possibly could, or fling itself forward in a spate of rapid hedge-hopping leaps. Not for those with sensitive stomachs, this was the best roller coaster ride you could ever hope for as the Lynx threw itself into tight left and right turns as it tried to grip the contours of the land, followed by a series of steep climbs to surmount the telephone lines, followed by an even steeper descent to avoid a clear line of incoming fire.

A few minutes later we landed in a field, close to a massive hole in the ground, near which a battered red car had been catapulted forwards. The next part of this story I only learned when we were back at base. The OC had gone immediately to the cordon area and told the corporal in charge to move it back – in case any secondary devices had been planted in the area. The RUC were responsible for setting up the initial cordon, but the OC trusted his gut, and had it moved back a further 200 metres.

My rapidly-assembled quick response team was patrolling the nearby fields when a loud explosion ripped through the air – its epicentre exactly where the first cordon had stood, and within 150 metres of the first blast. The timed explosive device, though smaller than the first, was planted to kill or maim our QRF personnel, and if it hadn't been for the OC's instincts and prompt actions, several of us would have perished that day, just doing our jobs.

Cheers, Major H, MBE.

It doesn't take long for a soldier's brain to adapt to the circumstances he's often thrown into, and then develop a warped and potholed sense of humour as a survival measure, because no tour is ever without its surreal and incongruous events. One night we were conducting snap vehicle checkpoints (VCPs) on the country roads around the base. We'd set up our position, with one GPMG forward and another rear of our troops to provide cut-offs. Our remaining guys were placed in cover, and the troop leader and I stood on the road sporting our special torches with the red cones on top. We'd been in position for quite a while, alone in the dark, wet, and seemingly-deserted South Armagh countryside, and were just thinking of moving to a different location when we heard a vehicle approaching. Even before it arrived, we knew it was in a poor state, as the blowing exhaust could be heard for miles. The tired engine sounds grew louder, and the boss and I stepped into the road, me making a circle with my red torch. We'd chosen a long, straight part of the lane to give drivers enough time to see us, but the car didn't slow down. I was close to jumping out of the way, when at the last moment the brakes were slammed on as if the driver had only just spotted us. I went over to check his wreck of a car, while the boss stepped forward to talk to him, and I couldn't believe what I saw. I had to bang my torch in the darkness to confirm it. The bloody thing had only three wheels – and while this might have been okay if it hadn't been designed and built with four in mind, the rear offside wheel (the driver's side!) wasn't there! How the hell the bloody thing had stayed upright was beyond me.

Wondering what our protocols were in this case, I turned to inform the boss, but he'd already started addressing me, stating that the elderly man was intoxicated. This was clearly a euphemism, as he was pissed all the way out of his head, but 'intoxicated' went on the incident record. The guy looked like Albert Steptoe, though more unkempt, and on the passenger seat lay a clear, near-empty glass bottle with a clear liquid inside. I took a careful sniff, and it definitely wasn't holy water. So I asked the old boy what his name was, and on getting his terse response, "Plunket Nugent" I nearly doubled over with laughter (did I mention that we had a deranged sense of humour for a reason?) I then asked him what was in the bottle, and he answered "Potcheen." Potcheen is a typical home-made Irish spirit made from barley and potatoes, and usually an absolute minimum of 40% proof"... Yes, that would certainly account for it. So I told him that he couldn't drive because he was too intoxicated and, besides, he only had three wheels – to which his reply was a tart "Feck off..."

Trying to suppress the schoolboy smirk that was attempting to commandeer my face, I repeated the statement because, seriously, the guy was a menace to himself and other road users, so with a stern look and voice I informed him that there were heavily-armed soldiers stationed further along the road, and would he please step out of the vehicle. "Feck off!" he shrieked again and, as an afterthought, "And they can feck reet off, too!" before stamping on the accelerator and speeding off into the distance, forcing me to radio the troops ahead to let him pass safely.

Scoring it up to experience, I have to admit that I admired the old codger.

Plunket Nugent: 1 – Y Squadron: 0

Another incident involved the whole troop and could have landed us totally in the shit. We'd been patrolling for hours, searching farms, and setting up snap OPs, when we came across a derelict house. The garden was way overgrown, most of the windows were smashed, and the odd curtain protruded through the broken panes. We were all knackered, so the boss instructed us to chill out in the garden and have lunch – to which we all happily complied.

We lay on the ground talking and, when lunch was over, Gus Ferguson, our troop corporal, had the idea to use the opportunity we'd been given (carpe diem!) and storm the house like the SAS would. He'd be the Blue Team approaching from the back door, and I'd be Red Team making entrance via the front. The boss's job was to command the house clearance, and to make it as realistic as possible he gave each of us a cobblestone to use as flash-bangs.

Ever the soldier, I set the scene – a derelict house in the South Armagh countryside, miles from anywhere. Twelve operatives to be deployed – six at the front, six at the rear. The troop leader thumbed the 'Push-To-Talk' button.

"Red Team ready. Blue Team ready. This is Zero – I have control. Go! Go! Go!" I slammed my size 10 against the front door, almost knocking it off its hinges, at the same instant as Gus did the same at the back. Then we lobbed our flash-bangs through the two remaining panes of glass at the front and rear, and with rifles at the ready we stormed into the house.

From the outside it must have looked brilliant, as we made a textbook entry into the premises. From the inside however, there was a problem.

In the front room sat a family, staring at us in utter silence, eyes wide with fear, their hands held trembling in the air.

I don't have the words to express how shocked we were, how apologetic we felt, and how badly it could have gone in every direction because we'd not done a proper recce. The boss immediately put his hand in his pocket to pay for the two broken panes, plus more to fix the others. We repaired the door and, still apologising profusely, made our way out, to put as much distance between them and ourselves as possible.

Personally, I blame the movie 'Who Dares Wins' with Lewis Collins, which was a major influence in the minds of many young men who enlisted after it was released. All I can say is, thank God we didn't try to stage the Iranian embassy siege!

> "I'm Andy Fisher, the guy that Wayne very kindly describes as a legend.
>
> Not a week went by without a different threat being announced, and we acted accordingly. But towards the end of our time in the Province, not an hour went by without a team(s) being out on the ground checking likely areas where the PIRA might set up a mortar. Ironically, the unit from the Royal Artillery that we handed over to had scoffed at the idea of the constant Mortar Base Plate checks, and did away with them not long after we left. I'll give you three guesses as to what befell them a few weeks later!!!
>
> The Tassagh Road bomb that Wayne also mentions happened towards the end of our tour, but the difference this time was that the two members of the RUC managed to walk away – albeit very shocked, cut, and bruised. This time the cordon operation fell to us and, thankfully, it was the last incident on our patch before we went home! As they used to say out there, the members of the Security Forces had to be lucky every day – but the PIRA only had to be lucky once!"
>
> Andy Fisher

Chapter 4

1993-94

Belfast

Just over a year later, with the 'active service' bug still buzzing in my system, I volunteered to return to Ireland, this time to Belfast with the 9th/12th Royal Lancers. Two things changed in my life during this tour. I transferred to a reconnaissance regiment – which allowed me more freedom as a soldier – and my passion for medical work got kick-started. We were based in a camp named Girdwood, just off the Crumlin Road in the northwest of the city, and connected to the main courthouse through a series of underground tunnels and heavy security gates on the surface. During the months of build-up training in Germany beforehand, we were kept updated on the various incidents that were happening within the province, and our area of responsibility towards them.

For the duration of this tour, the regiment would be broken down into different areas. I was attached to 'D' Squadron, patrolling the Shankill, which was mainly Protestant, and the Ardoyne (or 'the Doyne' as we called it) – a staunch Catholic enclave. We were also given the Ligoneil area, a mix of both Catholic and Protestant, to the north west of the city. 'A' Squadron got the New Lodge area, made up of several blocks of flats and properties which opened directly onto the pavement – and I later learned just how deadly this type of domicile could be.

In 1993 Northern Ireland was an especially dangerous area for our British forces. The IRA were making a final push for violence before the impending ceasefire agreement – the official end of hostilities – and they still had plenty of surplus anger and ammunition to use up. Which is why the RUC told us that they hadn't had it this bad since the 70's. Belfast was a completely different beast from the 'bandit country' I'd got used to a couple of years earlier. I'd only heard gunfire once in Armagh, and that was a negligent discharge, but in Belfast it became an almost daily occurrence. The atmosphere here was extremely volatile, and the tiniest spark was enough to incite and ignite an already unstable situation into a rampage of hatred and bloodshed. Most areas were known to be dangerous, but the Ardoyne and New Lodge areas were particularly nasty due to their layout. The Doyne was famous for its shootings, bombings and crowd-related violence, while the New Lodge had its own special kind of ugliness. It wasn't unknown for troops to be patrolling the avenues between the flats to have a washing machine or engine block dropped onto them from a roof or balcony above. Nevertheless, we learned to be patient and, especially, to avoid conflict with groups of people who, given a suitable stimulus or trigger, could spontaneously coalesce into an autonomous riot.

True to form, the tour wasn't without its funny side and one of my mates, Tom Kelly, had an uncanny habit of being in the wrong place at the right time. As team commander, Tom was patrolling the Lodge after the squadron had found a bomb-making factory there. Several hours of uneventful plodding later, Tom instructed his boys to chill out in one of the alleyways. To the untrained civilian eye this might have looked like skiving, but Tom referred to it as 'tactical repositioning'. The truth was that he wanted to go for a tactically prudent pee so, having left his team to their own devices, he jumped over a nearby wall – and landed next to a crate full of ready-to-launch petrol bombs. Needless to say, this was dutifully reported, and he received a personal commendation for his act of independent initiative and leadership!

Anyway, we'd flown from Herford in Germany to Aldergrove airport, from where we were bundled into the back of a removals truck to take us to Girdwood camp. This was supposed to be the first of many 'covert' operations, but by this time the IRA knew exactly what kind of transport we used, where and when we'd arrive, and on what dates our troops were rotated at the start and end of their six-month deployment.

Arriving at our new camp, I was amazed at its sheer size. The sports field alone had its own football pitch – though 'kiss-ball' was how our mud-hardened rugby players referred to the so-called 'beautiful game'. On the other hand, I was alarmed that our mortar-hardened accommodation at the bottom end of the camp was overlooked by towering blocks of flats and office buildings. The term 'fish in a barrel' immediately sprang to mind and, to reinforce the threat, a group of bullet holes in the wall at the front entrance door to our barracks served as a reminder of the soldier shot dead from one of the flats just a few months earlier.

Once barracked and billeted, our troop was informed that we'd be the camp guard force for five nights. As a lance corporal, I was allowed to be guard 2IC (2nd in command) with Dominic Keeney as the guard commander. Three sangers, 25 feet high, overlooked the north, east, and south of the camp, and my job was to post sentries to each of them every two hours. As I was escorting the first group of lads to take over from the day guard, we heard a burst of automatic fire from the New Lodge area. I reported this immediately to Dom, who in turn reported it to our squadron HQ. Several other towers also picked up on it, allowing HQ to triangulate the source to an approximate location within the Lodge – but with no troops currently out on the ground, we were told to just keep eyes on the area. We stayed alert all night, but over the next six months it happened so regularly – daily, even – that in the end it simply became background chatter, and we stopped reporting it.

Our time in-country was divided between guard duties, QRF, 'Greens' (mobile patrols in two or three Land Rovers, where you'd see two soldiers stood looking out the top at the back of each vehicle), and Saxon commanders – where we'd command the Saxon armoured vehicles to take troops out on patrol. We'd also attach ourselves to the 'Blacks', who were specialist RUC police officers. This would be in one green vehicle, and we'd follow the RUC to the incidents they were called to. This was always a good shift as these boys didn't take any crap, and it was extremely informative (and entertaining!) to watch them in action. We'd also patrol our own areas of responsibility, with either the troop sergeant or the troop leader being the multiple commander responsible for all the brics. Occasionally we'd be sent to Divvis mountain to provide security for the observation post there, and this was always a great week as we were totally self-contained, so we'd spend our time catching up on food, sleep, and the gym. Before every patrol there'd be an Int briefing, conducted by the intelligence corporal plus a senior member of the troop. Behind them was a large map of Belfast, with the Catholic areas shaded in green and Protestant houses in orange. Adjacent was the montage wall of known 'players' – members of paramilitary organisations – just in case we came across them.

We were always informed of what could happen, because although they knew of certain weapons extant in the Doyne, they didn't always know where they were. These scenarios included a long-barrelled weapon shoot against us, a car bomb on our route, fully-automatic weapons, and even improvised hand grenades. Bearing all this in mind, we'd then head out on our daily motorised or foot patrols. Each patrol would have a primary route which would be followed by the lead team, while satellite teams skirted around the outside to provide protection and deterrence against possible attacks. This was carried out in brics of four men, so you could have 16-20 guys patrolling an area, all looking out for each other. Occasionally we'd have a Gazelle helicopter, codenamed Alpha Whiskey (AW), providing overwatch and support for each team, and just the sound of it overhead made us feel safer. Team leaders carried a Cougar radio for instant communication with base, each of the other teams, and any assets – such as AW – we had at the time.

The squadron was blessed with incredible luck on many occasions – where shots were fired but missed their target, or IEDs thrown but didn't detonate, or exploded too far away from our troops to cause lasting harm. Good fortune protected us especially on 31st Aug 1993, as we patrolled the streets of the Doyne once more. We arrived at 13.00, with four teams spilling out of two Saxons. Troop Leader Jules Fuller led the primary team of the Two Zero Alpha (20A) multiple, with three satellite teams providing support. Each vehicle stopped briefly to let the teams 'bomb-burst' out – moving quickly to prearranged points to start patrolling, usually along side streets or alleyways. I always hated these, as they were usually strewn with overflowing bin bags and dog turds, but my team was still running parallel with 20A when we were told to 'go firm' (STOP!) Jules had passed a car which was reversed-parked up to the entrance of a property. He'd spotted the deformed boot and the inside filling with smoke, so he pulled us back, called in a 'suspect IED contact', and we started to cordon off the area.

The QRF arrived first, then several other teams from the squadron, followed by the ATO (Ammunition Technical Officer, or 'Felix' as we knew him). Dressed in full bomb-defusal armour, Felix cleared the car which was found to have 2.5kg of Semtex in the boot. This wasn't the commercial putty explosive used by construction companies, but the pro-grade stuff that gave you far more bang for your buck – and which, along with other 'specialised' items, the IRA had acquired from Libya. Unusually, it had been wrapped in a damp tea towel – presumably as an afterthought to make it look inconspicuous. A detonator had been inserted, and this was wired to a mains extension cable which ran from inside the house. Later, we learned that the IRA had commandeered the property, and had a spotter inside waiting for us to pass by so he could switch on the mains socket and light up the area. However, the water in the tea towel had slowly soaked into the Semtex, making it unstable, so when the circuit was triggered only the detonator had exploded, causing damage to the car only.

Had it gone as planned, there was no doubt that we'd have lost most of our primary team – but that wasn't all. Collateral damage was an accepted part of the IRA's modus operandi and, just as long as they killed the security forces, a few hapless civilians didn't matter. In this case they would have included a baby, asleep in its pram, in the front garden next door.

I kept a diary during my six months here and, reading the entry for this day, we'd returned to the Ardoyne soon after for a quick skirt around the outside to show our faces. This time Pete was the multiple commander. He'd been informed by a taxi driver that a gunman had been seen running along Etna Drive – the long road at the bottom of the Doyne – so we aimed to patrol the area quickly, then head back to camp past the Shamrock Club, which was a well-known, gated drinking den for IRA members.

In 4-man patrols such as this we'd have a point man at the front, guiding us along the planned route. The team leader would be in Position 2, supporting him, covering both sides. In position 4 was 'tail-end Charlie', who would walk backwards, giving us eyes at the rear, and he was supported by position 3, who also looked behind, and swapped places with him whenever it felt safe enough to do so.

At 21:30 we were the last team through. John 'Trigger' Horsley was point man and I was in position 2, giving extra cover by also walking backwards as we drew level with the bar. This was when two low-velocity pistol shots were fired at us from approximately a hundred yards away. You can't fire a pistol accurately at this range, especially at a moving target, but the shooter tried his luck anyway – and the problem with bloody amateurs like this one is that they can hit innocent bystanders by accident. We conducted a follow up, with no results, so we headed back to camp for the night. Just as we neared the entrance, a bright flash lit up the sky around us, followed by the faraway 'whump' of an explosion as a car bomb went off in the city centre.

At this point a normal, sane person might ask what the hell all this was doing to our mental health. It would be a good question today that might elicit an enlightened response, but back then a typical soldier would have answered, "Dunno what you're talking about, mate..."

It simply wasn't discussed. Nothing was taught. Nothing was said – even amongst your mates. We weren't aware of such a thing, and if you didn't feel right, you certainly didn't tell anyone. You carried on doing your job, keeping a brave face, a stiff upper lip, and cracked progressively inane jokes as you screwed down the valve of your mental pressure cooker a tad tighter – hoping that it would ease the pressure on the surface...

Our run of luck ran out on 21 Sept, less than three weeks later. This Tuesday morning started like any other, and at 8am we were called to the school on Crumlin Road, at the top of the Doyne. The children had found a suspicious package at the entrance of the main building. We were crashed out of camp, provided boots on the ground, and enforced the cordon until the ATO arrived.

Targeting innocent children may sound terrible – except this wasn't the work of the IRA. It was the schoolkids themselves playing tricks with us. They knew it took us at least two hours to confirm a genuine device. The IRA would normally call in a code word to the security forces, and this in turn would prioritise a response – but code words were never issued relating to the school.

A useful lesson the kids had learned was that an empty shoe box in a bag, with some wires sticking out of it, was enough to get them off school for most of the morning – and we'd play their game until they got bored and started chucking stones and bottles at us. More than once, I watched one of the RUC walk up to a suspect box, give it a tentative kick, then pick it up and stroll off to complete his bomb disposal report.

We collapsed the cordon just after 11:30 and, with a cheery "Same time next week, mister?", the children were allowed back into school. Back at camp we were given a debrief, and then told I could have the rest of the day off. This was great news as I felt mentally knackered, so I dumped my kit and headed off to the gym to beast myself, then to my room to try and catch up on some sleep. But I found it difficult to relax so, after a short time lying awake, I went for a run around the camp before returning to my room to clean my weapon. But even after this soldier's meditative routine I still didn't feel right so – I don't know why – as the team's medic I went to have a short talk with our Dr Meakin, and exchanged all our medical gear for new kit.

The lads had a full day of patrolling scheduled and, though I still had the day off, I volunteered to join the evening patrol into the Doyne at 20.00, a standard patrol with a vehicle drop-off and as many boots on the ground as possible. As the extra man, I was free to join any team I wanted, so I thought I'd flit between them all for the experience. The evening was warm and sunny as we left the chilly interior of the covered Saxon to start our satellite patrolling. I still had that odd, inexplicable feeling in my gut, but put it aside as I raised my weapon into my shoulder to scan the top windows and alleyways – always likely places for a possible attack. The usual traffic of people was present at our exit point, which was a good sign but, try as we might to engage them, they treated us like ghosts, totally ignoring our friendly greetings (we were here for their safety!) and even crossing to the other side of the road so they didn't have to acknowledge us. IRA members would often pull aside anyone who chatted to us, calling them 'touts' – informers – even if they were just being cordial and normal. There were even punishment beatings for anyone who got too friendly. We once pulled into the Doyne in two Land Rovers, with a police hotspur, and parked next to a group of young children no older than ten. I chucked several bags of sweets out to the youngsters, inviting them over to explore the vehicle, and pretty soon one of them was clambering all over the inside, wearing my helmet and looking out over the top – his boyish imagination running wild. To me, this is what the British Army is all about – people's hearts and minds, not dropping bombs on them – but my reverie was dashed when, as he climbed out, the other boys dragged him down and poured a bucket of their piss over his head, shouting "Tout! Tout! Tout!" into his face. The poor guy, who must now be in his forties, will have never forgotten this.

After several unsuccessful attempts to converse with civilians, I entered Etna Drive – and immediately felt something wrong. The street was totally empty, and most of the windows were open. Soldiers use the term 'combat indicator' when they feel something bad is about to happen. It's like when the sky darkens, and you know you need to get under cover quickly. If ever there was a mother of all combat indicators – this was it. I turned to my team to shout a warni… and the bomb went off. A huge flash not a hundred yards in front of me, followed by a massive boom and shockwave. I can personally attest to the fact that time slows down in a crisis, as your parasympathetic nervous system tries to help you make sense of what's happening within each discrete millisecond. As it tried to tell me that a blast of heat was passing over my body, I was already on my way towards its source. Jamie Smith, one of my best friends, lay unmoving on the ground with the bottom half of his uniform blown away, his boots gone, and two large clumps hanging from the massive trauma to his left leg. A nearby car's windows had imploded from the force of the homemade Mk 15 'grenade', the seats and interior in flames, and I didn't know if there was a secondary device nearby, waiting for idiots like me to show up.

Soldier of Conscience: From Fighting the IRA to Battling PTSD

The Mk 15 is made from a large catering jar, with half a kilo of Semtex down the middle, around which an assortment of nails and/or 1p coins are packed. The batteries and 'normally-closed' microswitch are at the bottom, so the simple act of the glass breaking triggers the detonator, making it a perfect, throwable IED that you could carry and even launch from a strong carrier bag – in a grim mockery of the term 'Bag for Life'.

I dropped beside him and started pulling my first aid kit apart *Shit! I need help!* as blood squirted up from the large hole in his other thigh. Instinctively I placed my hands over the hole to give direct pressure and stem the flow, then you fucking idiot realised that this wasn't the right move, because now I couldn't use my hands. My mate Scouse was sat against the wall, and I called him for help. But he couldn't – not with his knees pulled back to his chest in deep shock – and as the guys went into their contact drills I knew I had to continue on my own. I'd just pulled a field dressing from my pouch, trying to open it with my teeth *Shit! Shit! Shit!* when a female Royal Military Police (RMP) officer arrived and helped me apply it to the wound, which by now thank God! had settled down to a slow ooze.

Jamie had severe burns to both legs with associated blast trauma due to a variety of micro-missiles such as bolts, screws, nails and there's a fucking coin branded into his leg! so I used my two water bottles to ease the burns and wash away the blood to check what was left of his legs, and any further extent of the damage. An old lady, to all appearances a kindly grandmother, now stood watching by her gate just five feet away, and I asked if she'd please get me some more water to help. I'd severely misjudged the situation. Her lips tightened and, with a voice forged from cold steel plunged into liquid spite, spat, "Feck off! I hope he fecking dies".

My adrenal glands still pumping away, her words wedged like a dagger in my heart; several hours (which were, in real time, just minutes) passed until the Northern Ireland emergency services arrived and got Jamie into an ambulance, where I stayed with him for the journey to the nearest A&E unit. There, he was triaged, and a few days later transferred to the military hospital.

I wasn't aware at the time, regardless of how fast my mind was racing, of how much a lasting effect this would have on me for the rest of my life. For several days afterwards I'd see, hear, and smell every detail of the event whenever I closed my eyes. And though after a while I thought it had disappeared, I've learned that what your brain does is bury it for later processing, to help you get through the now. And the longer you leave it, like an odious job on your 'To Do' list, the deeper down it goes. But toxic waste, no matter how deeply you submerge it, still poisons the environment until it's brought to the surface and treated. Soldiers of today are encouraged to report any troubles they're having after such an experience, and counselling services are now on hand everywhere for any personal trauma. In the 90s, however, this would have been perceived professionally as a show of weakness, and unsuitability for the job.

A week later Jamie was med-evaced back to the UK for further treatment, while the RUC and military intelligence had worked furiously to identify who had thrown the device from the upper floor window. But instead of a name, they learned of an arms cache at a house in the Doyne. So, on 28 Sept, just as it was getting dark, several Saxons loaded with troops ready for payback arrived, and quickly set up cordons around the area while the search teams entered the house. Once inside, they found several weapons at the rear of the house, along with more coffee jar grenades and bomb-making equipment inside the coal bunker. The owners, a family, were arrested, but released after swearing blind they knew nothing about it and nothing could be proven. But two seized weapons, a 7.62mm AKM rifle and a .223 Ruger mini-rifle, were later forensically linked to seven killings and many more attempted murders. We knew it wasn't a plant, because our find created a tit-for-tat response two days later. I was commanding a Saxon with Trigger, and a para providing top cover. We'd just dropped off a patrol into the Doyne, and having been caught at the traffic lights we were now stationary at the junction of Crumlin Road with Tennent Street and Hillview Road. Behind us to the right was the old Flax Street Mill, which had once housed the British Army at the start of the conflict, but was now derelict. Thus stopped, and feeling safe enough on our journey back to the barracks, we were immediately shaken back to reality when a high velocity round passed between us all at head height. All three of us heard the *zzzzip* as it passed between us and we dropped inside the vehicle as one, before staring open-mouthed at each other, confirming it had been a shot, then collectively bursting into laughter because the stupid bastard had missed such an easy target!

There's a tendency for amateurs, when shooting at a group, to aim for centre mass in the belief that you're bound to hit one of them. Professionals know better, and take the extra split-second to aim for the leader in charge. An amateur with a powerful sniper rifle is a danger to everyone but, as we couldn't identify the firing point, there was no point in reporting it. It was just further proof that other exotic weapons were being stashed locally and available at any time to use against us. We did inform Dave Whalley, the other Saxon commander, because we had to drive the same route back for the pickup, but thankfully there was no second attempt – possibly because we drove the rest of the way with only our eyes showing at the hatches. But when we picked up the teams and got them safely back to camp, those who weren't wearing headsets confirmed that they'd all heard the shot, too.

> "It was in the Ardoyne, Belfast, and I was top cover, with one other, of a Saxon armoured vehicle. Wayne was the Saxon Commander. Our job was to drop a patrol off into the Ardoyne and have protection for them on the ground as they dismounted the vehicle and begin their patrol.
>
> Once happy, we started our drive back to camp. We approached a set of traffic lights and had to stop. Immediately the other top cover and I heard a high velocity bullet round pass near our heads. We immediately dropped into the vehicle, and so did Wayne as he heard it as well. The other Saxon vehicle on the patrol drop-off had already driven off, so did not hear it.
>
> We all looked at each other and couldn't believe what had just happened. In fact, I believe we actually started laughing. Thinking back to this incident now, it could have been a lot more serious – and even the death of one of us…"
>
> John Horsley

All in all, it was a good tour for the regiment because no one was killed, although we did suffer several casualties. Several regimental officers and soldiers received the OBE, MBE, or MID, and a good friend Andy 'Dyner' Dynes was awarded the Military Cross for an act of outstanding bravery. It was on 30 Dec, when I was on a mobile patrol with the RUC. At 22:30 we'd just entered the Doyne from Etna Drive, with the CO and RSM mobile patrols coming in from the Shamrock Club at the other end of the estate. We'd only got a few yards in when we heard several long bursts of automatic fire, followed by a loud explosion. The RSM's vehicle 33A had been engaged by an AK47 on full auto, followed by a failed attack from an improvised rocket launcher – otherwise known as a 'prig'. Under all this incoming fire Dyner jumped out the back of the vehicle and ran towards the engagement, before quickly veering around to the rear of the house to bar the path of any escaping terrorists. As he cleared the corner, he caught the gunman – still holding the AK – climbing over the wall at the back of the house. Dyner not only challenged and overcame him, but got both him and the weapon to the RUC, who promptly arrested the shooter and drove him away.

We arrived within seconds of the initial incident but, as always, a gathering of locals was assembling in the area. We had no way of determining if they were players, sympathisers, or simply curious – so our job was to keep them back, under mounting pressure, until a proper cordon could be created. The situation went on into the morning, as more and more troops were tasked to the area, where we'd become the natural targets for bricks, bottles, petrol bombs, and broken slates skimming through the air. The best part of the night was a confrontation between one of our corporals Pete 'Baz' Brignull, and a local IRA hardman. The IRA guy kept on goading Baz who, having the breaking strain of a brandy snap, agreed to the fight. Mr IRA, in a show of bravado, then decided to remove his coat behind him with both arms at once – probably the worst move you can make in the prelude to a fight. Using the tactical situation presented to him, Baz delivered a single, powerful right hook, knocking the guy off his feet and out cold. Then with a blown kiss and a "Goodnight, sweetheart...", Baz turned away from him to join us once more. To my incredulous surprise a rapturous outburst of laughter erupted from both the green and brown sides, and I recollected what I'd heard about the Irish loving a good fight! Baz had just demonstrated that infighting didn't just require energy and intent, but also insight and intelligence.

> "I was P-checking your man ****** and he started giving me shit. I normally play the really 'in your face' nice squaddie, with lots of 'Yes sir', 'No sir', 'Please', and 'Thank you', but decided that this knobhead was going down! We arranged to fight and, as you put it so perfectly, the rest is Northern Ireland history!
>
> I remember being given a pat on the back by the Troop Sergeant and Troop Leader, but also told not to make it so obvious next time!"
>
> Peter Brignull

Close to the end of the tour something else happened which left me ridden with guilt for years afterwards. I was manning the QRF at camp, and had been tasked with Jules to drop off Caroline – an RMP officer – at the New Lodge where she was due to join an army patrol. Just as Trigger, Josh Edge, and I were about to leave, Jules informed us of a suspect package in the waste ground outside the camp, and asked if we'd check it out. Suspecting another hoax, and not wanting to delay Caroline, Jules decided to take care of her first, then return to kick over a few old buckets before returning to base. We'd dropped her off safely and were headed to the waste ground to tackle the suspected device when I heard, "Contact! One man down! Steer New Lodge...". We immediately U-turned our Land Rovers and raced back to Spamount Street – just in time to see the RUC bundling someone into their hotspur and speeding off. As Caroline's main troop, led by the Troop Sergeant and Multiple Commander, had passed a terraced house directly adjoining the pavement, she had taken several 7.62mm rounds at extremely close range from an AK47 through a ground-floor window. The news report later used the word 'sniper attack' – but this wasn't sniping, which requires skill and patience to carefully choose your target. This was an arbitrary, close-up, fish-in-a-barrel shooting range, where you couldn't miss if you tried.

As we began to set up a cordon, part of her bric returned fire while the others got her out of further harm's way. As the IRA fled to the back of the house, Caroline's team followed them straight through the front window and the now kicked-in front door. For these angry men, the cowardly act of shooting-to-kill one of theirs, before doing a hit-and-run, was bad enough – but against a brave unarmed woman, with the guts to actually do this job, took it to a far deeper and more primal level. Moving quickly, they followed the escapees through the rear and into one of the many confusing back alleyways which interlace Belfast. Luck, however, was on our side as the gunmen had stepped in a large puddle while making their escape, and two sets of fresh wet footprints led to a back gate a short distance away. Though locked from the inside, that didn't stop it disintegrating from a single kick, allowing the pursuit to continue. These bastards were NOT going to get away.

Our guys burst into the kitchen, where two men were desperately trying to remove their blue coveralls to get them and their balaclavas into the washing machine. They were arrested immediately, and escorted to another hotspur with all the due care that could be mustered under the circumstances. There was no love lost between these two sides, because the IRA were Catholic, the RUC mainly protestant, and the IRA knew where each of them lived with their families.

But it didn't end here. During the pursuit our guys had spotted a suspect package stuffed under the settee of the first house. This turned out to be a bomb, so we cordoned off this area too and waited for the ATO to arrive. Within 15 minutes, national TV had appeared at the scene, and the whole place was buzzing with reporters and spectators. Sniffer dogs were with us on standby, and we were all stood beside the mine tape signifying the cordon when, unexpectedly, the device in the house exploded, turning the entire street into a dust cloud and completely obscuring him from view.

As first responders, we all raced into the haze to administer first aid, but fortunately no-one was injured in the blast. The other good news was that not only did Caroline survive, but she recovered. She'd sustained terrible permanent injuries to her face, back, and hand but, not only did she live to tell the tale, she continues to help the veteran/civilian community by telling her story and changing their mindsets. She is truly one of the pluckiest and most inspirational people I have ever met.

That night, and for many more afterwards, I cursed myself for getting her shot. For not stopping to look for a suspect device first, as we'd been asked – in what might have been an attempt at divine intervention. If I had – even if it had been a hoax – then she'd have been dropped off later, and maybe joined a satellite group instead, patrolling in a different location. Try as I might, I couldn't consciously or subconsciously process it to a satisfactory conclusion – where I'd learned from the experience – where I'd do things differently next time – where I'd make amends and everything would be okay again – before the next fucking job turned up. The pressure here was constant, with just no time nor opportunity. So, like so many combat soldiers before me, I simply added it to my mental 'To Do' list, and dumped it on top of the pile.

If anyone had told me back then that I was headed for a nervous breakdown – that I'd suffer for decades from something called 'PTSD' – I wouldn't have just not believed them. Neither I, nor any one of us, would have had a bloody clue what they were talking about!

Now, some 30 years later, while I don't believe I'm qualified enough to talk about the psychology of the subject, I do believe that I've earned, in blood, the qualification to discuss the causes and effects of prolonged paranoia – knowing that the only ones you can really trust are the ones fighting alongside you.

I no longer believe that some people are 'born soldiers.' Instead, I believe that some people are born good, brave, and honourable enough to take on the job when they're needed.

> "To be honest, the training scared me more than the tour itself. As the troop sergeant I knew it was down to me to bring these lads together to form a strong bond between us. For some of the lads it would be their first operational tour – and that was something never far from my mind.

Every day for six months prior to the tour we trained hard. Fitness, learning about the enemy, and the reason for us being in Belfast. Weapon training, new equipment training, patrol techniques, what to do in the event of an incident occurring, and the rules of engagement – something which I understood, but always felt that against a hidden enemy like the IRA seemed a bit one-sided.

Repetition, Repetition, Repetition – at the time it seemed like overkill, but I now know and understand why we did it. When something did occur the lads reacted instinctively, and I truly believe it saved lives.

It was mine and the Troop Leader's job to get to know the lads – what made them tick, what were their strengths and weaknesses, and also a time for them to get to know us. I always knew that whatever we thought of each other as individuals, we would be stronger together.

At the same time as bringing the troop together, I also had to manage my own personal life – trying to get my wife and two young daughters to understand that Daddy would be away for a while, but would be coming back.

But you know what? Despite the heavy responsibility – and boy, I felt it every day – I enjoyed every minute of it, and can think back of fond memories. Because despite the injuries to Jamie Smith as you've described, we all came home safe."

SSgt Pete Woods

Chapter 5

1994-95

Run Aground

Our Belfast tour ended in January 1994 and later in September I was asked if I wanted to join our sister ship HMS Brazen, a British Naval frigate at the Falkland Islands. It was to leave the Falklands, sail to Chile, through the Panama Canal to Nassau, then on to Washington DC where our soldiers would fly back. To me it sounded like the trip of a lifetime, and it certainly turned out to be.

For the first leg, we spent eight hours on an RAF flight to Ascension Island, which had played a massive part in the Falkland Islands war in 1982 as a staging post for equipment, spares, troops, and the take-off and landing runway for the unbelievably brave RAF pilots who flew and navigated the Vulcan bombers and their supporting fuel supply aircraft. A truly remarkable account of this event is captured in the book *'Vulcan 607' by Roland White.*

It's a fact that while most people have heard of the Falkands War, very few could point it out, let alone its key locations, on a map. Draw a horizontal line from Recife at the easternmost tip of Brazil, to Angola in West Africa, and Ascension Island is smack in the middle of the South Atlantic Ocean, just below the Equator. And as you can imagine, stepping off the plane was like walking into a blast furnace, because the average temperature there is 26-31 degrees Celsius all year round.

The second leg of our flight south took us the same route taken by the Vulcans, to the Falkland Islands near the tip of Argentina, though without the multiple mid-air refuels and bellyful of bombs. This took another eight hours, and we landed at Mount Pleasant airfield after being greeted and escorted in by two RAF Tornado jets, which are always a reassuring sight!

This was the closest I'd ever been to the South Pole in my life. It was the Falklands winter, bitterly cold, and we were issued with parka jackets like the ones you had at school, where the hood extends to form a 'viewing tube' with fur around the entrance. We'd wear this everywhere, even inside the cinema while watching a movie. To my surprise, everything seemed to be 'inside', with tunnels linking the cookhouse and the accommodation so that no one ever needed to go outside.

After a few days acclimatising we joined the ship but, I must confess, as soon as I set foot on board I felt claustrophobic. Not because I didn't like small spaces – if you can handle being closed down in a Scimitar tank, confined areas no longer worry you. What concerned me was being restricted to this hunk of metal which would soon be spending weeks on the open sea. I soon found out that, despite its bulk, the slightest ripple of a wave would send a surge of seasickness through our bodies, and I spent the first three days on my bed, turning fifty shades of green and throwing up constantly.

The beds – sorry, 'bunks' – were a wakeup call in themselves as to where we were. Each area was about five feet long by two feet high, the only visual and audible privacy was a curtain which you drew across to sleep, and it was obvious why it was known as a 'coffin bed'. Pete Smallsocks and I were messed with the communications guys – a great bunch of lads – and our place of work was on the poop deck. Yes, we spent numerous hours sniggering childishly whenever someone used the word in a serious context, making it clear that we were squaddies, and not matelots!

Prior to setting sail we spent several days aboard acclimatising to the vessel and crew, and I'd often chat with the naval divers (I was a keen diver at the time), asking them one question after another about their tasks and tactics. On the day before departure they invited me to watch them from the deck, as they checked the keel for anything suspicious. This procedure is always carried out before a vessel sails, for a general safety inspection/report and to check that no one had attached mines to the hull. Once they'd finished under the ship they came to the surface and shouted at me to watch. As the three of them trod water, they started slapping the water with their hands, and straight away several dolphins bobbed up beside them as if joining a well-rehearsed sketch. These beautiful, elegant animals then continued to swim around them, playing with their human friends in their aquatic playground. To me this was absolutely amazing to watch, and I felt a huge pang of jealousy because I'd have given a month's wages to do that!

For Pete and I, being on the ship was becoming monotonous, and we didn't really have anything to do other than get in the sailors' way. When positioned at our working location we could provide extra pairs of eyes on the bridge, which was okay during the day but incredibly boring at night – because all you could see against the stygian blackness of the open sea was the unadulterated open sky. Just one galaxy out of billions is enough to make you realise the sheer immensity of the universe and contemplate your own existence and purpose within it. But there's only so much soul-searching a man can do at a time and, while it would have been useful if either of us had the slightest interest in astronomy, we didn't, so instead we became 'tea bitches' for the officer of the watch.

After I'd got my sea legs, being on the ship became more bearable – enjoyable, even. We'd been at sea for several days now, well and truly in the middle of the South Atlantic. You'd look out from the deck to see nothing but an endless wall of grey in every direction – a vast and menacing ocean whose waves would regularly crash over the entire ship. When not at our allotted workplace we'd either be eating or in our self-made gym in an old storeroom. I must say though, that the food on board was amazing. How they cooked in these conditions I'll never know, but it was better than anything I'd come to expect while in the armed forces.

On 12 Sept I was due to supply an extra pair of eyes on the bridge during the early hours, as the next day was my birthday, the lads let me have time off. We were passing through the Strait of Magellan, the strip of water at the southernmost part of South America that separated mainland Argentina to the north, and Tierra del Fuego to the south. It was so narrow that, when I was stood on the flight deck, I could see both countries at the same time.

I was blissfully lying in my bunk, fast asleep, when a shudder suddenly ran the length of the ship and we were all thrown violently to the floor. The klaxons started up and the immediate response party sprang into action and locked us all in our cabins. This was to keep each part of the ship completely watertight, so if there was a hull rupture only those in the affected area would drown.

Type 22 Frigate HMS Brazen had run aground, stuck rigidly on a flat rock bed. I looked to the rest of the now-awake crew for guidance. Did they show any signs of panic? No, they didn't. What about the wireless operators with whom we shared a cabin? Were they worried, or even concerned? No, they weren't. They all knew something out of the ordinary had happened, so I watched, enthralled, as they opened a small compartment in the wall I hadn't noticed before, before proceeding to remove can after can of beer. They were only half the size of a normal can, but the concealed cache seemed to produce an endless supply. Once it was clear that nothing else could be done, Pete and I, the only pongos (the name given to soldiers by sailors) in the cabin, set up a video camera in the corner of the room to record Her Majesty's finest getting pissed up. It's one of the funniest movies I've ever watched.

Several hours later, after the ruinous ration of rum had run out, we were all allowed out of the cabin as the hull had been inspected and all leaks plugged. The crew and pongos congregated on the port side of the ship to look over the side barriers and find out what had happened, to be greeted by a massive hole that had been torn open in the bow, above and below the waterline.

We were stranded, crippled, for four days on this lump of rock, which was deep enough not to be spotted, but tall and massive enough to eviscerate a Royal Naval leviathan. We tried moving all the stores onto the flight deck at the stern of the ship to shift the weight. We even had the entire ship's company jump up and down while the engines were in reverse – but to no avail. In the end it was a Chilean tug, with the ship in full reverse, that got us off that bloody rock.

During the long wait I was standing on the flight deck with Pete, admiring the view of this desolate, frozen land when a puff of water about twenty feet from the side of the ship preceded a gigantic whale breaking the water, its tail slamming into the sea with an almighty splash, before dipping below the surface again. Yes, you see these images on TV, but it's impossible to portray, or even comprehend, the sheer scale and majesty of such an event without actually being there – which is why the natural history crew always look ecstatic afterwards when trying to describe what they've just filmed. Totally awestruck, all I can say is that I doubt I'll ever be lucky enough to ever witness such a magical, monumental experience again.

Two days after the rescue, we were able to sail on our own steam to Chile and dock in Talcahuano port. This amazed me, as there was still a huge hole in the bow, open to the sea and letting in water to this part of the hull, which must have made progress difficult, but we never saw nor felt this. The ship just glided through the water as if nothing had happened.

We docked several days later and, although we knew it was inevitable, we were still devastated to be told our trip was going to take longer than expected. We weren't sailors, so Pete and I asked if we could fly back to the UK via an Air France scheduled flight. This was finally arranged several days later, and we were conveyed to the local airport. Excited to be heading home and leaving our coffins behind, we boarded the plane and soon fell asleep in relative comfort, expecting to wake when the plane landed in Paris. Unbeknown to us, the plane had one scheduled stop – in Buenos Aires, where passengers were requested to disembark for a few hours. We didn't say a word to anyone, but our 'MOD 90' ID cards had been stapled to the front page of our passports. The customs officers' faces were a treat to behold, and they had to check and recheck to confirm that we were actually British soldiers before they let us through to the waiting lounge. Like a scene from a Benny Hill show, six

Argentinian military police officers followed our every move, and each time we stopped they'd also stop and start looking around everywhere to avoid suspicion, until we started walking and they'd follow us again. Mind you, we were probably the only British soldiers to reconnoitre their territory since 1982!

For me, life in the Lancers was brilliant and, true to their word, I was promoted, made a crew commander on a Scimitar tank, and alternated between playing rugby and deploying to Bosnia and Canada. In June 1995 I married Tracy, and had two wonderful sons, Harry and Toby. However, the marriage only lasted five years, but throughout the breakup and subsequent years we always put the boys first, and she has always been an exemplary mother to H and Tobes. I am extremely fortunate to say that Tracy and I remain friends to this day, and that she's also good friends with my wife Cara.

Back home again, in 1995 I found myself in another encounter with a group of drunken Irish nationals from Belfast. Not on the streets of Northern Ireland, but in a dance bar in Guernsey. Being in the military isn't all about going to war which – up until Bosnia, Kosovo, Iraq, and Afghanistan – had been a rare event for British troops. Most of our time was spent on courses, exercises, or adventure training – and it was during the latter that I was nearly lynched.

One thing the army teaches is how to build yourself into a small, successful team in difficult or stressful situations, and one of the best ways was to crew a small yacht. It was based in the Channel Isles, and its name was 'White Night'. We were stationed at Lulworth, Dorset at this time, so the six of us volunteered to learn how to sail in it.

We arrived in Guernsey on a Friday morning, after an overnight passage from Weymouth on the ferry. Dumping our kit onboard, and expecting to head out right away, we were gobsmacked when the skipper, also a soldier, told us that we were stormbound for the next 24 hours. To me, the water looked as smooth and level as a millpond, but he was adamant. However, he informed us that Guernsey had a reputation for its amazing night life, so as it was Friday, we were all going out tonight instead! We entered a bar which was quickly filling up with ladies, and soon became aware that they all had Northern Irish accents, so we made up a story that we were all visiting chefs. At this point the DJ called for two teams to stage a drinking competition, so four of us joined the four local chefs already on the stage. A group of drunken females had already formed on the floor below, which put them at waist level to our feet, and this elevation was to play a major part in the accident waiting to happen later on!

The game was to drink two bottles of wine through a hosepipe, with each team member taking his turn, against a clock. I was made 'team captain', and pushed to the front, just as the DJ shouted, "3,2,1, GO!" I swallowed as much of the bottle as I could – just over half – then quickly passed the pipe to the next man in line. Naturally, we beat the civvies hands down, but the DJ wanted his money's worth and called it a draw, which led to the 'Eliminator' round. This was where the team captains went head to head, and once again I was pushed to the front.

At this stage, it needs to be said that most of the ladies below me were now shouting "You'ze the fecking man!" So, with pride in my heart, and on the command "3,2,1, GO!" I downed another bottle of cheap wine through the same length of pipe. It was at this point I learned that the human stomach was not designed for this kind of abuse, that the inverse of 'What goes up, must come down' is also true, and where I blame the laws of physics for over-pressurising my digestive system. Stood like a god onstage, with multiple beautiful Irish women shouting that I was, indeed, the man, my overinflated ego quickly dampened as my overinflated stomach decided to dampen everyone in the mosh pit, as one and a half bottles of wine forced their way out the same way as they went in.

Anyone who's ever squeezed the open end of a hose pipe while water is pumping out will know exactly what happened next. I couldn't stop it, and even when I tried to shut my mouth the effect was even more widespread, as I projectile-vomited wine over every gorgeous woman stood in awe before me. And with the stage being at waist height – well, let's say that a little wine can go a long way. I was hurriedly dragged off by my mates who tried to manhandle me to the toilet, next to which was a small, occupied table. Unfortunately for the loving couple sitting together, and looking longingly into each other's eyes, my next negligent discharge scored a direct hit and ricocheted upwards into both their faces. I was on a roll and, once through the toilet entrance, the next round came up even faster than it had gone down. Contemplating the style in which I'd just redecorated the room, I realised that I was still sober – presumably as I'd not given it time to digest – so I rather stupidly followed with, "Well, that could have been a lot worse...". Because on exiting the toilet I was met by two burly door staff who promptly escorted me and my mates out of the building. Not because we'd done anything wrong per se, but because a mob of irate Irish nannies wanted blood and – not to put too fine a point on it – it was mine they had in mind.

I'm sure that most people would have had a great week sailing around the Channel Isles, learning how to go hard to starboard, and recognise the cut of someone's jib, but not me.

We'd just left Jersey one morning in rough seas when, unusually close to shore, passed a catamaran which we later found out to be the 'St Malo' on its voyage to Sark. The captain informed us it was rather tight but, as landlubbers, we were too busy laughing at Tiny Tilney hanging on for his life as we crashed through some seriously mountainous waves.

We'd just rounded the island when we came across the catamaran with most of its stern below the water and the bow pointing upwards. Yep, not content with being aboard one sinking ship in a lifetime, I had to witness another, and I realised why I'd not joined the Navy. Our skipper skirted around the distressed vessel as its crew got into life rafts, and called in the incident.

Ah well, another tale for the grandkids...

"I was blissfully unaware that anything was wrong. Blissfully unaware, that is, until 'Emergency Stations' was piped throughout the ship, and the shouting started.

Just to be clear – it wasn't panic, and it wasn't chaos. It was simply shouting of the type which is designed to get a message from one part of a 130-metre warship to another. It was gone midnight and into the early hours of 12th September 1994. I had just finished my stint on the Bridge as 2nd Officer of the Watch, and climbed into my bunk for a few hours sleep, only to be rudely awoken by the Tannoy and the commotion going on outside my cabin. Most of the 9th /12th Lancers on board HMS Brazen had spent time in Belfast less than a year earlier, so we weren't at all fazed by a sudden commotion. It was more curiosity as to exactly what was going on…

I stepped out of my cabin and watched with bemusement as people formed a human chain, and started passing long pieces of wood from hand to hand. I later learned that the wood was for the chippies, a crack bunch of part-time carpenters whose secondary function (everyone on board ship has more than one job) was to shore-up bulkheads in the event that the hull was breached, and restrict the flow of water from one compartment to another. I asked what was going on, and received the quickest of quick responses – we had run aground and I needed go to my muster station and pick up a lifejacket.

This was the opening act of a play that would last three and a half days, and which would contain everything from embarrassment, to dark humour, to camaraderie the likes of which you very rarely experience. In short, we were stuck, on a rock, somewhere in the Magellan Straights in Patagonia and we weren't going anywhere fast. The subsequent courts martial found that the Captain and the Navigation Officer had failed to properly plan HMS Brazen's passage through notoriously difficult waters. We had been steaming too quickly, in a narrow channel, and in weather conditions causing poor visibility. We missed a vital turn and the resulting understeer took us onto the rock which would become our home for the foreseeable future.

Into the third day, and a much larger salvage tug arrived from Punta Arenas which had ten times the bollard-pull of the smaller tug (30 tonnes as opposed to 3). At last, we could see some light at the end of the tunnel. Type 22 Batch 1 frigates like HMS Brazen had two sets of engines. Rolls Royce Tynes (9,700 hp) and Rolls Royce Olympus (54,000 hp). The Olympus engines were the marine equivalent of the Concorde aero engine, and used sparingly because 54,000 horsepower requires an exceptionally high amount of fuel consumption. However, in this instance the horses were not to be spared. Two tugs, 220 people jumping up and down, and two Concorde engines in full-astern finally got us off that rock.

We had been there for 83 hours. Eventually, after what seemed like an eternity, we felt the engines roar back into life and we set sail for Talcahuano. The distance to our next landfall was just over 1,000 nautical miles, which gave us all time to reflect on what had happened and what was yet to come. I didn't know it at this stage, but we would be losing Wayne Ingram and P.A. when we arrived in Chile, and they would be sorely missed. The rest of us would just have to make up for their departure by throwing ourselves into life on board ship, for the month that we would be laid up for repairs. This is another story, and just as memorable as the above, albeit for vastly different reasons..."

Keiron Russell -Troop Leader HMS Brazen

At the time of our venture to the Channel Islands I was a troop sergeant, based at Lulworth. The trip offered a relaxed atmosphere to learn the basic skills of sailing a small vessel. We were all surprised when the skipper told us we would be spending our first night, Friday night, in Guernsey, especially as the weather was fabulous, but with the guys in high spirits I accompanied them to the local bar to keep that 'fatherly figure' eye on them. The latter came into effect when four, including Wayne, had entered into a drinking competition against four civilian chefs.

This was all light-hearted humour with the troops winning by a gulp; however, as Wayne was smothering himself with rapturous applause, he responded by spraying the crowd with 1.5 bottles of white wine. Thankfully I was still sober and was able to guide him to the toilet, and safely out of the bar, so the throng of wet, angry women didn't take their pound of flesh!

The other thing which springs to mind from nearly 30 years ago was witnessing the catamaran sinking, after hitting submerged rocks. Thankfully, rescue efforts were in full force on our arrival."

Lee Barnett Lt. Colonel

"As I remember it, most of the crew were from C Sqn 9/12L, and at the time we had the honour of being the support squadron at Lulworth ranges. The skipper, who had been seconded from the RDG to look after the Royal Armoured Corps yacht 'White Knight' was Kev Smith. While we are talking about individuals, we bumped into Gary Stunell, an ex-Lancer, in a pub on Guernsey. Was that coincidence or had somebody called him? I do not know, but it was definitely in the pre-smartphone era, so I put it down to a fluke.

At some point on the passage, we were caught out in a channel squall with far too much sail. The winds appeared seemingly from nowhere and whipped the seas up. The boat was keeled over too far, and the danger with an inexperienced crew was that something was going to break. This meant that we had to reduce sail, and this was done by clipping on and developing a spiderman-like grip to the deck of the boat, then moving forward to bring down the head sail, and putting reefs into the main sail."

Dave Aslin

Chapter 6

1997

Mass Graves

In December 1997 several squadrons from the regiment were sent to Sipovo and Mrkonjic Grad in Bosnia-Herzegovina, the deployment coming under the umbrella of Stabilisation Force (SFOR). The war had officially ended in December 1995, with NATO taking over duties from the UN, and the British troops now stationed in the country changed from blue berets in white vehicles to standard-issue helmets in camo-covered conveyances.

As a corporal, I'd been allocated to B Squadron which, beyond all doubt, was the best squadron in the regiment. Its reputation was captivating – that anyone who joined would never want to leave – such was its high standard of leadership, professionalism and camaraderie. Mind you, it had some real characters within its ranks. Major Crash Charrington was our squadron leader, Charlie Cheery the squadron sergeant major, Lee Barnett backed him as the squadron quartermaster sergeant, and Captain Jules Fuller was the 2IC.

These sturdy bricks were mortared together by sergeants Mick Cowles, Steve Buckley, Mike 'Sherlock' Holmes, Carl Stone, Don Keeney, Harry Wragg and Dave Clarke who, between them, managed the five troops of twelve squaddies plus the support staff. The squadron's ethos was 'Work Hard, Play Hard', and the latter usually involved alcohol, often a 'smoker', and always the Poo-Bah. The Poo-Bah was 'born' while the squadron was completing an escape and evasion exercise run by the SAS on Dartmoor. One of our lads, Daz Martin, had kept the pelt of a rabbit which we'd dispatched for food during the exercise, plus a massive staff he'd found and carved. Its large bulbous head, plus the necklace of barbed wire he'd wrapped artistically below, made it both a mascot and primitive symbol of authority.

That night, after the exercise officially ended, the squadron leader decided to round off the event with a smoker. This was not, as you'd imagine, a group of squaddies sitting around smoking cigarettes together. In fact, all of Support Troop (otherwise known as 'Boot Troop') smoked pipes, obtained locally, just to be that little bit different... No, a 'smoker' was a massive campfire around which we'd all sit to unwind, drink, and share stories and memories. It was on such an occasion that the Poo-Bah made his first appearance.

Dressed informally, the pelt on his head, and grasping the hefty, imposing staff of office, the Poo-Bah perched himself, god-like, upon a makeshift throne made of logs, and flanked either side by the squadron leader and the 2IC. On seeing this, the other ranking officers arranged themselves in descending order around and away from him. Thus, it was decreed that from here on, at every smoker, the Poo-Bah was king – to be worshipped and obeyed by all ranks – and this mandate was never questioned, not even by Crash. The Poo-Bah's word and deed were law, so when he commanded us to cross the flames, that's exactly what we did, taking the fiery red logs in our stride as a single, united body. We were a brotherhood, we knew that we'd live and die for each other each and every day, and that this level of comradeship could not be bought by any army at any price. Naturally there were arguments, and different points of view, but none of us ever wanted out, and no one could ever get in unless invited.

A prime example of this esprit de corps was when, just before our deployment to Bosnia, we had a battlegroup parade on Salisbury Plain in an area named Imba Village. Our squadron had already formed up, with the remainder of the regiment alongside us, then next to them stood all the other arms including a Guards battalion. Well, I had two pieces of adhesive sideburns, which I stuck above my upper lip to create a large, bushy moustache. Then, once I'd checked they looked the business, I took on the alter ego of 'Tracker', a legendary SAS trooper.

Crash noticed the imposter in the parade immediately, and came straight over to me. 'But instead of reprimanding me, he asked if I wanted his major's rank slide and officers' beret to inspect the battlegroup. With surprise, but without hesitation, I accepted and the squadron formed a tight circle around us while we exchanged ranks. Then, sporting this massive moustache and major's regalia, I marched out to the front of the squadron as the sergeant major brought them all to attention, and followed me as I brazenly inspected the entire front rank of the squadron. How Lee, Steve, and Carl didn't burst into outright laughter is beyond me. But now, fully into the role, I strode over to the other squadrons of the regiment who, realising it was a 'Class A' B-Squadron prank, brought all their respective soldiers to attention for me. But my problem now was that I was about to leave the regimental guys, who all knew me, and move on to the other attached arms, who didn't. My saluting was going further and further to the back of my beret, and the crusty 'ahem' I'd affected for the occasion was becoming increasingly more pronounced and annoying. To make things worse, the first of these attached arms was *oh, shit!* a company of Guards so, quickly checking my big, brass balls were still bolted firmly in place, I strutted over to inspect them too and, to my joy, the company sergeant major brought them all to attention. Clearly, he was in two minds, but he wasn't going to argue with the rank and beret of a superior officer. His men, of course, were immaculately presented, but still I picked them up on all sorts of misdemeanours from berets raked a full degree out, parade-ground dust on their boots, and anything else I could think of. But when I stopped before a fresh-faced young soldier to lambast him, the terror in his eyes told me that he was more afraid of me than anything he'd ever seen in the field. At this point I knew I'd gone too far, and that was when I saw the brigadier arriving with his entourage.

I made a quick about-turn, and my way back to the squadron where we formed a circle once more, so that Crash and I could swap over and get that bloody moustache off for the real parade. I was also sent to the back, which was for the best because as soon as it was over, several senior ranks from the Guards made an angry beeline for me. However, our Support Troop stuck together as always and, while the others created a barrier, my mates Mick Cowles, Jess James, and Tim Godfrey got me out safely. However, the Guards had their own code of honour, and this led to a retaliatory incident later on.

The squadron was tasked to repel an enemy attack on our location. Our Boot and Guided Weapons troops were based in the village, while the other troops would fight a rolling recce screen rearward towards our location. Near the end of the exercise, and the day after our smoker, I found myself with Carl and Nick Galley in an upper room overlooking the main road, with my weapon of choice being the GPMG.

This fully-automatic machine gun is belt-fed, usually from 200-round links. We had seven of them, so Carl decided it would be fun, as a show of force, to join them all together. But with great firepower comes great responsibility, so he also agreed to help feed them into the gun for us!

The infantry eventually found and attacked our position, giving me a good reason to unprofessionally unleash fourteen hundred rounds of 7.62mm blank ammunition in one continuous, two-minute torrent of raging fury – just like in an action movie! I say 'unprofessionally' because it should be used in short bursts; the barrel was now glowing red hot, and we couldn't use it again. Yes, standard operating procedure necessitated that we carry a spare – but without more ammo, there was really no point. The infantry overwhelmed us and started to clear each house one by one. We were supposed to lie still so they could train to check our bodies and so on, but when they recognised the loudmouthed twat who'd made them look like fools on the parade, they decided on revenge. Realising I was about to get a good beating, I stopped playing dead and got up to face them. Nick and Carl did the same. The standoff lasted only a second, but when they realised that we weren't prepared to back down, and were ready to reciprocate, they wisely acknowledged the situation and left.

As well as patrolling the streets and local areas around Sipovo, we'd occasionally be tasked to a week at Red Dragon, the troop house based in the small village of Strojice. This was a welcome break from the confines of camp life, and our patrols were directed by troop leader

James Gasson-Hargreaves (GH) and troop sergeant Mick Cowles. There, we were totally self-reliant, and we loved it. We all took turns to cook, with some incredible dishes served up by the junior troopers.

We spent entire evenings playing strategic battles of Risk, or huddled around the TV watching videos of 'The Fast Show', even though we'd seen them all before. It was the camaraderie that made them feel brand new each time, and this was non-stop during our week off, during which Boot Troop took on the name 'Borg Troop' from Star Trek – suggested by Carl and Alex Mallin, the senior corporal of 1st Troop – because of the collective mindset that characterised everything we did.

To top off the week, James and Mick had proposed a formal dinner evening, for which we'd all prepared by having our suits posted from home to Bosnia. Once we'd all showered, shaved and dressed, the scene looked like a something from a mafia movie – a classy dinner table around which sat twelve burly men, all dressed to the nines, each with a military-grade weapon by their side! To us, though, it was simply a group of mates making the best of a bad time, before they got all thrown back into the fire again.

Mick was a no-nonsense soldier who, we believed, if you were to cut him open, would have been camo'd up on the insides too. Both he and James were amazing leaders who insisted that every soldier in the troop should know everyone else's job within our recon role and learn from each other. As a result, every man's weapon handling, map reading, advanced first aid, fitness, and recon skills – including how to create a sub-surface observation post (OP) and conduct a close target recce (CTR) – were exemplary, because we'd all learned from the best.

This proved extremely useful when we needed to carry out a CTR and insert an OP against a district police force who were reported to be using excessive aggression against a minority ethnic group within the local populace. This came from the UN International Police Task Force (UNIPTF), and their intel showed that these atrocities were being committed at a specific roadside checkpoint, a few kilometres from our camp.

For several days we sat around a table in a 'Chinese Council' – where any member of the troop, regardless of age or rank, could say what they thought the best plan would be. How were we to learn, otherwise? Sometimes a senior officer can miss a simple or local aspect of an operation while trying to see the bigger picture so, even though the final decisions on how, who, what, where, and when rested on James and Mick, it made the whole operation highly inclusive.

The final plan was for insertion 15 kilometres short of the location via one of the squadron trucks, followed by a tab on foot by two teams to the target location. James and my team would form Team 1, with Mick and Dave Halliwell in Team 2. Team 1 would insert on target to conduct the CTR and OP, with Team 2 providing support a few hundred metres south of us. The job would last four days, after which we'd go overt, and meet at a different location for helicopter extraction back to camp for tea, biscuits, and medals.

Mick decided that we'd take everything with us to conduct the OP – comms, batteries, binoculars, notebooks, water, rations, and enough ammo for a small war if it all went wrong. We even took the laser target marker (LTM) just in case – even though the only plane I'd seen here was the one we'd flown in on – but it all went into our bergens. The insertion went to plan and, just as the sun was setting, we were dropped off and both teams said our goodbyes, with Team 2 starting their tab sixty minutes after we'd left. We set off on our pre-determined route and, though point man Nick Galley did his best to guide us through uninhabited territory on his map, wherever we went there was always a small hamlet with a dog waiting to bark sharply at us.

Several hours later and knackered, we arrived at our rendezvous point, where James, Nick, Jess and myself left our bergens with the lads while we went forward to see if we could get eyes on the location and if their checkpoint was set up. Thankfully, the area was still deserted, so we were able to get to the designated area unobserved and then across the road to a derelict barn. On the map it had looked like an ideal spot, but close up it was too exposed and, if spotted, we'd have been totally screwed. Instead, we all agreed to move up onto the hill at the side of the road, where we could still get excellent eyes-on while remaining unseen. By this time it was the early hours so, satisfied with our choice, we made our way back to the RV, collected our kit, and proceeded on foot to our intended spot. After a quick call to base with our location, we started digging into the hill to make ourselves a home for the next few days. That's to say, we dug a hollow into the rear side of the hill to form a flat base for us all to live in, since there was already natural cover from the front. Also, this being an active OP, it meant hard rations – no hot food or water – for us all, but at least the weather was good for this time of year.

Anyone who's ever done an OP will agree that, other than the insertion and the exfil, the rest of the job is just tedium. Days are spent alternating between watching the objective, radio stag, admin (tidying up and cleaning weapons), eating, and sleeping. Thankfully, I didn't snore like I do now, otherwise I'd have constituted a major threat to our safety and security.

I loved it when night fell as, being in a wood, we'd hear the occasional rustle of animals passing by while hunting. Hell, we even heard wolves calling to one another. It started with the howl of a lone wolf somewhere in the distance, which was picked up and echoed by another wolf in a different location, and so it carried on. We might have preferred total silence at the time, but the sheer captivating beauty of the experience played a major part in why I still enjoy living, sleeping, and simply being in the woods today.

An unforgettable but essential part of OP life involves ablutions, while leaving no trace that you were ever there, so our kit included empty 2 litre plastic bottles to hold four days of urine each, and strong plastic bags for the other stuff. Using these is definitely not for the self-conscious, or those who get embarrassed easily – because it's not a job you can do alone, and it requires an extended leap of faith. Your mate would hold the bag open until the process was complete and could hopefully be trusted to keep the bag still. If not, revenge could be served by slipping your filled bag into their bergen whilst they slept so that they carried it home for you.

The next morning the police arrived as we'd hoped, and set up their spot not a hundred metres from us, giving us clear view of their movements. Over the next four days we manually recorded all their stop-and-searches, smashing of headlamps, demanding fines for driving unfit vehicles, and beating up drivers and passengers with their heavy truncheons – the usual Serb vs Croatian crap we were still getting used to.

We kept notes on everything we saw and, on the day of extraction, James instructed us to go overt as planned. As eight grimy, smelly, camo-creamed soldiers with several days of facial hair growth appeared from the woods, and sauntered confidently past their checkpoint, the realisation hit them hard. No words nor shots were exchanged, and we knew we'd done our job perfectly. We made a comfortable 10km stroll to our helicpoter extraction point and, once back at base, handed in our notes and recordings to UNIPTF for their assessment and action. Though we knew we'd never get to learn the outcome, it didn't stop us from speculating loudly about each bent copper involved over drinks afterwards.

A far more sobering mission was to help recover and identify bodies from mass graves. To this day these are still being discovered, and in 2017 at Vlasenica, between Sarajevo and Tuzla, a cluster of 137 bones – including 86 skulls – was unearthed. I accompanied Toby Masterton, our intel officer, to a burial site at the south east of Sipovo, to help oversee the identification. I don't know what I was expecting – it's not what you plan for – but what I saw *and smelled!* went beyond anything I'd ever witnessed or even imagined before. The site was believed to contain many war dead – including civilians – and I expected precautions regarding privacy and security to already be in place. But I was wrong. I'd driven us there in one of the squadron Land Rovers, and I always enjoyed Toby's friendship and insights into the work. He was a no-bullshit officer who'd chat with anyone at any level, regardless of age or rank. There was also a rumour that he was 22nd Regiment SAS, but of course you never asked. If they wanted you to know, then they'd tell you.

We arrived at the site to find there was no cordon in place. No sheets erected around the site to prevent passers-by from looking in. No police to prohibit the press or anyone else from entering. Just a huge digger at the side of the road, and two civvies carrying a club hammer and a long hollow steel pole, two inches in diameter and about six feet long. Civilians passed by constantly within mere feet from where we sat observing. Children, satchels over their shoulders and swinging at their sides, walked to school. Everything was in plain view of everyone – but this wasn't all. We were about to exhume bodies which had lain under the surface of this soil for months. Bodies which once had parents. Bodies which once had been parents. Bodies which left behind brothers, sisters, and children. Bodies which once lived and breathed the same air as us. Who had the same dreams and aspirations as us. Who just wanted to enjoy life, be loved, love and help others, and teach their children to do the same.

Those who walked past us didn't take a second glance at what we were doing. Even the natural morbid curiosity of children just wasn't present here – because war and its consequences had stolen their innocence, forcing them to grow up before their time. For these kids, this was normality.

The other sad reality was that, as the first body was found, Toby and I were sitting on the Land Rover's bonnet eating our packed lunches. And as they kept on coming out of the ground, we just exchanged the odd glance, with an occasional shrug of our shoulders. It's only now, with 28 years of hindsight, that I realise my brain had also detached itself from the reality of which I was an active part – treating the events as a normal working day *Hi mum! Good to hear you again! Guess what I'm doing for a living!*

I know from friends who've almost died that, at the moment of expected death, your brain appears to shut down, effectively fading all your senses to black before it happens – like falling asleep instantly so you feel nothing after your climbing rope snaps, as you're pulled underwater, or as your car hits the tree. Is this how the brain copes with expected emotional circumstances, too? Is this its natural way of protecting us from what should not be experienced, let alone remembered, by any human being?

Both men held the pole perpendicular to the ground before ramming it down hard into the soil, and then banging it four feet further in with the hammer. Then they'd take it in turns to smell the open end of the pole – long, careful sniffs – to find out what they'd hit. Then they'd wiggle the pipe around to remove it, knock out the soil, and try again somewhere else – and this carried on until they stopped thoughtfully, looked at each other, and nodded, which was the signal for the digger to move in. After a brief consultation with his supervisor, the digger operator set about removing the soil from the hole, gently and gradually, into a spoil heap on the right, until after several minutes one of the two men started waving his hands frantically. Toby and I made our way down to the exposed hole, and saw two green body bags lying beside each other. Both bags had been opened up, and the white waxy face of a forgotten soldier, skin taut over the bones, stared up at us with sunken eyes, while the other's massive facial trauma revealed the cause of his death – an indiscriminate shot to the head at close-range. These were brothers in arms, even in death.

Ever since the Great Plague of 1665 – the Black Death – corpses have been buried at least six feet under soil to prevent scavengers – both animal and human – from smelling and digging them up. These guys were lucky if they'd been given half this measure. I returned with Toby to our vehicle – our ringside view – unaware that I was becoming increasingly inured to the macabre proceedings, just like everyone else here.

After an hour of the digger carefully removing thin slivers of earth, and men with shovels doing the finer work, the gruesome tableau beneath was finally revealed – row after row of long, sealed plastic bags laid side by side.

After the photos were taken came the next stage – proving the contents. Each bag was opened to reveal the remains of a soldier. Some looked like waxwork figures, while others were simply skeletons in uniform. At this point there was no way of knowing what ethnicity they were, or when they'd died, but it was very clear that some were far more decomposed than others.

My mind recollected pictures I'd seen in military history books, which portrayed fallen soldiers in previous conflicts. Somehow, they always looked dignified, though I now suspect that these bodies had been carefully chosen and then cleaned up before being laid out respectfully for the photos.

Real corpses are different. Photos or videos can't convey everything, and looks are only part of the tableau. What gripped me horribly, inducing the worst fears about what had happened to them, was the smell (your nose is the most primal sensory organ of your body, and can convey crucial information from afar well before you can see or hear it). The stench tainted the air and assailed my nostrils and, while it was to be expected (these neglected cadavers had lain beside their comrades for far too long), it seared my psyche and membranes so deeply that I thought I'd never get rid of it.

Several years later, I was on the shores of Portland in Dorset, looking for crabs with my sons Harry and Toby, when I turned over a rock – and was immediately transported back to Bosnia. The smell hit me like a hammer to the head. That black sludge, sometimes found under rocks on a sandy shoreline, is actually dead and rotting organic matter, with exactly the same odour I experienced those many years ago when standing over the hole. It's the smell of death – of decomposing flesh. It's the smell of mass graves.

We continued to overlook the site for several more hours, watching bodies being exhumed and documented, until Toby decided that we'd seen everything and we should return to camp. Afterwards, however, we learned that beneath these soldiers was another layer – the bodies of children, adults, and elders from the village – and that this was done purposely. Having soldiers of another religion lying on top of you ensured that, in the afterlife, you knew who was still in charge.

To keep going we continued to work hard and play hard. The squadron was based inside a disused sawmill in a valley, with our offices adjacent to the car park, and the warehouse at the bottom now used as a garage for our tanks. Just above us on the hill was the bar, which was frequented by doctors and nurses from the military hospital located further up the hill. They were just as stressed out as we were, and they knew we ran bloody good parties to deal with it. One of these events was promoted by the troop and, in typical Borg fashion, ours would be a military affair. This time it was a Vietnam war-themed 'Nam Night'.

In preparation we declared the bar out of bounds and then, over the course of several days, stuffed a stack of sawdust-filled sandbags inside to turn half of it into a GI den. The other half was converted into a jungle, created from hessian sheets draped around the walls with tropical vegetation painted on. We even made a small bamboo hut in the corner, and before long everything was looking really good for a great party.

The problems started when I decided that a proper jungle needed animals, which led to Mick and I visiting a local farmer and using our accumulated goodwill to borrow his singular pig and two of his chickens, with the promise to return them intact and unharmed the following day. It sounded simple at the time.

After collecting them from the farm, the animals were carried to the upper floor of the bar (which, with hindsight, was probably not a good idea) and let loose in an artificial jungle that to me, finally looked like a Vietnamese homestead. After making sure they were content in their new environment, we all left to prepare ourselves for the upcoming fancy dress do.

However, my world was turned upside down when I returned to check on the pig, and found it lying dead on the floor, and the chickens gone. Without a clue why, nor what to do next, I informed Mick and Nick who were coming up the stairs after me, and Nick's solution was to splash fake blood over it – as if it had rushed the GIs from the jungle, and they'd shot it dead in its tracks.

I still had so many things to arrange before the party started, but my world continued to crumble when I saw that Mick had not only cut off one of its ears, but now had it dangling from his neck alongside his dog tags. With scenes from 'Apocalypse Now' running through my head, I knew that this had gone too far, and I'd ruined everything again due to my over-powered imagination and underwhelming lack of foresight.

But in the end no one said anything and, other than me, the dead pig, and the missing chickens, everyone had a great time. They'd all put in the effort to dress up – Boot Troop as GIs, Guided Weapons Troop the Vietcong, the doctors and nurses as the HQ staff – and the legend of our 'pull out all the stops, then add some more stops and pull 'em out too…' parties continued.

The next day I asked the squadron leader for money to buy a new pig and, to my dismay, but not my surprise, he said no. So, as our troop was on camp guard that week, I made a large 'hearts and minds' billboard about replacing a local farmer's lost livestock, and took a collection from every vehicle entering the camp. The true meaning of the word 'livestock' stayed strictly between ourselves, and by the end of the week we'd made over DM 500.

Mick and I walked apprehensively to the farmer next day to discuss compensation for his loss. To start off he wasn't overly pleased, but when we asked him how much a new pig would cost, he tentatively suggested 100 marks, which even we knew was over the odds. So when we offered him the DM 500 to cover everything, his attitude changed abruptly! Out came the Slivo in a one litre bottle and, between the three of us, we got through the lot. In fact, we had a triangular conversation in which Mick talked to the guy in German, the farmer responded to me in Serbian, and I translated to Mick in English. I'm not saying it was the Slivo, but by that point we had no problems understanding each other! Soon after, his sons and daughter-in-law arrived and he proudly displayed his financial windfall. Mick and I made our excuses and got up to leave, but thankfully one of his sons offered to drive us the short distance, which saved us an embarrassingly drunken lurch into camp. We were also extremely lucky that our troop was on duty because, later on, while Mick and I were sleeping off our stupor, the same son made a return trip with a delivery for us. We'd left our SA-80 rifles in his car.

NOTE: This incident has been included to pre-warn all new recruits of the dangers associated with alcohol, especially Bosnian Slivo which, when brewed locally, is over 60% proof.

It's not big, clever, nor grown up to drink on duty – and as 33% living proof, I only managed to achieve one of the above!

> "In 1997 I was Troop Sergeant of Assault Troop, B Squadron of the 9/12 Royal Lancers. The Troop was

responsible for dismounted operations within the Formation Reconnaissance role, including Close target reconnaissance, rear-guard actions, demolitions, or being tasked against High Risk / High Payoff Targets. The troop was commonly referred to as 'Boot Troop' within the Armoured Corps, and within the regiment had come to be known as 'The Borg' (A like-minded group or 'collective' of individuals with a hive mind against whom 'Resistance is futile'!)

When we deployed in '97, the fighting had ended, and our role was 'stabilisation of the peace' – a mix of tasks including providing an active, credible deterrent to ALL former warring factions whilst providing a neutral presence; local intelligence-gathering, including such things as locating minefields, former warring faction positions, weapons, etc; identifying sites where atrocities had been committed, enabling the International Police Task Force to carry out their evidence collection and investigations; and assisting humanitarian organisations with aid delivery and repatriation of displaced people. Our biggest threat was from land mines, of which hundreds of thousands had been laid, and often unrecorded.

The Troop was a well-trained, determined, tight unit – forged through challenging, realistic training. As Field Marshal Erwin Rommel (the Desert Fox) said "The best form of welfare for the troops is first-class training, for this saves unnecessary casualties".

Morale was high, and the troop had a 'Work Hard – Play Hard' attitude. As the Troop Sergeant, my biggest concern was boredom and complacency... Mines are the best soldiers in the world – they never sleep, they never rest, and they'll kill or maim you!

My thoughts on our deployment are mixed – the Squadron (and Regiment) did its job and, most importantly, brought everyone home alive. I am proud of how the troop conducted itself, with every man a professional soldier and a brother to his comrades.

Our presence was necessary, stopping a war in which the innocent were targeted and atrocities were carried out – often the targeting of women, children and the elderly by war criminals. Assisting in the gathering of evidence leading to the prosecution of perpetrators and justice. Helping people who had nothing, by delivering humanitarian aid, and making a difference, especially in the Bosnian winter.

All forgotten by the politicians who ordered them to go, as everyone who deployed to Bosnia saw something and experienced something that will stay with them forever – stored in that place in the mind labelled 'Not for general discussion'. For some, it is still locked in there..."

Mick Cowles – Sept 2024

One last thing I'd like to mention was the birth of my second son, Toby, while I was still deployed. I'd just returned from R&R (two weeks at home) with Tracy and Harry. Tracy was pregnant and had another four weeks to go, so I was confident I could get another few weeks in with the troop up to this date.

The day after I returned, I met the troop, which was in the middle of completing a firepower demonstration with the Americans. I was really made up about this, as we'd be flown to the target in Blackhawk helicopters, and GH would call in gun support via two US Apaches!

It all went brilliantly – with full tactical getup, our faces smeared with camo cream, and loads of shooting. The Americans were amazing and, as our guests, gave us anything we asked for. However, as soon as we landed a burly US officer walked over to us asking if a Corporal Ingram was around *Shit, what have I done this time?* I owned up immediately, and all he said was "You're going home, son...".

Without changing or washing, I was bundled into a Lynx helicopter that was already waiting to take me back to Sipovo. As we landed, my mind was still going at full revs *what the fuck have I done?* as the pilots said they'd shut down and wait inside the cockpit, because Charlie Cheery was already there at the landing site for me. He informed me that Tracy was in hospital, but they didn't have any more information, so they were going to fly me home ASAP on a compassionate flight. Alex had packed a travel bag for me, which I received at the Lynx, then I was on board and flying as fast as it would go to Split airport. The crew gave me a headset, and the pilots wanted to know what was happening, but as I didn't know much myself, I simply asked what time the flight home would leave. To my amazement, they said that they'd grounded the outgoing R&R flight until I'd got on.

I knew there'd be plenty of pissed-off soldiers on the tarmac, and hoped to hell that none of them knew me. The tension grew as the Lynx landed 50 meters from the RAF plane, and I was quickly ushered off to be met by an RAF cabin crew sergeant major. He took one look at me, still in full camouflage gear, cam-creamed up, and fully loaded with my belt-order kit, before taking my bergen and escorting me into the aircraft. Then he carefully put my bergen on the seat beside me and said "Look, I know it must be top secret, and you can't tell me, but I know you boys are always hungry…" And with that he gave me two rounds of sandwiches and two cups of tea. Bless him, he really thought I was SAS.

Once I was on board, the rest of the passengers were allowed on. Fortunately, I didn't know any of them, so I was able to milk my short spell in the Regiment until Quennie, one of our lance corporals, got on the plane and called me a total wanker.

We landed at Brize Norton where a car was waiting for me and, just like a scene from 'An Officer and a Gentleman', except in dirty camos, I was whisked away to the hospital in Dorchester to meet our beautiful new-born son, Toby.

NOTE: This incident has been included to point out that, although my career with the British Army ended extremely bitterly when I was discharged without support after sustaining an injury on duty, whenever anything happened to their troops on the ground – no matter what the situation or location – they spared no expense to get them back to their families.

1997: Mass Graves

"In 1997, when we deployed to Bosnia, it was my second tour. Prior to that I'd deployed in 1992 during the first initial deployment of British troops – the Cheshire battlegroup commanded by Lt Col Bob Stewart.

I expected much of the same as my first tour, but how wrong was I. We had trained hard for the tour as all soldiers do and, as a support troop in a reconnaissance regiment, we were capable of numerous tasks – close target recce, demolitions, OP's (both mounted and sub-surface) as well as being trained to an extremely high standard in your usual skills – arms, map reading, first aid, etc. We'd even earned the nickname of 'The Borg' – a single collective – and we relished it, especially the camaraderie and the friendly rivalry with the other support troops in the regiment.

We were deployed to be a visible force – a deterrent to the local factions who hadn't gone away, but had just stopped fighting and gone home. So just like the terrorist organization in Northern Ireland they were in the local population, hiding in plain sight.

We would regularly go out on patrols, either in Land Rovers or our armored vehicles to show a presence. We would stop and chat to locals, who would willingly offer intelligence even if they didn't realize it. On occasion we patrolled on foot in the hills surrounding Sipovo, and were often the first British troops villagers had seen since the end of hostilities. We were never idle, and even at the troop house 'Red Dragon' or 'Delhi Spearman' we would patrol or be conducting troop PT, much to the amusement of the locals – one even asking why we were being punished! We had to explain this was standard physical training for the British Army.

We played hard too, and as a troop and squadron the ethos was 'Work Hard Play Hard'. Obviously, the squadron bar was the focal point of numerous social events – these occasionally being in fancy dress, the standard only limited by the individual's imagination. We earned a reputation, and other visiting units even asked about the tales they had heard about the Reece Sqn in Sipovo, particularly the 'pig incident'...

We did our job and we did it well. Morale was high in the troop and the squadron for the whole tour, and everyone came home. I have mixed emotions about Bosnia, having seen both sides of the coin – the violence and ethnic cleansing in '92 to the stabilization in '97. It's a beautiful country, and the people are so welcoming and resilient. It seems our presence was welcome, as peace remains but the factions are still there. Hopefully, the political stability in the region will remain"

Dave Hallewell – June 2023

Chapter 7

1997–2003

Stefan

Over the ensuing years, life carried on as normal within the regiment. Squadrons were sent to Kosovo, where we lost a comrade to a 'mine strike'. This is when your armoured vehicle drives over a landmine, and you experience the devastating effect the shockwave has on the fully sealed-in, cramped space above. I attended one course after another with a view to gaining promotion, and this finally came in 2000 when I was posted to Lulworth to undertake training as a Schools Gunnery Instructor.

This was an intense time, being scrutinised daily on my ability to deliver lesson plans on ordnance from 30mm Scimitar guns to 120mm Challenger 2 tanks. In addition, I was new to the mess etiquette of senior non-commissioned officers, so not only was I studying hard each night in my room, but I also had to prove I could do the right thing at the right time in front of the RSM!

On top of this Tracy and I had separated, and she'd started divorce proceedings. Though still totally naïve, and not understanding why at the time, I had to contend with this too. My mind and mental state were starting to cause me problems – sleepless nights, excessive alcohol, periods of feeling depressed and isolated – but I put it all down to the stress of training and didn't say, let alone do, anything about it. Instead, I spent my evenings in the tank park hangers, or in classrooms standing over 30mm guns, or machine guns taken from the inside of a turret, and stripped down to show their working parts while training rounds were being fired from them. I'd watch soldiers revising, parrot fashion, what they had to say in their lesson. Occasionally I'd see a soldier talking to an imaginary class, extended pencil pointer in hand, asking questions of an empty space, and even replying to a question answered correctly or incorrectly.

Thinking about this now, the word 'cuckoo' springs to mind, though this was our normality at the time. Each lesson I delivered was graded from A to F, and enough 'F's would not only get me returned to unit (RTU'd), but also back to the rank of corporal. I was so incredibly relieved when I passed the course and went on to spend two wonderful years in the Dorset countryside meeting people who were happy to chat with me. This was a far cry from the streets of London I'd known, where natural landscapes had been replaced by high-rise buildings, and clean fresh air by exhaust fumes.

The Army was generous in providing married quarters at the camp, so Harry and Toby could stay most weekends – and towards the end of my deployment I even managed to get my foot on the property ladder, buying a small, end of terrace, 'two up/two down' house in Weymouth.

I returned to the regiment in 2002 to take over 1st troop B Squadron. This was a really lucky break for me as I'd not been a troop sergeant before – but I gained two amazing corporals, Roger Jones and Daryl Gibson, both of whom worked tirelessly behind the scenes, keeping me up to date on what was needed to keep life in the tank park running smoothly.

The regiment was based in Hohne, near Belsen in Germany, and needed to be available for fast deployment anywhere it was needed. We had the usual posting to Batus training area in Canada for several months, but in 2003 we were pencilled in for another tour of Bosnia. I really wasn't looking forward to this and, even though it had been ten years since the regiment had first set foot there, the memories were still traumatically vivid. Somewhat apprehensively, we landed at Banja Luka airport in March 2003 for the start of a six-month tour, based at the metal factory just outside the city. This was the home of SFOR, where British troops mixed with American, Dutch, Canadian, and Italian forces inside this extensive compound. To my enormous surprise, I was given my own ISO container for accommodation, complete with TV, fridge, and sofa kindly left behind by the previous sergeant. The lads were given the same, though with two to a room. This was a far cry from previous tours where it was not uncommon to barrack 4-5 soldiers, complete with their bergens, webbing, and civvy clothing all in one container!

B Squadron had its own compound, away from the Highlanders to whom we were attached, and at the end was the communal shower and toilet block. An hilarious episode happened in this area, but we'll come to that later.

After Sarajevo, Banja Luka is the next largest city in Bosnia and Herzegovina, and its history can be traced back to the Romans, whose ancient ruins were still on display. It's a vibrant place with its own university and a young population just short of 200,000, and life there in 2003 seemed idyllic to me. Or so I thought.

A new troop leader, a great guy named John Farrer, had been posted to the troop, and while he fulfilled his role superbly, he was always keen to get as much advice as possible from me – his troop sergeant. As a troop we were given an area of operation to patrol and, most importantly, win the hearts and minds of the people. Whichever country, city, or town we were sent to, we would respect the local community and their customs, and this included learning their language, their greetings, and their ways of life.

1st troop was given Laktasi, a small municipality 20km north of the city. Intel reports from the area were pretty sketchy, so we set to work with an open mind, patrolling out daily from our base in Scimitars or Land Rovers, with a pre-determined set of goals to achieve. One of these was organising arms amnesties, with the intention of removing the plethora of live weapons which still remained in the community. To this end, we headed out north one morning into the hills and forests, with no set location, but to try and speak to as many homesteads as possible. We tried many places, but old memories lived on, and most of those who actually admitted owning weapons were unwilling to relinquish them. One family, however, agreed to hand over an old hunting rifle, before inviting us to stay for lunch. Their house was in the middle of nowhere – their nearest neighbours several kilometres away – and pretty soon they had Scimitars parked one after another on their front lawn, with the entire troop sitting under a huge homemade parasol which sheltered the massive wooden table in their garden. The weather was glorious, the sun beat down, and a soft breeze blew through the forest surrounding the house as plates of food were paraded out to us – meats, cheeses, breads, vegetables, and pieces of their own free-range chickens that had been running around a day earlier. Their hospitality was absolutely amazing, and we were greeted as if we were family members returning home.

It was during this celebration that something magical happened. Seated at the end of the table was the grandfather of the family who, other than the occasional utterance, had been very quiet so far. All of a sudden, he raised and pointed a finger directly at me, and said something for the interpreter to explain. Several exchanges took place between them, and I could see the interpreter becoming interested, then fascinated, by what was being said.

The interpreter then addressed me, saying that the old man had lived in this house his entire life. He remembers that, during World War II, two British airmen were being transported back to England via the local resistance. They'd been shot down somewhere close by, and had ended up at this house. As a child he'd been seated at this table when his father and grandfather had hosted these two brave men, who had been seated exactly in the same place as I was now. He went on to explain that Yugoslavia had been an ally to Great Britain during WW2, and how Josip Tito had come to power leading the partisans, one of the most effective resistance movements in occupied Europe. The whole troop listened intently to every word, and you could have heard a pin drop as story after story flowed from his lips, tales of real wartime exploits and the hardships experienced by everyone during the recent fighting. This was raw history, from a man old enough to have been there and understand, yet young enough to still remember. It was one of the most amazing and memorable experiences of my life, and one which I have told and retold many times over.

Another regular task was arranging meetings with key personnel, from restaurant owners and church leaders to government ministers. A particularly difficult target was the chief of police, who would always find a way to cancel our pre-arranged appointment at the last minute. He turned out to be the slipperiest eel I'd ever tried to net and, like the elusive Pimpernel, I needed to think smarter to nab him! Which is why, on the day of our next planned meeting, I arrived at the police station a full hour early and, as I entered the lobby, we caught each other's eye along the corridor. Immediately he made a beeline for the back door, and I shouted, "Hey!" after him while vaulting over the counter in pursuit, which made him quicken his pace to avoid and evade me. The next scene was like a James Bond movie as I gave chase along the corridor and burst through the back door – only I tripped on the raised lip at the bottom and rolled arse over tit across the baked soil of the car park, before coming to a stop in a sprawling heap, feeling like an idiot.

I'd missed my chance, and his patrol car was already speeding out of the parking lot, but at least, I thought, no one had seen my glorious sortie – until I heard two men giggling behind me. Still lying bruised on the dusty ground, I turned over painfully, looked up at them with an innocent expression, and said, "Dobro jutro" ('Good morning') as if I did this all the time. They both burst into laughter, and I joined in too. After they'd helped me up and I'd brushed myself down, I introduced myself to these merry gentlemen (God bless them...), unaware that several lives were about to change forever.

They turned out to be Dragolslav Kovacevic – Minister of Defence for Laktasi – and his personal assistant Milos Savic. The minister invited me to his office for coffee which, under the circumstances, I readily accepted. There's an old military saying that 'when one door closes – there's usually a window left open...', and I was never one to miss such an opportunity!

The minister spoke perfect English, so I quickly went to tell the two troopers, who'd travelled with me in the Land Rover outside, to chill out while our impromptu meeting was being held, and Jevena, our interpreter, that her services wouldn't be needed. The two gentlemen then escorted me to their office, which sported bare walls with plain painted surfaces, and a small framed flag of Bosnia Herzegovina hanging on the wall – typical of all the official buildings here. I was served Bosnian coffee and, once the three of us were seated comfortably around the table, we made our introductions.

I started by telling them how we worked, about 'hearts and minds', and the problems I'd faced with the police chief, while trying to obtain snippets of intel from them about illegal weapons and anything else of importance. Thoughtfully, the minister produced a picture of a young, smiling, fair-haired boy about 3-4 years old, and I was shocked to hear (and see!) that this toddler had been born with a rare and severe facial cleft. Where his nose should have been was a large, protruding knob of flesh-covered bone which was slowly working its way into his nasal cavity and forcing his eyes further apart each day. The image took me completely by surprise, and I just stared silently, heartbroken but mesmerised, at this poor, innocent child. Holding back the tears that were forming, I forced myself into a professional composure, and asked who this youngster was. And was shocked again as Milos responded that the boy's name was Stefan Savic – his son.

Milos took the picture in his hands for several long seconds, staring into it, and I suddenly felt the man's character – a stalwart father, a proud and decorated war hero who had been severely wounded in his country's conflicts, and had gone on to experience a new depth of parental heartbreak, far beyond anything I could comprehend. He had tried, unsuccessfully, to do everything he could to give his only son a normal life. And he would clutch at any straw, no matter how small or flimsy, to achieve this goal. He looked at me with the ghost of a hopeful smile, and asked if any of the hearts and minds in the British Army could do anything to save his son's face?

I didn't know what to say, so I asked if they'd done any research, and the minister explained that they'd approached a specialist hospital in France which could perform the requisite series of operations for 30,000 euros. But this was Bosnia, and an a injured veteran like Milos hadn't a chance in hell of raising anywhere near this sum.

What could I say? I was genuinely devastated, as my Achilles heel was children in need – especially those who were ill or, even worse, had been abused. I knew this wasn't my job, nor was it within my authority, so I had to be professional about it. Even though I just wanted to go back to camp and do anything I could to get the money, I already knew that in our role there, getting the permissions and funding to help one child would be an incredibly difficult, if not absolutely impossible and unprecedented, task.

Still emotionally shocked by what I'd seen and heard, I told them that I'd talk to some officers back at the camp and, while I couldn't promise anything, I would let them know the outcome. As I stood to shake his hand, Milos gently took mine and placed the picture into it, insisting that I keep it as a gift. I thanked him for this, saying that it would help greatly, and left the office still contemplating the problem. We drove back to camp in silence, and fortunately our troopers knew that when the sarge was quiet, there was usually a bloody good reason for it.

As soon as we were within our own lines, and our weapons back in the armoury, I went to our Squadron Leader's office to discuss what I'd just experienced. Major James Farrer (no relation to John) was a young, energetic, and honest leader who was liked and supported by every soldier in the squadron and regiment. He was sitting behind his desk perusing some local maps, which he quickly rolled up as I entered. I didn't ask him what operation was about to go down but, instead, showed him Stefan's picture. Like me, he was visibly mortified and wanted to know more. I made us both a brew and we sat for some time discussing what we could do to help get this child a better start in life. He asked me if I realised what this would entail, and innocently I said that I did. After all, with the massive military budget available to run our operation here, raising 30,000 euros shouldn't be that difficult, should it? There was a long period of silence as he held the picture, staring intently at the small, cheerful face. Then he put it down, tapping his desk while looking intently at me, before finally stating that he would grant his permission, but only after running it past the colonel first. After thanking him, I went straight to the interpreter's accommodation and asked her to call the defence minister with an update – and that as soon as I heard anything I would let them know.

Next day, James called me back into his office and gave me the permission I'd been hoping for. The colonel had approached the brigadier for the final nod, but with the go-ahead from these three officers we were set to go. I thanked him profusely but, just as I was about to leave, he warned me, "Sergeant Ingram, be careful. This has the potential to become a gargantuan task for you…" I just grinned at him with my usual cheeky charm, and replied, "No worries, sir!"

Little did I know that he would be chillingly correct, and that this would be the first day of a 13-year lone, uphill struggle, during which my emotions would reach immense highs, followed by long, dark descents into self-doubt, where I'd feel totally out of my depth, with no idea how to make it to the next stage. Even worse, and despite my confident promises to his trusting parents abroad, that my naivete and inexperience could eventually, inexorably, and inevitably let this child down.

I went straight to the troop and told the boys what had happened, then explained to them how I was going to raise the funds needed for the operation. My plan was straightforward – I'd write to a multitude of celebrities and, before the end of the week, the funds would have arrived in an account all ready to be handed over to the family. See? It was so simple – it couldn't possibly go wrong!

At the time we had these 'bluey' letters, specially printed for service personnel abroad, and which we could post free of charge as long as they had a BFPO address (British Forces Posted Overseas). So for several days I sat writing the same lines over and over, ready to send to various offices in the UK where, I'd been informed, they'd be forwarded to the right people for redistribution. We also arranged a meeting with the family at their house, so I could tell them what was going on, and to finally meet Stefan. It was the obvious next step, and the first of many to come. I knew that, to progress further, it needed to happen, but I kept putting it off due to the emotional conflict I was in. It took me a lot of effort to reach this conclusion, but in truth this 210 pound, 6' 2" lumbering lump of a sergeant was actually terrified of meeting a small 4-year-old child.

The next day I took along the entire troop to visit the family, and as they lived up a steep hill in the middle of nowhere, we decided to go in the Scimitar tanks. Yes, writing this now, it does sound like a ridiculously excessive exercise in moral support, but I still remember how extremely nervous I felt at the time, wondering how I'd react to meeting this little lad. I've always had a soft spot for children caught up in conflict, in wartime or at home, and their stories always bring me to tears. My heart was pounding, causing adrenaline to course through my system, and if I'd known then how to be honest with myself, I'd have already realised that my greatest fear was to turn up at their house as a blubbering wreck.

They lived up a long dirt road, halfway up the hill, in a beautiful scenic area surrounded by trees and extensive panoramic views of the Bosnian landscape. Milos was there to meet us as we pulled up, and the moment I emerged from my 12-ton armoured security blanket, he put me at ease by immediately wrapping me in a big brotherly bear hug. He then shouted for Stefan, who was playing with a football in the yard, to come over – and suddenly here was my first memory of him. The little chap started to run excitedly over to me, before pitching headlong into the dirt track a few feet from us. A sudden intake of breath broke from the whole troop as we all watched, horrified, at what had just happened, and I suddenly realised the true courage and determination of this boy. He simply got up, brushed his slightly bloodied knees, and carried on walking towards me with the happiest, most adorable smile I'd ever seen in my life.

As I knelt down to meet him on his level, he greeted me with "Hallow…" in a small, broken-English voice, and then reached up to kiss me on the cheek. And that was when our collective nervousness evaporated as we all saw that, apart from his physical deformity, he was just like any normal boy. And in that same defining moment, I instinctively knew that I would protect this beautiful child with my life, while doing my utmost to ensure that his operation went ahead.

I was introduced to his mum Slavenka (familially, Slava), his slightly older sister Nina, his aunt Dzejna *(pron. Jaynah)*, and his grandparents. Then the whole troop was shepherded to a table outside, where dish after dish of food was brought out for us. I'd rarely encountered this level of generosity and hospitality anywhere in the world, but I was to experience it many more times afterwards.

After we'd all finished, and washed it down with bottles of Pivo (a Bosnian lager), Milos, Slava and the grandparents listened intently as I explained the details of what we'd done to date. I'd written to many celebrities, we would plan a football match between the locals and SFOR troops, and numerous fundraising events were being planned around the camp. While we were engaged in conversation, several younger members of the troop were playing football with Stefan, gently kicking the ball to him to kick back. But at one point my father's intuition kicked in as I picked up on the lack of noise from that area. I broke off talking and turned around to see Stefan, wearing his small-scale boxing gloves, sparring off against Chris Harris, one of our troopers. Chris was sportingly taking jab after jab on the chin from Stefan, who was giving his all, but I called a break when Chris pretended to land a gentle right hook in return!

> "In 2003, and whilst out on a routine patrol as part of SFOR, Wayne Ingram became involved in a series of events which lead him to meet Stefan (a small Bosnian boy) and his family. When Wayne returned to the Headquarters, he explained the background, the situation and the need for our involvement. It was clear that we would support at least his initial investigations in what, if anything, he could achieve. It quickly became clear that Wayne could achieve a huge amount.
>
> There was still significant tension between the various factions in Bosnia, and this story bridged many of those divides and gave an opportunity for the broader community to come together and support Stefan on his journey. With

unrelenting compassion, grit, and determination, Wayne initiated a process to help Stefan which took years to complete. The success of this story is beholden on Wayne, Stefan, Stefan's family, GOSH, and all the sponsors and stakeholders who have given their support and time for a genuinely excellent cause.

It is truly humbling to see what they have all achieved, and it both restores faith in humanity, and shows that there are good people that can, and will, help in a time of need."

James Farrer

Chapter 8

2003

Amnesty

Although my personal goal was now set on raising money for the operation, I still had my duties to the troop. The amnesty was still in place, and our patrols continued to gather intelligence and collect illegal weapons. Rog and Daryl took on the work leading some of these, allowing me to continue with the mundane tasks of running the troop, inspections, servicing, and training.

One morning I received an informal letter addressed to me, and was *Wow!* surprised to read that it was from David Beckham. He'd written that, while he'd been genuinely moved by my appeal, he unfortunately had to decline his help because he'd already directed his charitable donations for this year. I learned that he received regular requests like mine, so he studied each one and chose several worthy causes each year, and was unable to help at this time. He went on to wish me luck, and asked me to contact him next year if I still needed help.

His was the only response I received, and I would like to thank him via this book for not only taking the time to reply, but also for his honesty and candour. I was unaware of the numerous donations he makes each year, totalling hundreds of thousands of pounds, to good causes.

Sir, I salute and thank you for your kind, honourable, and great-hearted response, your philanthropic work, and for the many thousands of people you help each year.

It was a start, though not the one I'd naively hoped for. But it had put the bit between my teeth, and I knew I had to change my tactics –

because at this rate the money was not going to come flooding in as I'd originally thought.

Rog, Daryl and I sat around a table one night discussing how this could be achieved, and Daryl suggested a football match between the locals and the B Squadron troops. This seemed a great idea as I knew that everyone loved kiss-ball *(Sorry!)*, so the next day we took the troop to visit the local football team, and our interpreter explained what we were trying to achieve to their manager. He turned out to be extremely passionate about football and good causes, and said that he had several talented players – so he'd not only produce a formidable side to play against SFOR, but also stage a fundraising barbeque afterwards!

If I'm honest, although my fundraising for Stefan evolved into a love for a family that has continued ever since, I originally saw it as an exercise in 'hearts and minds' – doing what we could for the local populace – and a football match would be an ideal way to bring a community together for a united cause. To make my point, I took out Stefan's picture and left it with him.

On returning to camp, I asked the interpreter to inform Slava of what was happening, and the following day we visited them with a fuller explanation of events. Once again, enormous quantities of food were bestowed upon us and, as we finally arose to head back to camp, Slava handed me a huge hock of smoked ham and a crate of Pivo for the troop. I passed these dutifully to the lads on my return, then dispiritedly went to see James to update him on how much we'd raised so far – exactly £0.00, which wasn't exactly the nice round figure, nor the number of zeroes at the end, that I'd hoped for...

The squadron wanted to cut down on the opposition's penalty chances, so I was placed in goal with Roger, also a keen rugby player, in defence. The weather was glorious, Stefan was on the side-lines with his family shouting their support for the locals, and the football skills displayed on that historic day were amazing – though sadly not from SFOR. We lost 7-2 to Bosnia, but in addition to raising a whopping

6,000 euros for Stefan, a post-warring community had triumphantly united for a common cause.

Watching afterwards at the barbeque, I was happy to see every single player, along with every spectator, having a great time – as if old friends were recalling their history, and the fun times they'd had together before the ravages of a bloody war had torn them all apart.

I was discussing the match several days later with the defence minister and Milos, and we all agreed that it was a tremendous start for the community, and already a fifth of the way towards our financial goal. The minister then asked if there was anything he could do at this point to help us, so semi-seriously I said that we could do something similar for the arms amnesty, as we needed to get as many deadly weapons off the streets as possible. I was surprised when he and Milos turned to each other and started a discussion, before turning back to me and stating that he would help. He knew that word was already spreading about British soldiers attempting to help a local boy, so the minister said that he'd circulate news of the amnesty too, and also set up collection points around each municipality. This would take place the following Saturday and, at the end of the day, any weapons collected would be taken to a central point for B Squadron to collect. To me this was amazing as, not only did it have the potential to remove more firearms from the community, but now the initiative was being led by the locals – and not forced upon them by SFOR.

On the Saturday morning, Milos told me to bring a vehicle to the centralised area for 5pm. Although the amnesty started at 7am we wouldn't be needed until the collection time, and I guessed that it would look better if we weren't there standing in plain sight all day. However, I was certainly not expecting what we found when we got there. Along with several troopers, Daryll and I arrived on time in two Land Rovers to a scene of utter amazement. Eventually finding my voice, and mimicking that scene from 'Jaws', I turned to Daryll and said, "We're gonna need a bigger truck…"

Laid out tidily before us were nearly two hundred assorted rifles, from hunting to military spec, including AK47, AK-74, and AK102, plus several mini-machine guns including two UZIs and an Ingram (no relation!) In a separate pile were over ten thousand 7.62mm cartridges, and around thirty handguns with countless small boxes of 9mm rounds. In one corner stood two RPG7 rocket launchers with twelve rockets stacked neatly alongside, and in another were several boxes of hand grenades, plus fifteen anti-tank mines!

We all stood transfixed at this significant arsenal and, once we realised the gravity of the situation, I called for an explosive ordnance (EOD) representative to ensure that everything was safe to take back to camp for decommissioning. An hour passed before Dez Henderson, the squadron sergeant major, arrived with a 4-ton truck, and even he was gobsmacked when he saw, first-hand, what a tremendous gift we had ready for him.

Milos and the minister stood there throughout, smiling at their achievement and the joy on our faces. The sobering thought, though, was that while a massive arms haul such as this (which had been under our noses all this time) had now been removed from the community, we were certain that this was just the tip of the iceberg, and there was much more work to be done. My only regret now, recalling this impressive haul, was not informing the colonel or the brigadier, because this would have been an imposing feather in the squadron's collective cap!

The weeks rolled on with a variety of fundraising events taking place, including pulling a Land Rover around the camp for 10 miles, positioning barbecues in strategic areas throughout the camp for everyone to enjoy and donate, and even several games nights in the sergeants' mess. The balance in the 'Stefan account', which I'd set up with the regiment for this specific purpose, now stood proudly at over £10,000. We were a full third of the way there, and we were just getting into our pace.

The PR side was building, with reps from 'Soldier' magazine accompanying us to the family home. The photographer took shots of Stefan seated on my lap, for which they granted me unlimited permission to use in any future fundraising exercise, and when the magazine finally arrived we were all overjoyed to read their article – especially the details of how to send donations to the account!

For the first time in my life I learned about 'syndicating' – where newspapers share articles with each other – because the story started to appear in other periodicals, with different slants. First in women's magazines, and then the national tabloids, each time with details of the fundraising account. The balance continued to rise steadily without us doing a thing, and I took note of how, once I'd got the ball rolling, the press could be used to our tactical advantage – one which I'd continue to channel over the next thirteen years.

I also learned that reporters changed certain elements of the news to suit their own needs, and this became apparent when I was introduced to one from a well-known Scottish tabloid. We were attached to the Highlander battlegroup at the time and, as they wanted to capitalise on any PR opportunities, they invited this reporter to the camp.

Now – I understand that stories are written to sell newspapers, and although it was English soldiers who had met Stefan, and English soldiers who were fundraising to help Stefan, stories about English soldiers would not sell a single, solitary newspaper in Scotland!

Which is why I stormed into James' office and started raging about a picture of Stefan, on the front page of the paper, wearing a Tam O'Shanter on his head! Highly protective of this child, whom I now felt was being exploited, I didn't hold back, and James sat back patiently as I fumed, vented, raved, and ranted, with expletives included in every sentence for good measure.

Once I'd stopped, still breathing heavily, and he was satisfied that I'd thrown my last toy out of the pram, he quietly told me to sit down, and then asked, "Is the story bringing in money?"

To which I hesitantly replied, "Well, yes…"

He then leaned forward, smiled softly, and asked, "So does it matter who gets the story, as long as Stefan gets his operation?"

And that's when I realised, he was right. I'd made it too personal. Too prideful. Even made it my story. While in fact it was bugger all to do with me. From here on, I decided, I'd just let them do their job, and crack on with any story they wanted to write – just as long as it helped Stefan.

During my time in the Army, serving with the 9th/12th Royal Lancers, I had the pleasure of serving in Bosnia on two occasions – first in 1997 and secondly in 2003, both from Banja Luka metal factory. During the 2003 tour I was a troop corporal, my sergeant was Wayne Ingram, and the troop leader was Lt John Farrer (JF). The second troop corporal was Daryl 'Gibbo' Gibson. I worked with the Tp Ldr, and Gibbo worked with Wayne.

Because JF and I were out in different areas around Banja Luka, we never really knew what the others had got up to until the end of the day's tour, when we would discuss our day's events. I remember on one occasion Wayne stated that he had bumped into a bloke called Milos. They got chatting and the conversation got on to his family, his wife Slava, his son Stefan and his daughter Nada.

Stefan was eventually taken to GOSH, where the surgeon assessed and agreed to do the operation. Due to this, Wayne continued to raise money through various means for Stefan, as the flights weren't cheap. Stefan has been back to GOSH on several occasions for follow up operations and check ups. On one occasion I met up with Slava, Nevena, and Stefan in London for the day, and it was great to see them. Nevena is Slava's sister, and Stefan's auntie.

From the initial day of meeting Milos, Slava, Stefan, and Nada, the whole troop has stayed in close contact with them, and they have become good friends of a few of us. Several years later, I even rode my motorbike from the UK to Bosnia to see them. With the help Wayne had sorted out for Stefan, Milos reciprocated this by assisting Wayne and his section recover a massive number of weapons that were hidden/dumped, used in the war, and no longer needed. This helped clean up the local area, and reduced the chance of the weapons being used again in anger – a fantastic result.

The first time I saw the weapons was when I returned back to Banja Luka from patrol, to find Wayne, Gibbo, other troop soldiers, and the squadron sergeant major laying them out for a photo opportunity, as it was quite an achievement! There were rifles, pistols, and a variety of other weapons systems that had been adapted to fire a bullet or projectile. I seem to remember it as being the biggest haul of collected weapons ever found.

I would like to take this opportunity to say that I thoroughly enjoyed my time working under Wayne and JF. Wayne is an inspiration to lots of people, and has a heart of gold.

Well done, Wayne, I salute you! Even though you weren't commissioned LOL!

Roger Jones

My Memories of Bosnia...
Meeting Stefan

Meeting Stefan and his family pretty much changed the whole tour as, up to that date, it was pretty mundane with Int gathering and business surveys and the odd OP Harvest. Getting to know Stefan and his family, and feeling the hospitality of people who, compared to most of us, had very little to give, was very special. Considering the condition he was dealing with, he was a nice and pretty happy little lad.

The Football Match

Having been tasked with picking the side for the football match, there really was only one decision when it came to Wayne playing – in goal as 'Chopper Harris'. Otherwise, he'd have definitely have broken a few shins, and possibly Anglo-Bosnian relations, partly down to his ability to run around like a headless chicken, and his complete lack of skill."

Darryll Gibson

Chapter 9

2003

David Dunaway

As most of our funding was coming from the UK, I wondered if it would be possible to get Stefan's operation here, too. As long as we could get the proper standard of treatment, it would be brilliant for further publicity should we need it, it would eliminate another language problem, and it would be on home turf, making it easier for the British Army to stay involved. The obvious place to start asking was the world-famous Great Ormond Street Hospital (GOSH) for children, in London.

Dez gave me permission to use the squadron's telephones for long-distance calls, and I explained to the receptionist who and where I was, and what I was trying to achieve. Maybe it was my attitude, or my inexperience, but I got the impression that she thought I was a prank caller. In desperation I went into more and more detail until, after several long minutes, she heard the plea in my voice and gave me the number of David Dunaway, a cranial facial consultant.

David wasn't at the hospital at the time, but I eventually managed to reach him at his surgery at Harley Street. Thankfully, GOSH had already alerted him to expect a call from an odd squaddie in Bosnia. This had already piqued his interest, and he started by asking me about our military infrastructure here, how the citizens were managing after the war, and if the hospitals were coping. As I did my best to explain everything I knew, I became aware that this Harley Street specialist was giving me no impression that I was wasting his time. He was genuinely concerned about the people here and, to my great surprise, actively and attentively listening to every word I said. Little did I imagine then, that David Dunaway would not only become a good friend, but also ending up saving Stefan's life.

He then asked me about Stefan – everything from his age and social circumstances to his medical history and the local facilities available to him. Finally, he wanted to know how Stefan looked so, holding the picture in front of me, I did my non-expert best to answer all of his queries down to the last tiny detail.

When we'd finished, and he'd considered all the circumstances, he said that he might be able to help, but he'd have to see the computerised tomography scans before meeting Stefan in person. This was the breakthrough I'd been hoping for, so I thanked him profusely and said I'd do everything I could. As I put the phone down, I was buzzing with excitement. Yes! Not only had we got specialist advice from a hospital and a surgeon, but I now knew specifically what needed to be done next. Stefan's once-speculated operation was slowly becoming a reality.

I went to the family home to inform them how much money we'd collected so far, my conversations with the UK, and that we'd need a CT scan. Stefan's aunt Dzejna had been an interpreter during the war, for the Americans, and understood English perfectly. She said that the CT scanner had been looted from Banja Luka hospital, but knew of another (or quite possibly, the same one) at a different address in the city. Not wanting to lose momentum I asked if she'd contact them and, if an appointment could be arranged, Slava's permission for us to take Stefan.

We got an appointment, and the following day I met Slava and Stefan with our interpreter outside a large, nondescript, detached house in the streets of the city. Ascending a flight of stairs to two enormous front doors, we entered a spacious foyer with a single desk in the centre, and a man sitting behind it. Our interpreter started to speak, but the man interrupted in English and asked us to fill out the forms which he said were necessary for a private procedure to take place. He then guided us towards a flight of stairs down to the waiting room, where he said the CT engineer would meet us. We thanked him and followed his instructions, and were soon sitting in the waiting room gazing expectantly at the door to the CT Room. When it finally opened, we looked up in astonishment. Wearing a white coat and holding a clipboard was the same man we'd met upstairs, who was now audaciously asking if we were here for an appointment.

Wondering if we were in a scene from a 'Carry On' film, I confirmed that we were, indeed, here for a CT appointment – to which he informed us that the scanner was currently being calibrated, and would we please wait? With the door still open, we watched him go into the CT Room, remove his white coat, put on a brown one, pick up a mallet, and start to hammer gently at part of the scanner. Once he'd completed his task he removed his brown coat, put his white one back on, and re-entered the waiting room to tell us that the calibrations were complete and we could continue with our consultation!

As Slava, Stefan, and the interpreter stood up, I held back and motioned them to go on without me. Call me a coward if you want, but at this stage of my life I had two children and I certainly wanted more. Imagining that the radiation leakage from this 'private practice' probably exceeded that of Chornobyl, I excused myself on the grounds of checking my guys waiting outside, and immediately reverted to my military Nuclear, Biological and Chemical (NBC) training – that of personal protection, exposure time, and distance.

After treating my two troopers to a coffee in a local shop – which ideally would have been located several miles away in an underground, lead-lined bunker – I returned to the consultation building, this time imagining us taking bearings using nothing but the clicking of our Geiger counters, until we finally gazed upon the unearthly, tell-tale glow of ionising radiation in the distant sky.

The session was over and the same guy, now the receptionist, told me that everything had gone well, the cost was 250 euros, and I could collect the copies in two days. To my surprise he kept his word and, by the end of the week, I was in possession of two scans which I could send to David Dunaway on my return to the UK.

I returned home for my two-week rest and relaxation (R'n'R) break, well and truly set on keeping the fundraising going. As soon as I arrived in

Weymouth, I contacted my friend Mark Vine, author of 'The Crabchurch Conspiracy', who reported Stefan's story to the Dorset Evening Echo, our local newspaper. The staff really took it under their wings and, soon after, broadcasts began running alongside it on our regional radio station, Wessex FM. This resulted in a meeting with Calvin Stone, owner of the well-known Weyline taxicab firm and who, I quickly realised, was not a man to be messed with. But he had an enormous heart where children were concerned, and I consider myself extremely fortunate that we've become great friends. Calvin made me aware of various avenues along which I could raise money, and put me in touch with Kim Llewellyn and Sandra West, the charity coordinators of Weymouth's main Asda store. Both ladies agreed to have buckets positioned at the end of each till, with a large picture of Stefan and myself stuck to the outside, so that shoppers who already had their wallets and purses open could donate. They also allowed me to cook a barbecue at the main entrance, and provided the meats, bread, and condiments for free. I set up a stand there, with a picture of Stefan for reference, but local media coverage from the paper and radio had already got the ball rolling, and now everyone could see and hear first-hand why the money was needed.

Calvin arranged for me to appear at a local football stadium, featuring Weymouth FC, and it was there that a group of us stood, buckets in hand, on their Saturday afternoon match day collecting more money. I was even invited to the Weymouth Pavilion where, after reading the article, Jim Davidson had generously donated a four-figure sum. Several locals had taken it on their own backs to do their bit too, and held bric-a-brac sales, or staged their own barbecues to help. Funds continued to flow in from all directions, and were fast becoming a flood. I was beginning to see how generous the Great Brits really are.

My leave was soon over but two things happened near the end. Our international work hadn't gone unnoticed, and one evening I received a call from James Farrer who said that he'd just been in front of the colonel, who had been in front of the brigadier. Our PR was now making national news, and potentially involved the hearts and minds – the very core – of the British Army, and if I did *not* make this work then we would be well, truly, and royally fucked – and that losing our jobs would be just the start.

No beating about the bush there, then, and the old saying 'shit always flows downhill' immediately sprang to mind. I realised that if, for any reason – including my inexperience with international medical aid, the handling of funds, and the national media – things did go wrong, and I failed to deliver on my promise, then the Army would treat me like an unexploded bomb, and I'd be on my own to deal with the national and personal shitstorm that would bury me deeply. Though desperately tired after jangling yet another tin all day, I didn't sleep well that night.

More happily, the next day David Dunaway called to say that he'd received my recorded delivery, and could we discuss the scans? Although they weren't the best quality (I hadn't gone into detail as to how we'd acquired them) he said he might be able to help, but needed to see Stefan in person before making a firm decision. *Oh, thank God! We're moving forward...*

Having spent my entire R'n'R meeting the press, doing chat show interviews, cooking burgers, talking with the public, and attending various public and private events (including a garden party), I was back in Bosnia preparing for the forthcoming visit of Pope John Paul II to Banja Luka. Briefing after briefing ensued, in which we covered how, why, when and where troops were to be positioned, and what we'd do if and after an assassination attempt occurred.

There were the usual rumours of a possible attack against His Holiness, but I just told the troop that if they continued to act in the same professional manner as always, then everything would be okay. For the event, however, we were to be deployed only as reinforcements, sitting at a roadblock several kilometres from the city centre.

During the planning period, when things were a bit quieter, I arranged to meet Milos and the minister at their local coffee shop in Laktasi. The threat level was low, so I drove there in one of the squadron Land Rovers accompanied only by Chris and an interpreter. Chris stayed in the vehicle as I sat in the coffee shop, dressed casually in army-issue shirt and trousers with the mandatory pistol on my belt. I updated them as to the amount of money raised, what David had said, and how we were going to tackle getting Stefan into the UK, which would likely involve a lot of wheeling and dealing. And it was then, while we were chatting, that the American military entered the city. I knew the Pope's visit had heightened everyone's awareness of security, but this was just sheer overkill. Four Humvees (High Mobility Multi-Purpose Wheeled Vehicles) were moving slowly and deliberately down the street. Standing out of each was a soldier scanning the area with a .50mm machine gun. Either side, on foot, were soldiers patrolling in full battle order – helmets, body armour, weapons in the shoulder and, of course, black sunglasses. The five of us just sat aghast at this excessive show of raw military force and firepower, which would have been over the top even in Northern Ireland.

As they patrolled past us one of the American soldiers spotted me and did a double-take, surprised at a soldier being so under-dressed for the occasion. In response to my fellow comrade-in-arms, I gave him a smile, a wink, and a cheery "Alright, mate…"

This really brought home to me how much the British Army is head and shoulders above all where hearts and minds are concerned. Fighting, shelling, and bombing is not our goal, and we'd rather abide by the rules and customs of each country we enter and show respect to everyone we meet. Having said this, anyone who wants to try their chance, and poke a docile hornets' nest, can expect long-lasting and indelible consequences.

Anyway, on the day of His Holiness' visit we set up and manned a roadblock, where absolutely nothing whatsoever happened. Except that after several hours of attentive boredom an old lady approached our vehicles carrying a tray of drinks and several small, homemade cakes. Through the interpreter she asked if I was the soldier who was helping the local boy. Having received affirmation, she came over, kissed me on both cheeks, and thanked me, saying that the drinks and cakes were for my soldiers in gratitude for their help.

It goes without saying, though I'm going to say it anyway, that this small but wonderful act of appreciation made up for the entire wasted day, plus many others here, too.

Epilogue

When the papal visit was over, and we were all back to normal, Milos invited the troop to spend a night with him and his friends at a hunting lodge in the middle of a forest north of their house. We arrived at the designated area in our Scimitars to find the campfire well-lit, and several small groups of Bosnian men sat around it drinking Pivo. After locking all our weapons (hearts and minds, remember?) in the vehicle, we joined them around the fire drinking beers with each group, and singing song after song well into the early hours. Eventually, with everyone but the designated drivers totally intoxicated, we all went to sleep fully-clothed on the dry forest floor.

In the morning we woke as normal and, after a communal breakfast cooked on the open fire, said our goodbyes as friends and returned to base. I was feeling a bit under the weather, so I instructed the lads to chill for the day and then walked to the communal shower block (the one I mentioned earlier) to clean up before heading back to rest for a while. And that was when I noticed my chest was covered in small parasitic ticks, all heartily feeding on my O-negative blood. There must have been twenty of the bloated little bastards, so I called the troop out of their rooms and asked if they had the same, with most saying that they did. This necessitated a troop meeting in the shower room, where we all stripped naked to buddy-up and check each other all over. Ticks can spend hours searching around for the warmest and cosiest dining areas before settling down to feast, which means exactly what you think it means.

Incongruously, it was at this precise moment when a British military chef walked in to use the urinal, only to have a room full of naked men turn around as one and stare up at him – half of them bent double having their bum-cracks inspected, the other half on their knees behind them, grimly spreading apart a pair of arse cheeks, as if to say, "I'm going in..."

Unaware that he'd walked into a perfect Monty Python sketch, he just stood there, open-mouthed, taking in the situation before his lips tightened and, uttering a peremptory "Hmmph", did an abrupt about-turn, and exited the block considerably faster than he'd come in.

And that's when the entire troop erupted into a collective, uncontrollable fit of laughter because, like a startled rabbit caught in headlights, the expression on the guy's face had been absolutely priceless.

My Memories of Bosnia… (cont.)
The Ticks
"The thought of a hog roast and a few beers out in the forest, after a day going house to house trying to collect weapons during OP Harvest, was something to definitely look forward to – knowing what Bosnian hospitality was like. Luckily, some of us had the common sense to set their bed up on the roof of the Rover before getting a few Pivos down our necks – as the forest floor isn't the best place to kip… Can't say I was sad about missing the butt-naked bendover inspection most of the troops went through, though I'm sure that Chef enjoyed it!"

Darryll Gibson

Chapter 10

2003

The Operation

Back in 2001 at the Gunnery School, I'd stupidly broken my right lower leg and ankle in five places, which required two weeks of intensive surgery, and having plates and pins inserted. It didn't help at the time that I was probably the fittest I'd ever been in my life, so having my leg in a cast was a major hindrance to everything I did back at the camp. My mental state was still in tatters after the divorce, and physical exercise had always been my panacea for this sort of thing.

After eight weeks of this I was going nuts so, as soon as the cast was removed, I celebrated with a 5-mile run on a familiar course. I knew it wasn't going to be easy, and I was going to have to push past the initial pain, but instead of easing up it got steadily worse and, around the 3-mile stage, it became so unbearable that I had to stop and walk the rest of the way. When I say 'walk', it was more of a stumbling, lop-sided gait as I received a severe stabbing jab each time I transferred weight to my right foot.

After a two-mile hobble, furious for not completing something I'd normally find easy, but also with a creeping suspicion that I'd fucked myself up badly, I limped embarrassingly back to the hospital. They took one look at my freshly swelling ankle, and I had to confess what I'd done. I received a severe telling off, another healthy dose of radiation in the X-ray room, and a new cast. Not only had I undone all their good work, but I'd also broken and weakened the bones even further at the site of the original fracture.

This really came back to bite me when I slipped on patrol in Bosnia. I didn't say anything to anyone, and instead ingested loads of Ibuprofen to cope with the pain, which I felt certain would soon recede. Most soldiers will tell you that Brufen is the first drug of choice for army medics and quacks (doctors) to prescribe, usually in a little brown bottle full to the brim with little pink tablets.

A few days later, jumping onto a Scimitar tank to help service the gun, I banged the bloody thing again, converting the chronic pain to biting agony, so I returned to the med centre where the doctors referred me immediately to the field hospital in Sipovo – the home of my last tour in Bosnia. And here, the surgeon told me I needed yet another operation, which they carried out under general anaesthetic. Once I'd come around and got my head together, the Dutch doctor asked me how I was feeling, to which I said I was okay. He told me that the operation had gone well, he'd cleared out some loose bony matter and had removed the old pins and plates. I thanked him profusely for this, unaware that the events leading to the end of my career had just begun.

With an open wound on my lower leg, I was sent home for another two weeks' recuperation, but while arranging my flight home I had a brainwave. Even though the Stefan account now stood at a healthy £40,000, I knew we were going to need every single penny and more for the operation to become a reality – especially in transporting him and his family to the UK, and getting accommodation for them *Hmm...*

I was good friends with a movements clerk in the RAF, a top guy who used to facilitate fast jets for our recce exercises. This was always a win-win situation, as we'd get to practice our forward air controlling (FAC) and laser target making (LTM) skills, while the pilots got to hone their flying manoeuvres.

I phoned the guy and, thankfully, he was still in post. He'd seen our fundraising efforts on TV and understood exactly what we needed, while warning me of the Gordian Knot of red tape we'd need to cut through before going ahead. He asked me if they had their travel visas, to which I happily told him (a white lie) that they were safely in my possession back at camp – *this needs to be my next job...*

Several more minutes passed before he agreed to get them quietly onto an RAF plane, which would take them from Bosnia to Brize Norton – but only if:

1. I could prove they had a return flight booked, and
2. I promised that nobody would know that we'd used an RAF plane!

With the outbound flight now sorted, I approached Dez to tell him what had occurred, and what was needed of him. Then, once he'd promised to organise it all at our end, I booked my own flight and went home, feeling pleased as a pig in his own shit.

True to his word, Dez helped to get visas for the Savic family in Sarajevo and, in July 2003, our RAF colleagues flew them to Brize Norton. Dez had pre-warned me that this was a one-off situation, which needed to be kept very hush-hush. But of course, someone had tipped off the British Forces Broadcasting Service (BFBS), who were set up exactly at the right spot to film the arrival. I hurriedly briefed them on the situation, giving them permission to get their footage, but insisting that the plane had to be kept *strictly out of shot* at all times.

Later on, I wished that I'd got someone higher up to supervise them. On the BBC news that evening was an image of Stefan, Slava, and Dzejna descending the steps of a grey plane, its RAF emblem clearly in view. Even worse was that the entire regimental recruiting team turned up with the BBC news crew to welcome the family as they alighted, giving the situation further credibility and publicity – wanted and unwanted. Little surprise then, that my RAF mate never accepted a single call from me again…

The following day we made our way to Great Ormond Street Hospital, where we met Prof. David Dunaway for the first time. I was humbled by his composed nature, his gentle mannerisms and the ease with which he made everyone feel, well, at ease. He was the perfect dad, grandfather, and favourite uncle all rolled into one!

He admitted Stefan into GOSH for four days, during which thorough examinations and another CT scan were carried out – this time without the unregulated radiation leakage! Slava was allowed to stay by Stefan's side throughout, while Dzejna and I made the daily walk to the hospital and back. Now that we were finally at this point, the one shared by thousands of people in hospitals every single day, there was absolutely nothing military involved and everything was down to me – and as we sat in silence I felt just as nervous as the others. *Shit, what if it can't even be done?* as we awaited David's final prognosis.

Once the tests were complete, the Savic family went for a walk around the local area while I chatted freely with David. He said there was a high probability that he could do something, but as Stefan was only four there was no way of avoiding further operations on his face as he continued to grow. Every such operation carried a risk, and operating so close to the brain each time would make the job more difficult, so I had to keep in mind that something could go wrong at every single stage. He then asked me how much I'd raised to date and, when I told him, he smiled and told me that he would not be charging for his services. I just gaped at him, astounded, because this was the kindest bombshell that had ever been dropped on me in my entire life. *He'd done this before!* Not only had the operational costs had just been scaled down astronomically, but I'd just witnessed a spontaneous and voluntary act of humanity that would change my way of thinking forever.

Two days later the family flew back to Bosnia via British Airways, and I did the same the following day. Several more days of anguished waiting followed before I received the call from David, who finally confirmed that yes, he'd be able to operate on Stefan, with the first requirement being the removal of all his teeth. This was to give David more flexibility while deconstructing the skull, and reassembling it correctly afterwards.

Next, he warned that although the main operation would pose a considerable risk to Stefan's health, other facts would need to be considered by his parents. He'd found that essential bone matter was missing from Stefan's forehead, which not only increased the potential risk of infection from meningitis in future, but that the disease's proximity to his brain would almost certainly be fatal. He'd also identified that the nasal airway had never formed properly, and this would need correction along the way. Like any layman, I was blissfully oblivious to the enormity of what he was describing. Not comprehending most of it, I simply latched on to his conclusion that, once the operation had been completed successfully, it would unquestionably save Stefan's life.

With this basic understanding, I drove confidently to the family and told them everything I could in my own terms, then waited patiently while they discussed it together. It couldn't have been easy for them. *Is it ever?* But, thankfully, the overall decision was that the surgical procedures should go ahead. I then informed them that, as I'd just been promoted to Staff Sergeant, I'd need to return to the UK within the next two weeks. However, I promised to keep them up to date via Roger or Dez, and that I'd see them again in the UK once everything had been arranged.

Back at Gunnery School I was able to get some hands-on training prior to my new cadre starting up. The PR juggernaut was still rolling, with the Dorset Echo displaying Stefan's face in almost every issue. Wessex FM, too, continued to host regular petitions for donations. In my free time I continued to raise funds at garden parties and barbecues, and the Stefan account grew increasingly in stature.

Weeks turned into months and, in the background, arrangements for surgery were being made. As visas had already been granted for the previous trip, this was no longer a practical issue, and I used my natural charm to secure accommodation near Kings Cross, a short walk from the hospital. It wasn't the Dorchester by any stretch of the imagination, and at night my digs felt like those American movies where the main character opens his window to hear the ambient sound of traffic, screams, and gunshots. Okay, this wasn't the Bronx, but it was certainly Mecca for the homeless, traffic noise was 24/7, and drunken swearing with the occasional scream littered the background. I'd lived in worse, though, and it was cheap enough to cover all of Stefan's future operations in the years to come.

The date was finally chosen for Monday, 13 October 2003, which required Stefan, Slava and Dzejna to stay in the UK for over a month.

My job was to meet them at Heathrow and accompany them to their accommodation. Calvin agreed to supply all the taxis free of charge during this time and, for good measure, all the journeys we'd ever need to make afterwards.

They arrived in early October, giving them time to settle in, arrange all the pre-operational appointments, and have time for sightseeing in between. Despite what was to follow for all of us, this was the first time any of them had seen the centre of London, and it was pure joy to watch little Stefan's excitement shine through in everything we did and everywhere we went. The greatest astonishment for them, I noticed, was the fast pace of life here compared to the relative tranquillity of Banja Luka. Well, except for Dzejna, who was already well-travelled and took it all in her stride.

I was approached by 'Soldier Magazine' who wanted to continue their coverage of the story, so on a free day we met up with a reporter and cameraman to discuss a schedule of ideas. Portentously, the day was gloriously sunny with a clear blue sky, so first stop was the London Eye, which gave us a mind-opening overhead view of the city. Next was Hamleys' toy shop, where the manager escorted us personally around the entire store. It was a child's paradise, and the icing on the cake was when he invited Stefan to choose any toy he wanted, free of charge. Of course, the store had everything, including huge construction sets, the latest electronic games, and the most popular action figures from the big screen. We spent what felt like ages going up and down the escalators until Stefan finally made his momentous choice – a cheap, battery-operated toy chainsaw. I was surprised at his decision (as a somewhat older child, I'd have gone for the biggest and most expensive!) but when I asked Dzejna why he'd chosen this, she said that it reminded him of his father, cutting firewood back home.

Stefan was admitted to GOSH's children's ward as planned, to have his teeth removed prior to the main surgery two weeks later. As always, the care and attention bestowed on him was amazing, and he was bedded in a single room which allowed Slava to stay by his side throughout. While I was relieved (and excited!) that we were finally about to start, I couldn't help but feel worried about the potential risks involved. However, what Stefan was about to experience was classed as minor surgery and, as he still had his milk teeth, their removal wouldn't be as bad, nor have the same potential consequences, as the permanent removal of adult teeth.

As soon as he was admitted, and the door swung closed behind him, Dzejna took Slava's hand and guided her out of the building. Nothing like this had ever happened to my own boys, and I couldn't imagine what was going through her mind right now.

We sat in a coffee shop near Russell Square Gardens, drinking one cup after another, and the two ladies practically chain-smoked while they called the ward every half-hour for updates. Finally, we learned that Stefan was out of theatre and in recovery, so we hastily made our way back to the hospital to await his return to the ward. I don't know what I was expecting but, other than looking very sleepy, he didn't look any different. *What goes through the mind of a 4-year-old child when the adults around him pull out all his teeth?*

Dzejna and I left Slava to be alone with him while we went for more coffee, and I continued to feed my newly-acquired passive smoking habit. The hotel was only a few miles away, so we went back to freshen up, and for Dzejna to collect the necessities for Slava's overnight stay in the ward.

I have always been amazed at Stefan's courage throughout every one of his procedures, and Slava for her calm support under pressure, but I remember that first day clearly. I didn't know how Stefan would be taking it by now. Would he be crying, nervous, fidgety? To my great surprise he was none of these. As I entered the ward, he was sitting on his bed playing with hospital toys, and as soon as he saw me his face lit up and gave me the biggest, happiest, gappiest smile I'd ever seen in my life. He was discharged from the ward next day, and advised to rest until he was needed again the following week. This allowed everyone to relax and enjoy London, and for me to return to Gunnery School for a few days of finger-pointing and talking to myself as I prepared my lessons. However, my return wasn't quite as quiet as I'd hoped, as

I quickly learned that media coverage is always a double-edged sword, and the saying 'Sleep with the devil, and wake up in hell...' cuts both ways.

I couldn't blame the Echo for pushing their local good luck story, but this had now spread to the women's magazines, the national tabloids, nationwide news, and breakfast television. My bloody mobile never stopped ringing, with constant offers of special-interest stories and TV appearances – and while they continued to bring in much-needed revenue for any future operations, they went on every day from early morning to late evening, with each caller trying to catch me when I wasn't busy!

I really felt for Slava and Dzejna, who were supposed to be relaxing in the capital of an unfamiliar country, but here I was, phoning them every hour requesting permission for stories to be written on their behalf, and informing them that TV shows wanted them in the studios. I now felt desperately uneasy about this national public side-show, and with myself for asking these questions, because I knew that they hated press intrusion into their family affairs. But I couldn't see another way of funding Stefan's operations, other than through public support. And if you don't inform people, then you deny them the opportunity to get involved.

On the 25th I booked myself back into our 'Kings Cross Hilton', and met them all in their room there for Bosnian coffee. I have to say that Slava makes the best coffee I've ever tasted – and for those who've never tried it, here's her recipe:

- Get a tiny coffee cup, and a metal coffee pot, like the ones you see cowboys boiling over an open fire in a movie
- Boil some water (not in the pot!)
- Put your ground coffee granules into the bottom of the pot, and pour the boiling water over them
- Now bring the pot to the boil
- Scoop off the foam and drop it into your tiny, empty cup
- Pour the boiled coffee into the cup on top of the foam
- Enjoy, and imagine yourself as a cowboy...

Bear in mind that the ground granules won't dissolve like instant coffee, and you'll inevitably get some in your cup, so when you're nearing the bottom don't down the rest in one go! You can trust me on this one because I did just this, on my first tour in the Balkans while on patrol and meeting a Serbian colonel. His soldiers made us coffee and supplied the Slivo while we got to know each other through polite conversation. But at the end of the meeting, I instinctively downed the dregs of the small cup – and immediately wished I hadn't. My mouth was suddenly clogged with a thick brown sludge, which was too viscid to swallow, but too embarrassing to spit out. Unable to speak without gobbing all over the colonel, I turned away with my glass of Slivo, swilled it quickly around my mouth, and swallowed the bloody lot. For the remainder of the conversation my teeth looked like they'd never been brushed in their life, and I couldn't sleep for days afterwards!

This time we were joined by Milos and Nada, Stefan's younger sister, both of whom I'd arranged to be flown over for the main operation. I knew the mammoth task that lay ahead, and felt it only right that the family be united before it happened. It was great to see Milos again – this great bear of a man with a constant, reassuring smile on his face. The kind you earn by experiencing everything, and still rising above it all. We chatted for a few hours in their room, and I was thankful that I'd returned to Dorset when I did, as the ladies had spent the entire time walking around London exploring one shop after another, which would have been my idea of hell. However, Slava knew that I'd be returning today and had bought cold meats, chicken pieces, bread and pickles for us all to share, which I thought was a wonderful gesture. They'd also started referring to me as their brother, including me as one of their family, which completely bowled me over with the sheer honour of it. *But would they still feel the same way after the operation?*

That evening, I went for a couple of quiet beers in a pub along Euston Road. This was after I'd already gone to my room for a good night's sleep but, instead, found myself pacing the room, switching the TV on then off again several times, then lying on the bed, then getting up and sitting in the chair to read a book, then putting it down after reading several pages without absorbing a single word.

Have I done the right thing? I'd involved an entire family from another country in my own nationalistic passion project.

Who the fuck gave you that right? I'd got permission from the British Army, hadn't I? *Yes, but these are civilians, and this isn't a military operation.*

The entire country is on my side. Surely that makes it right? *Maybe, but right or wrong is decided by motivation. It's all about you, isn't it? What you want. Isn't it always about you?*

And what if it all goes wrong? A loving, trusting child would be dead, or disfigured helplessly for life. How would I answer to his family, who trusted and even loved me? How would I face the nation? *Alone, mate – that's for sure...* As I sat, my head went down, my hands came up to my face, and I wept uncontrollably. Actually, that's the wrong word. What's the word for when you cry your fucking heart out and you can't stop and you're a grown man but no one can see you so you keep on crying and crying until there's absolutely nothing left?

It was only then, in this now-empty mental void filled with nothing, that I realised... What must the family, and its individual components who did not have my luxury of solitude, be feeling? For them, it would be all about Stefan – their son, their nephew, their family. So why should I be any different? Hadn't I just been made an honorary member of that family, bonded by the love and heartbreak we all shared for that wonderful little boy? I knew, there and then, that deep within my heart I had an eternal, inseparable bond with the Savics, and this included an overwhelming sense of love and protection for Stefan, for whom I would willingly die, over and over again in any battle, to make things right for him. And that's why we're doing this, together, as a family.

Sunday 26th Oct. The Day had finally arrived, and we had to be at the hospital for 9am so that Stefan could book in for his pre-op. Pulse, blood pressure, temperature, and even temperament – everything needed to be checked by the medical team. The paediatric nurse, the anaesthetist, and

David Dunaway himself, this incredible cranial facial surgeon who had steadfastly refused to charge for his services, all had to be 100% certain that everything was in order before surgery could go ahead, because it was scheduled for the very next day.

Later that morning David visited Stefan, and met his father Milos for the first time. The whole family was gathered in the single wardroom where Stefan was staying. Slava asked question after question, and I listened as Dzejna interpreted David's answers for her. I can't imagine how challenging it must have been for both parents, even after all the preparation. Not only were they fully aware of how desperately their son needed this critical surgery, but they had so little control over it, and had to put their trust in a complete stranger.

David was amazing, as always. He knew the high risks involved, but at no point did his body language or vocal tone suggest anything but confidence. I've known a lot of soldiers, many of whom gave their lives in action, and David is one of the coolest, talented, and professional men I have ever had the good fortune to meet.

Thankfully, due to his age and innocence, Stefan seemed oblivious as to what was about to happen to his face, taking it all in his stride and trusting us totally. He just sat on his bed, playing with a cuddly crocodile that the children's ward had given him. When I say 'playing', I was pretending to attack him with it, which made Stefan laugh in the same room as other, more serious conversations were taking place. Was I trying to take Stefan's mind off the impending events, or my own?

When every possible question and outcome had been discussed, David and I left Slava, Milos, and Stefan to talk. David had come in on his day off, and left to go home. Dzejna and I went for another coffee. I thanked her sincerely, and she returned to the Great Ormond Street family accommodation. I went to the pub on Euston Road again for some quiet time, and to drown my apprehension in a few real ales. I knew absolutely nothing about surgery, but I'd been helping to publicise and raise money for this child – if anything happened to him, it was all on me.

I arrived again at 9am the following morning, and found Dzejna and Milos already there. I'd arranged to meet BFBS TV in a coffee shop

Soldier of Conscience: From Fighting the IRA to Battling PTSD

next to the hospital, to do an interview for their documentary 'Stefan's Story', which would be aired several months later on the Forces Network TV. I think the interviewer's name was John. I don't remember. We sat drinking coffee while he asked the usual questions – How did I meet Stefan? Why did I decide to help? How many operations had he had so far? And so on until he came to the question I'd been dreading – How was I feeling right now, on the day of the most crucial operation? I froze, and had to take several deep breaths, scrunching up my eyes, while my mind tried to come up with an answer for which there were no words. Still going around my mind was everything I'd heard could go wrong. And this was a child... My body started trembling. *Oh fuck, not again.* I knew I was about to make an absolute idiot of myself on camera. This was worse than last night. My stomach was churning, an emotional time-bomb was about to detonate inside me, and I felt so indescribably scared.

I've always been a moron when it came to hiding emotions, and I've never been a good liar (*isn't that an oxymoron?*) so I asked to stop the interview for a toilet break. As soon as I entered the single washroom, even before I'd locked the door behind me, I burst into tears – big, unstoppable, uncontrollable tears. I couldn't hold them back, so I tried to keep them silent so as not to alarm anyone outside, and this just made it worse. It must have taken me several minutes to purge the stress, and wipe and wash my red and swollen eyes with cold water, before I looked presentable enough in the mirror to face John again. For fuck's sake, I was a man, a soldier, and we're not supposed to cry! But this is the price men pay for being human, too.

As soon as I entered the ward, I felt the tension in the air. It wasn't just me, but from everyone but Stefan, and even he must have felt it. I don't know how long we waited, in heavy silence, but finally the anaesthetist arrived and asked Slava to sign the consent forms, before the porters came to wheel Stefan to the operating theatre. Slava, Milos, and Dzejna followed them to the anaesthesia room, and I respectfully stayed behind to give them family time, despite their kind attempts to invite and include me.

They returned some forty minutes later, and it was the first and only time I'd ever seen evidence of Slava crying. She was a brave lady from a war-torn culture where survival depended solely upon strength of character, and to me this was the ultimate proof of how critical and distressing this event was in their lives, so far away from home.

Such memory I have from serving in the Balkan regions is a story from several British troops from the same infantry battalion. Where the alleged atrocity took place will stay anonymous, but it wasn't far from where I was stationed. They said they'd been on patrol and entered a burning village. Some homes were already completely gutted, while others were in their last throes of smoke and flames. Oddly for this kind of recent event, there wasn't a single person around. But on passing through the village they found a mine shaft, with multiple grenade pins scattered around a ventilation hole in the ground. Clearly this was suspicious and needed to be reported, to account for the unexploded ordnance. However, as the hole was near-vertical they couldn't descend into it without the proper equipment. Several days later a Royal Engineers team followed up on their report and made their way down into the shaft. What they found was carnage beyond their worst expectations, because at the bottom of the shaft lay the recent remains of the entire village. From what evidence they could gather, live babies had been dropped straight down the shaft first, followed by infants, then children who'd been shot once in the head. On top of them were adults, also shot in the head, and at the top of the heap were the village elders, who had been forced to watch every last one of their descendants executed as their village was razed to the ground. To destroy any evidence, and ensure that not a single soul survived to tell the tale, upwards of sixty live grenades had been dropped – one by one – down the shaft after them.

This was ethnic cleansing at its dirtiest, and though I never actually heard if it was true, it was never refuted. No report was circulated, and I never saw anything on the news – but the sad fact was that no one questioned its authenticity. So many such atrocities happened here, left unreported by the world's media, that it could only be true. Think about it – if this kind of event happened repeatedly in your own community, and no one ever said or did anything about it, how could you not become inured, blasé, or emotionally-hardened, in case you were next in line?

Another reason nobody questioned it was because we'd all seen similar villages, one after another, during our tours here. Boot Troop had been placed in a village named Blagaj, after a reported threat of a Croatian force planning to come back across the border to finish what they'd started. The leaders of these pogroms – the deliberate, systematic and violent eradication of a different class of human – knew that any displaced families from here would be allowed to return, and our job was to make sure they had a fighting chance.

Thoroughly ravaged by war, this small town was totally devoid of life except for an elderly couple, living in their wooden shed, literally trying to pick up the pieces of their former existence. After ensuring that it wasn't mined, we commandeered the largest house overlooking the border crossing point. Mick had us set up the GPMG in an upstairs window, and to park our vehicles strategically around the property for fast access and egress. He and James then gave us instructions to stay within its grounds, which had also been checked for mines and cleared for safety. Left to our own devices, we did a recce of the premises, found that it had a cellar, and went down to check it out. From the numerous used and bloodied field bandages and dressings littering the floor down there, it was joltingly clear that it had been used as a makeshift field hospital.

That night we set up a small fire in the front garden, donated a few boxes of rations to the old couple who were without food, and slept alongside the village ghosts. After a couple of days in situ, Mick was called back to Germany to brief the unit taking over from us. GH was still in charge, so I became acting sergeant and, rather than the strategic fire which Mick had allowed, I organised the building of a huge bonfire on all the nights he was away. Totally unprofessional, for sure, but a great morale booster for us all. When Mick returned and saw what we'd done, he had us build a Yukon stove in the enlarged fire pit we'd created. This type of stove is made out of mud and chicken wire, shaped wide at the bottom and narrow at the top, allowing plenty of room for wood to burn inside but channelling all its heat upwards into a smaller area. However, while it's a superb way to stay warm, cook food, and boil water, it's not as much fun to sit around as a roaring campfire!

2003: The Operation

The ward staff told us that the operation would take at least ten hours, and there was no point in hanging around worrying. Reassured that we could call them at any time, we took their advice and left the hospital, because at least outside in the fresh air we could smoke. I then did something utterly stupid, which I still regret to this day. Making the excuse that I had to meet someone in town, and would return later, I left them to be alone – which I thought was for the best at this time. Dzejna looked daggers at me as she translated, but said nothing. In truth, I knew I couldn't deal with the situation (*did I think that they could?*) and instead of staying to share the weight of their burden, to be their strength in their ten hours of need, I left them alone with it and walked away from them like a coward.

Thinking that separating from them would somehow lessen the impact of what was happening to their child, I mentally went through what he was going to experience over the course of this day before the evening's dark curtain brought it to a close. This operation would be a massive trauma for anyone, let alone a small child, which naturally carried additional risks, especially with anaesthetic medicine. David would start by cutting into the facial skin, before peeling it back to expose the skull. Next, he would remove the top of the skull, draw out the eyes, and deconstruct the bones around them – all the while with both eyes and the brain totally exposed. He'd then reconstruct the skull to a normal shape, before re-securing it to the head with titanium plates held together by small metal pins.

Easy to say, but I couldn't allow my own brain to imagine this happening to myself – thus creating a memory. It was much easier, and safer, to imagine it happening to someone else, despite the risks, and all I could think of was how I'd feel if anything went wrong. Yes, I was looking out for Number One, and it was incredibly selfish of me. Why wasn't I with the Savic family, giving them everything I had in support? I knew why then, and I know even better now, that mentally, and emotionally, I simply didn't have the strength nor the capacity, and I'll try to expand upon this later.

BFBS continued to film 'Stefan's Story', and had been allowed into the operating theatre for the first part of the operation. Several days earlier I'd watched as they interviewed David, where he explained what would occur, while showing them scans of Stefan's skull. On a computer screen, he pointed to where several large pieces of bone were missing from the front of the head which, if not treated, would lead to infection and possible death. He went on to describe how the operation would be conducted, what he'd be doing and looking out for throughout the procedure, and the risks likely to be associated with each stage. I just sat there in dumb awe, watching him chatting away like the professor he was. I dare say that if you'd taken our pulse readings at the time, his would have been in the low fifties, while mine would have been thumping up in the hundreds!

Common sense finally took over from nervousness and, knowing that my absence had already been far too long, I met up with the family where they were waiting for me in the park near the hospital. The look I received from Dzejna stripped me bare, but Milos and Slava just gave me another big hug. They'd all been out shopping, without buying anything, while Dzejna had stayed in constant telephone contact with the ward. It had been ten hours, so we all returned to the hospital to wait in Stefan's room, but even this was premature. Two hours later a member of staff arrived to tell us that Stefan was out of theatre. He was now in recovery, before being moved to the High Dependency Unit. This 4-year-old child had just undergone an intense 12-hour surgical procedure, which would have been difficult enough for a grown adult. It had certainly been bad enough for us. How would Stefan take it?

We got up and stretched our legs, ready to make our way to the HDU and await Stefan's arrival. Again, I tried to hang back. *Surely this is a family matter?* but Slava was adamant, this time, that I join them. *They must have been talking about me.* The sight which greeted us was truly remarkable, and will forever be embedded in my mind. Stefan lay in a massive hospital bed – a tiny figure surrounded by an expanse of white sheets into which small patches of blood had seeped into the fabric. Either side of him were tripods supporting equipment that monitored his diminutive body, and informed the nurses and doctors of his vital signs. Attached to his little arms and chest were a multitude of wires and tubing, including a blood pressure cuff which manually inflated every few minutes until it reached its optimum pressure, then deflated in a series of small hisses. Two plastic bottles, full of fluids, were attached one to each arm. From the top of his head, over his eyes, and down to just below his nose, he looked like a mummy, with bandage after bandage applied to the massive wounding underneath. But even with all these dressings applied, I could see that the shape of his head had changed, and looked far more normal than it had in his previous life. Slava's tears gushed at seeing her son lying there, not because of all the medical paraphernalia, but because she could finally see the face with which all children should be born. She looked up at me, gave me a massive hug, and sobbed in English, "Thank you. Thank you. Thank you…"

Stefan had been highly sedated and was still asleep, so I rose to leave them all in the room, which would now become Slava's for the next few days. And that was when David, having changed into his suit, popped in to see us. He told us that the operation had gone as planned, and that the reason Stefan had so many bandages over his eyes and face was to allow their natural healing, and for his eyes to rest and settle into their new positions.

Leaving the family with this good news, and fearing the wrath of Dzejna, I left to return to my digs, stopping at my usual pub along the way. I must have been in there far more often than I'd thought, because the barman pulled me a pint of ale, the second I stepped through the door. I also asked for two double whiskeys for starters.

"Bad day, mate?" He asked, in his broad cockney accent.

"Mate, you don't know the half of it…" was all I could say before quickly downing both shorts, followed by the pint in four huge gulps. After one more pint down-range, I returned to my room, stripped off, and got into the shower. The blessed relief that poured out of me, to disappear forever down the plughole, was overwhelming. As I moved around, letting the hot water pour over my body, I felt the stress flow out of me – from my head, my shoulders, my back – as I stood there facing into the torrent, my body shuddering, and crying my heart out.

All these months of preparation, the fundraising, the media, the potential loss of career, the hopes of a family, and – most importantly – the life of a small child. All these issues had been resolved in one go, and a clear future lay ahead. The main stumbling block was finally over… I don't remember what time I eventually got to bed, and I must have fallen asleep as soon as I'd pulled up the covers, but I stayed in this dreamless slumber until Dzejna knocked respectfully on my door at 8am the following morning.

Stefan stayed in the HDU for three days but, true to his amazing courage and internal strength, he returned to the general ward sooner than expected. We carried on our daily visits to check his progression, which improved each time, and of course Slava was always there by his side.

David did tell us of a concern that Stefan's eyesight could be affected long-term by the operation. He'd had to reconstruct both orbital sockets, which had moved both eyes from their former positions, and he didn't know if Stefan's brain would adapt to this sudden change. There was still a possibility of permanent visual problems, and a worst-case scenario of losing his sight altogether. He believed that everything had been done properly, but couldn't know for certain until the bandages came off.

On the fourth day post-op, I walked into the ward to find Stefan sitting on his bed, his face unmasked, and playing with his toys. As he heard me come in, he looked up, and as soon as he recognised me his face lit up, creating the biggest smile he could form over the pain. I was gobsmacked because I'd not expected this, and turned to Slava who excitedly explained, through Dzejna, that David had been to check on them earlier that morning, and was so impressed with Stefan's progress that he'd asked for the bandages to be removed.

So used as I was to Stefan since I'd first met him, I couldn't believe that before me, at that very moment, was an even-more-beautiful-than-ever little boy with a normal, standard-shaped face, in which the eyes were perfectly positioned within a natural-looking skull. He even had a little button of a nose. In fact, the only evidence that Stefan had recently had his entire skull taken apart was a multitude of stitches forming

2003: The Operation

a cross from his nose to the midway point of his skull, plus the ones running diagonally across his forehead. David had already conducted a basic eye test, which Stefan had passed with flying colours but, as his body was still recovering and adapting, he'd need to do another assessment in a couple of weeks. But this was truly amazing. David had achieved everything he'd promised, which was more than anyone could have ever hoped for. Slava and Milos now had their beloved son returned to them the way he should have been born. He'd go on to lead a normal life through school, get his chance to wear spectacles, and never be bullied for his looks.

I could now present a glowing report to the media, I'd get to keep my job, the British Army could sport a new feather in its cap and, as an added bonus, Dzejna had forgiven me – at least until I messed up again!

Chapter 11

2003

Post-Op

Several days after the operation David was ready to chat with me about the procedure. It had taken almost 12 hours from start to end, during which he'd removed bones from the top of Stefan's skull, and parts of his ribs, to engineer a normal facial structure. He then showed me two CT scans, taken pre- and post-operation, and the difference was astonishing. The former showed a small skull with huge orbital sockets and three holes in the frontal bone that shouldn't have been there. The latter, however, could have come from a different child – the eyes were now settled closer together, the holes had gone, and a bone graft from a rib had been reshaped to form the bridge of a new nose.

Two weeks passed before Stefan was given the all-clear to leave the hospital, well ahead of schedule due to his youthful speed of recovery. Slava had spent the whole time beside him during this period, venturing outside the hospital's front door for a cigarette only when she was certain that Stefan was asleep, or another family member had taken over her vigil. The mental and emotional toll on her had been immense, and it showed.

The day of his discharge was another checkpoint reached and, as always, the little guy took everything in his stride. Armed with as many toys as he could carry, and sustained by copious kisses from the nurses, we were able to grab a taxi for the quick trip back to our accommodation. Once there, mandatory Serbian coffee was boiled up and, with several cups of caffeine now coursing through my veins, I made my excuses and headed back to Lulworth, and work!

A few days later, however, I returned to London to sit with Eamonn Holmes and Fiona Phillips on the famous 'Good Morning Britain' sofa. Stefan, Slava and a male interpreter answered their scripted questions, about how we met and what had occurred to get us this far, and I was pleased as Punch to be on national TV for the first time. However, the moment I left the studio I was bombarded with a plethora of idiotic phone calls from the lads in the regiment! Initially I thought they were calling to congratulate me on the interview, until every single one of them castigated me on the deadpan brown cardigan I'd been wearing which, they said, made me look like a large turd... To be honest I'd given no thought to dressing specially for TV, which is why my favourite casuals went on parade before the UK's entire breakfast-viewing audience. I've since learned (from my wife, bless her), that I have no dress sense whatsoever, but at the time I felt as though I'd served amongst a bunch of philistine fashion hooligans.

Throughout this jubilant period, the gunnery school hierarchy allowed me all the time I needed away from the unit – though this was definitely helped by the BFBS constantly asking for me to attend photoshoots in London, for the documentary they were making for the British Army around the world!

Before leaving, Stefan had his final consultation with David and, as he'd already got the provisional go-ahead, I'd arranged for the homeward flights the day after. The usual media frenzy had been scheduled in, including the BFBS and a well-known national newspaper, and we arranged to meet them in a park, close to the hospital, once this all-important meeting was over. David was reliably thorough in his examination, and reassuringly approachable for the family, answering every possible question they could think of. He told them that everything had gone as planned, and that Stefan had made a remarkable recovery – though he'd need further treatment over many years to correct his nose as he grew, and to remove several pins which would start to protrude as his facial bones matured.

Then that was it, and we were officially discharged. As the family left to go outside, I held back briefly to say a personal thank you to

David for his help, kindness, and compassion. But instead of the grand finale I'd been preparing – the stirring speech at the end of the movie – I just choked up and no words came out. I finally blurted that he was the kindest man I'd ever met, and that nothing could possibly express the gratitude I was feeling. I ended on an anti-climax as I handed him a bottle of red wine, and a promise to bring the family back when Stefan's next surgery was needed.

It's strange, but while the mundane has stayed with me, other memories from this period have faded much faster than the rest. Maybe it's old age, but maybe it's the mind's way of coping with extremely stressful situations. Over those few months my stress levels had been treacherously high, while Slava's must have been so far up the scale, there could be no common ground for comparison.

While preparing for this book I re-watched the BFBS documentary, where it showed us entering the park for the photoshoot. Stefan was in combat clothing, I was in uniform, and there were several pictures of me pushing him on a swing, plus the now-famous one of him sitting on the top of a slide next to me sporting my 9th/12th Lancers' beret. Until this stage – the final part of the proceedings – I hadn't realised just how pushy, insensitive, and harshly uncompassionate the news media could be in getting their 'pound of flesh' from us. Maybe it was just me. Maybe I was blind to the fact that, oblivious to the day-by-day complexity of everything that had happened to us all, over a period of several months, all they really wanted at the end of the day was the 'money shot' in the park.

Depending on the lighting and background Stefan and I were shepherded from one location to another. Directed to push the swing in this way. Stand next to the slide in that way. Smile for the camera here, now there, now here… and on it went as I fought back the urge to batter the bloody lot of them, sweep Stefan up in my arms, and get us both the hell out of there. Thankfully, travel deadlines ended our performance, as the Bosnia flight from Heathrow had its own agenda.

As promised, Calvin's taxi showed up on time to whisk us all to the airport, before taking me to Weymouth. We said our goodbyes in the departure lounge, exchanged kisses all round, and I promised to see them in a few weeks to continue the documentary at their home. Then their flight was called, and I watched them depart – signifying the end of an extremely long and emotional era.

On the 6th December that year BFBS flew a cameraman, a reporter, and myself back to Bosnia to reunite me with the Savic family and complete 'Stefan's Story'. It was only for a few days, but we were treated like royalty. Plenty of Pivo was consumed in the process, and it was good to catch up with the family and their entire support network.

At the end of a mammoth night's drinking, lifts were arranged home for everyone except for two uniformed police officers, both of whom literally staggered to their patrol car. After a heated argument with the keys, they got the car going, and then started searching for the exit at a speed that would have been deemed reckless anywhere in the world. Having seen so many disastrous consequences during my career, I'm strongly against any level of drink-driving and I am not exaggerating when I say that those two were totally incapable of driving in a straight line – *to protect and swerve?* As they finally careened out of the car park onto the main road, I had grave concerns about the other drivers and pedestrians using it. Incredulously, I turned to Milos and asked him, "Are they safe?" He smiled and said they'd be okay. The passenger was the Chief of Police, and the driver his Second in Command – so if stopped they wouldn't get into any trouble.

Chapter 12

2004

The Final Cut

I was finally free to focus on other matters. My ankle had been steadily getting worse, and I was referred to Headley Court Rehabilitation Centre in Surrey for a programme to strengthen the ankle. But as it was now November, I was only there for two weeks before everyone was sent home on Christmas leave, and the rest of the treatment would need to wait until after the holidays. Typically for the Army, this was for most of December and into early January.

Since our split, Tracy and I had agreed to spend alternate Christmas periods with the boys, now 6 and 8 years old, and this year was my turn. On Christmas Eve, having checked they were asleep, I laid all the presents out under the tree, before chomping on the carrot, downing the mince pie, and drinking the glass of whisky they'd left out for Santa. Our boys know that we're not like other households who, for whatever reason, always leave sherry for the big, red-suited guy who comes ho, ho, ho-ing down our chimneys each year. No, I have top-secret government information that what he really enjoys is a good old single malt, without water. But just imagine what would happen if they all did that.

Like every other parent in the world, I woke early on Christmas morning. It was still dark, and the boys still asleep, so I crept downstairs to make sure I'd done everything possible to make it a really magical day for them. But as I put my foot down after the last step, my world literally turned upside down as I realised I'd missed one. There was no time nor room to compensate, and I landed badly – which rarely ends well when you're over six foot tall and weigh 15 stone. I knew as soon as the pain hit that I'd incurred serious damage, and my ankle immediately started to swell up again – just like it had done every previous time it fractured.

Oh, shit! Shit, shit, shit! I didn't want to wake the boys, and had to bite my upper lip to stop myself crying out in agony and despair, because I knew what would come next, over the time they'd be with me. I knew where my ankle supports were, and positioned myself carefully before tentatively pulling on one over the other, while knocking down Ibuprofen to suppress the pain.

For the next 24 hours I didn't say much. I just focused on giving my boys the best time possible while rapidly reducing my stock of Brufen. I was grateful when Tracy collected the boys earlier than planned on Boxing Day, which allowed me to get to the hospital. Now several sizes larger, my ankle had turned an ugly black and dark blue and, even before they did the X-ray, I already knew it was broken.

They found another fracture at the joint and I spent the rest of Christmas back in crutches, plaster, and bad spirits because I'd buggered up my ankle yet again. As I was still under treatment at Headley Court, they advised me to stay at home until the plaster was off and then return, which I did. The physio sessions recommenced but the pain was much worse than ever. After several more X-rays and tests, they concluded that there was nothing more they could do to strengthen or improve it in any way. On the last morning, I was on the couch being examined by a Colonel surgeon who, after extensive prodding and poking concluded, "Well, it's pretty useless. I can remove it for you, if you want…"

I looked him straight in the eyes, and asked him, "Will it stop the pain?"

"Hmm, I can't completely guarantee that, Staff," he responded, positively, "But we'll give it a bloody good go!"

Sod that! I thought. Giving him my most stalwart impression of the British Empire, I declined.

Out of options, I got put on the Y list, which basically meant go home and wait. To be honest, this was brilliant to start with as I was being paid as a Staff Sergeant with Local Overseas Allowance enhancements. LOA was paid to service personnel abroad and, as my base was officially in Germany, this still counted. Soldiers appreciate any addition to their standard pay packet but, as the days turned into weeks, and then months, I really started to miss the army life. I phoned Manning and Records every other day, and wrote several times to the regiment asking if they had any news for me, but each time encountered a stony wall of silence. It took until October for the world I knew to come crumbling down around me. I answered a telephone call from a civilian surgeon, who told me that I'd been selected for medical discharge from the Army and he needed to chat with me about it. *What the hell?*

My last confidential report had me down as outstanding; I was recommended for promotion. I couldn't have asked for more, and I'd been considering life as a WO2 (Warrant Officer Class 2), then later as an LE (Long Enlistment Officer). This could *not* be happening, and half my brain concluded that it was one of the regiment lads having a joke. The other half told me that this guy sounded like the real thing, but I just couldn't believe it. He must have realised this because he apologised for disturbing me, asked me to give it some thought, said that he'd be in contact again, and then put the phone down.

Several weeks later, after making an appointment, he arrived at my home to explain what would happen to me, starting in December. For the past few weeks I still hadn't processed it, and a million and one things continued to run through my head, creating more questions and permutations than my brain could cope with. I was 35 years old. I had a mortgage to pay. I had kids to support. All I'd ever wanted to do, and had trained to do after I'd left school, was to be a soldier. *What the hell would I do now?*

He told me that I'd get 18 years of my 22-year pension, plus a small lump sum and a war pension, so I'd be okay financially. In monetary terms I could just manage without having to work, but mentally I was sliding downhill, unable to stop. The military, the regiment, the lads – I was physically and emotionally bonded to them all. I'd have willingly given my life for them. And now they'd flung me away like a scorpion you'd just found in your boot. I knew that there were two massive conflicts now going

2004: The Final Cut

on in the world, in Iraq and Afghanistan, both of which were devouring huge amounts of resources and manpower daily. I knew I was a ridiculously small piece in a colossal machine – but it's all these small parts that make the machine work. Remove them, and even the biggest parts would stop moving. I told him that this was my life. That I'd do any desk job, in any conflict zone in the world. I even pleaded with him. But there was nothing he could do – because he was just another small piece. The decision had been made based on facts and factors, which by design didn't require my input, and now he was just doing his job to help me as best he could.

It didn't take long before insult was added to injury. I'd not heard a thing from anyone in the regiment since I'd been away, and felt I'd become 'out of sight, out of mind'. Until I was contacted by the then current Regimental Sergeant Major, who told me that he'd been saddened by the news of my discharge on medical grounds. My hopes were now raised. *Thank God, a friend! Someone who understands!* I appealed to him to try and find me a desk job anywhere in the regiment, to which he explained that, regrettably, he could not, as the decision had been made by Manning and Records and, as such, was irreversible. He then moved on to the main reason for his call – that I had an unpaid 275-euro bill for mess silver (the fund which covers the upkeep of flags, medals, and other ornaments in the sergeants' mess). Well, that payment is supposed to come out of my monthly wages, and I'd not used the mess for over a year, so I told him to firmly shove it up his arse – along with my payment. He reminded me, calmly, that I could not speak to an RSM like that, so I just said that the way I was being treated, there was no way in hell I was paying that bill! He told me that I was being treated as fairly as anyone else in my circumstances, and if I chose not to pay then I would not qualify for a departing gift from the regiment. Still fuming, I told him to keep it, knock it off the mess bill, and give the lads my best. That was the last time we spoke, and I heard nothing more afterwards from the mess, nor from the regiment.

On my day of discharge, I had to hand over my uniform to the kit store at Bovington camp. This was run by civvies, who issued and collected clothing daily from the junior leader regiment, and only on rare occasions like this would they encounter a Staff Sergeant. At this exalted level the unwritten rule, while you're stationed with a regiment, is that the store only takes back the kit they absolutely need, such as expensive ceremonial garments. Everything else would be trashed, so they usually let you keep it.

I arrived, stupidly expecting the elderly guy behind the counter to recognise my rank, give me a knowing nod, and tell me not to bother. But instead, he started treating me like a rookie, painstakingly explaining how to lay out my kit and then stand still while it was being counted. After telling him to wind his fucking neck in, that he was talking to a senior soldier and not a teenager he could treat like shit, he finally realised the error of his ways. But he wasn't going to let it go, and I remembered that civvies don't answer to senior soldiers. This jumped-up jobsworth systematically took every single piece of kit from me, one by one, examined it in detail, and then threw it onto the pile behind him. Whenever I asked if I could keep it, for old times' sake, he just said "Sorry, staff, but rules are rules…"

Then he pushed it too far and asked me where my army-issue PT kit was. Infuriated, I told him that those red and white T-shirts and blue shorts had been issued to me eighteen effing years ago, when I was on basic training! He said nothing in response, but I'm sure I saw him smirk as he added them to my bill.

Still fuming, I went upstairs to the admin room to hand in my ID card to another civvy, who had barely started shaving. Clinging to the only military connection I had left, I stood to attention before him across his desk, and announced that I was Staff Sergeant Ingram, here to be discharged. Okay, probably over the top, but I was still a soldier. In response he didn't stand, nor salute. Instead, he picked up a pair of scissors, and deftly cut my MOD 90 in two.

And that was it. The end of an era. The endless operational tours. The laughs. The tears. The fights. The cold nights on duty waiting for the Russians to invade. The bodies of the dead and wounded. The countless hours spent guarding people like him across the continent. Staff Sergeant Ingram had gone, and had been replaced by a disabled has-been. He'd become another archived record *and a broken one at that…* A veteran of war who'd travelled the world doing as much good as possible. Who, along with countless others, had been shot at, more than once, with the intention to kill or maim him, simply for doing his job. He'd seen more corpses than most civvies will in a hundred lifetimes. But who'd also saved as many lives along the way *including having to piece some of them back together...*

Which is why it didn't feel right that an 18-year life of military service had just been taken – by a civvy, from behind the safety of an office desk, armed only with a pair of scissors...

Chapter 13

2004

Broken

◇◇◇

All service personnel eventually leave the military and take their place alongside their civilian counterparts – usually on their own terms when they feel it's the right time. But for me, it wasn't. Far from it. Ever since I'd learned to think for myself, I'd known only the discipline of the cane or the Army to keep me on course, and now I had I no structure in which to move, learn, and develop. In my Game of Life I was used to climbing ladders, one step at a time, and now I'd stumbled and landed on a very, very long snake.

But after falling 18 years I wasn't just back at the beginning. I'd been booted right out of the game – with no way back in, past my prime, and injured *in more ways than I knew at the time*. And what did I have to show for it, at the age of 36? A disability pension!

In most modern adventure stories, the male hero is around my age. Mature, self-confident, world-wise, financially secure, and a professional in his own field of expertise. This is how he's able to meet adversity head-on, outwit the bad guys, save the world, and win the girl. The End. Which is why I felt scared. And devastated. And so miserable that after waking up each day I just wanted to cry. This wasn't just unemployment. This was a bereavement. When the very foundation on which you've built your life has suddenly crumbled as in an earthquake. When you realise that everything of importance to you was actually beyond your control. And that all around you now are just fragments.

Looking back while writing this narrative, this feeling actually stayed with me for the next ten years. I'd loved my career in the Army. I was proud to have served Her Majesty, my Queen, with an exemplary service record modelled on her own. And this must be why I felt so betrayed, so let down, and so extremely bitter at the way the MoD had treated me after nearly two decades of devoted service. Now severed from the global support system in which I'd spent my entire adult life, this institutionalized individual now had to learn to look after himself in a big world. But right now, a 17-year-old student, just out of school, would have been far better prepared and qualified than I was.

Chapter 14

2005-2010

The Beginning

There were, indeed, many more things I needed to learn about life. Including that wherever people, especially individuals, are concerned, unexpected events tend to happen for very specific reasons.

A few days later I drove into my local shopping complex, and parked close to an ambulance with two large uniformed guys in the front seats. On an inspiration, and seeing as they weren't doing much, I walked over, knocked on the passenger window, and asked if they'd take me on after being medically discharged from the Army. The guy turned to his right and pointed his thumb, "See that fat fucker? He's had two heart attacks. If they'll take him on, they'll take anyone…"

To which the driver's succinct and witty repost was "Fuck off, Fatso…"

I smiled broadly, instantly recognising the humour and camaraderie I sorely missed. That was my introduction to the Dorset Ambulance Service. As soon as I got home, I was on the phone to the local station, and a couple of days later received an application form for the role of ambulance technician.

It was still December, and my training course was set for February. However, one of the January course participants dropped out, and I jumped at the chance to fill their place. The universe really does work in mysterious ways, and it was during the first morning's induction that I clapped eyes on a beautiful blonde student on the same course, who had introduced herself as Cara. When my turn came, I looked directly at her, smiled, and said, "My name is Wayne, and I'm single…"

To be perfectly honest this was only technically true because, to me, girlfriends were like collectables, and I already had several irons in the fire. I was in a failing live-in relationship back home and was also making moves on a teacher in Cambridge. Yes, you're right. Having three women on the go at the same time, let alone two, was a completely heartless thing to do to any of them – but my heart was being overruled by my baser instincts.

As our friendship developed, I told Cara that I'd been going through a difficult time at that point in my life, and was really confused – which was my time-honoured 'get out of jail free' card whenever I got into trouble with a woman. The reality was that, like most of the men I knew, I was a total tool when it came to opposite-sex relationships. But Cara was having none of it. She knew I was being a knob, and set about putting me straight. Cara and I married in 2006, and have stayed happily that way ever since. But it nearly didn't happen, as she likes to remind me of my fateful words one morning together. We were holding hands while walking to the pub to retrieve her car, and the conversation suddenly turned serious. The last thing on my mind was a stable, full-time relationship and, in response to whatever it was she'd just said that had taken me by surprise, I blurted out "So, what do you want from me?" Believe me, these are not the words a lady wants to hear from the man who's just slept with her, and her icy reply was "Marriage, kids, and your life…". On seeing my vacant yet horrified expression, she pulled her hand away, glared at me, and told me I was a 'pompous arse'. That's when I realised there was something really special about this one. She was a fighter, she was tougher than me, and I had no choice but to give in to her demands. In my defence – though I don't dare say it – I still like to think that she'd been caught hook, line and sinker by the Ingram charm!

Ambulance Technician training involved three weeks of blue-light driving, followed by a 9-week course of anatomy and physiology (A+P). If you pass at the end you're allocated to a base ambulance station on a relief rota system, where you're teamed up with a proper paramedic.

You're then given a portfolio of tasks you need to record, to ensure that you're reaching your correct educational standards – such as in cardiac arrests and heroin overdoses. You have one year to record all these types of incident, during which time you have to write two dissertations – one on an incident that you've attended, and the other on a medical subject of your choice. It's also stressed that no confidential medical information can ever be kept by a member of staff.

I was based in Weymouth ambulance station, where I got to know the two guys who'd 'recruited' me into the service. Despite their deranged attitude and sense of humour, Nigel Cowan and Pete Owen were two highly competent paramedics who'd seen every bizarre situation a person was capable of getting themselves into.

I saw my own fair share of incidents, ranging from the simple and the serious, to the downright unbelievable. Cara, on the other hand, was based in the sleepy town of Shaftsbury in Dorset, and spent most of her time just sitting around waiting for an incident report to come in!

I'll share a few of mine from this time, as they don't involve confidential information as such. Early in my career, all communication to the crews was done by phone or vehicle radio. I was sitting in the cab with Jay Mercer, my paramedic mentor and friend. Jay was driving, and asked what kind of job I wanted us to respond to that day, to which I said that I hadn't yet seen a hanging. At that very instant, Control called us to report of a man whose brother was trying to hang himself. Our eyes opened wide, we both turned to each other, and said "Spooky"...

We arrived at the open front door to see a man at the top of the stairs with a massive knife in his hand, so I shouted that we couldn't come in while he was holding it. Right away he put it down safely, apologised, and explained that he'd just taken it off his brother, who'd smashed up the house and was about to hang himself. The stairs led up to the front room, kitchen, and bedroom, but as it wasn't this guy's house, we needed permission to enter the bedroom where the owner was in the process of tying a length of white string around his neck.

Seeing us at the door, he shouted at us to get out. This was his house, and he could do what he wanted in it. We were, indeed, trespassing, so I turned to Jay, who said that we had to respect the gentleman's wishes and needed to call the police for backup. Now, at this time I was becoming known as 'Captain Slackbladder', due to the amount of tea and water I was constantly drinking, so I took the liberty of quickly using the bathroom opposite the bedroom before leaving. As I finished and flushed the toilet, remembering that I could now technically be sued for stealing water whilst trespassing, I heard a loud, dull thud and a snapping sound. "Shit! He's jumped!" shouted Jay. The three of us instinctively burst into the bedroom, just in time to see the guy's legs, then feet, disappearing downwards through the first-floor bay window. We rushed over to look, and watched agog as the man picked himself up, then started running away down the road, a length of string trailing from his neck, and being chased by three police officers! He'd taken the trouble to climb a stepladder, open the loft space, tie the string to one of the roof beams, and then jump off. Thankfully, the string had snapped under his weight so, to finish off the job, and himself, he'd opened the window and, head first, manoeuvred himself out of it. (Un)luckily for him there was a thick bush below, which broke his fall before he hit the ground. We took him to A&E and, though we'd normally have collar-and-boarded him first after such an array of physical trauma, this guy was having none of it, and a police officer had to accompany him in the ambulance to ensure that he didn't escape en route! Sadly to say, I have since witnessed the results of several more hangings – all of which were considerably more successful in their execution.

Another incident, which created much subsequent laughter at my expense, occurred in the early hours of the morning. Some jobs are classified 'Urgent', and usually when a doctor refers a patient to a hospital or respite area. An ambulance is then tasked, due to either the frailty of the individual, or if they have no other practical means to get there.

At around 2am we were sent to a care home to transfer an old lady to the local hospital. While Jay was doing a verbal handover with the care staff, I asked which room the lady was in so I could go and get her ready. I was pointed to the room and, after quietly knocking, I entered. The lady was asleep in bed, so I woke her gently, apologised, introduced myself, and told her that we were going to take her to hospital. "Okay, my dear," was her willing response and, as she got up to sit on the side of the bed, I explained that I was just going to get a special carry-chair for her. But on exiting the room I saw Jay and the care staff laughing in my direction. To my horror I learned that I was in the wrong room, and needed the next one along. So, in trepidation, I returned to her room to give her the good news, that she was okay and the hospital no longer needed her. Bless her, she just said, "Oh, alright dear", rolled back into bed, and fell instantly asleep.

One freezing cold and wet November morning I arrived at work to start a shift with Jimmy Ryan, another paramedic mentor. Jimmy was well known to drive, let's say, a little over-the-limit on occasion. We'd just clocked on when we received reports of two people in cardiac arrest, and were sent as part of a double ambulance crew. We were the first truck out of the station and the roads were empty, so we were able to make good time down Weymouth Way – but at the bottom of the hill we hit black ice, and the tyres lost their intimate connection with the road. Now, a sliding ambulance weighing several tons is not an inspiring sight, especially from the inside. We glided into the central reservation, continued into the opposite carriageway, and careened into the far kerb without slowing down. The truck flipped over onto its side, rolled downhill, got itself trapped in a mass of thick brambles, and came to a shaking halt partway down an embankment. The good news is that – had the local flora not broken and cushioned our descent – we'd have likely ended up in, and probably under, Radipole Lake. The ambulance was trashed, its back and sides bent and dented all over but – to give the manufacturers their due – all the important, heavy items had stayed secured to the main bulkhead. Thankfully, the only part of the superstructure not broken was the windscreen which, after checking we were both okay, Jimmy and I kicked out.

The second truck, with Andy Crawley and Mike Ellis, arrived within seconds and, as they jumped out to see if we were okay, Jimmy and I waved and shouted them to carry on to the job, as we were both fine.

Okay, if this had happened to anyone else, both driver and passenger would have been 'collar-and-boarded' and sent to the local A&E for review. But we weren't anyone else. We were just us. So, when the duty officer arrived to check how we were, we asked him to take us to St Leonards so we could collect another truck. Yes, we could have gone home, and no one would have argued, but we still had a 10-hour shift to finish.

I passed my paramedic pre-test exactly a year after completing my Tech Training, and a few weeks later started my full 9-week Paramedic Course. Then immediately this was over, I started training as a retained firefighter with the Dorset Fire and Rescue Service, as a second job to keep myself busy.

I've always been a keen motorcyclist, passing my test in 1993 while on tour in Belfast. Those were surreal moments, patrolling the streets and taking on the local hardmen during the day – then riding past them later on, without a weapon, dressed in civvies and crash helmet, hoping I wouldn't be recognised. A year after getting my professional paramedic registration I was invited to join the motorcycle response unit – the MRU. This was the best post-military job I ever did, as it combined three of my greatest loves – motorbikes, all things paramedical, and being in the thick of the action, because the bikes were sent mainly to Category A (life-threatening) jobs. So, no pressure there, then.

In this role, one sunny Saturday afternoon I was dispatched to the Harbour Master's office in Weymouth, where reports were coming in that a female had collapsed in the shower. I parked the bike outside and was directed to a French couple, both in their early 40's. Thankfully, the lady was now out of the shower and in her dressing gown, sitting on the floor and resting her head against her husband. I quickly learned that neither spoke English well, but with my pidgin French and hand signals I gathered that they'd just arrived from St Malo on their sailing vessel. While her husband had been navigating the route between our respective countries, the wife had been busy with a different type of port, and had subsequently passed out while showering after their arrival. What I really needed was her prior medical history, and that was when a member of staff showed up and earnestly asked if I needed a translator. Always receptive to professional help I gratefully accepted, and asked if he could find out if she had any special medical conditions I needed to know about. He looked at me with a serious expression and said "No worries, man," before directing his full attention to her. Taking her hand gently, and looking her directly in her eyes, he said slowly, in his best French accent (I wish that everyone reading this book could have been there to hear…)

"Azz youze enny meddykel condishons I nead to knowz?"

The lady just gaped at him, open-mouthed. He then turned back to me and, just as earnestly, asked, "Need anything else, mate?"

During this bilateral intercourse the husband and I just stared unbelievingly at each other and, doing my best to stifle an impending burst of laughter, I asked, "Please, would you just find out if she's taking any medication?". "Yeah, sure" he responded, before giving her his undivided attention once more. With a penetrating gaze, borne from long experience of dealing with French tourists, he asked her, "Azz youze enny meddysenz?"

Neither her husband nor I could hold back any longer, and both of us erupted into fits, and then gales, of laughter. Tears started flowing freely down our faces, and even the wife started laughing, drawn into the infectious hilarity of the scene playing out around her. The only one who didn't see the joke was the office manager, who gave me a 'What the hell's going on?' type of look. Barely able to speak, I managed to convey to him, between gasps, "Mate… Even I can speak better *beep!* French than that!" before stopping to heave in another deep breath of air.

At this revelation, the manager took extreme umbrage and promptly told us both to fuck off before stomping away. Eventually I had to make the 'all-clear' call back to control, but the memory trigger was still there, my gut was aching, and it was only under extreme duress that I managed to get the words, interspersed by unrepressed hoots and chortles of laughter, out over the bike's radio.

Another episode which, if you wrote as fiction no one would believe, occurred one evening between Christmas and the new year. During this period, coachloads of elderly people arrive in Weymouth and happily spend their time with friends at local hotels on organised coach trips.

Just before midnight, Andy Randell and I were called to one such hotel, where the staff had reported a male having collapsed on the premises. On entering Reception, we noticed two old ladies pressing the button to call the lift, which would take them either down to the bar or up to their rooms. While Andy obtained information, I continued to watch these old dears repeatedly pressing the button. The patient was reported to be downstairs, so we made our way past the ladies to the staircase, respectfully resisting the temptation to suggest that maybe the lift was out of order. Before I reached the bottom, I heard Andy ahead shout, "Bloody hell!" and then I saw why. The reason the lift wasn't moving was because the guy we'd come to check was lying on the carpet with his head in the lift entrance – and each time the doors tried to close they'd hit his head on both sides like a vice before re-opening!

Standing round him were half a dozen pensioners from the coach party, who were either unable to move him clear, or unwilling to do so in case they caused further injury. Straight away Andy and I grabbed him firmly but carefully, sliding him away from the doors, and laying him out flat, away from the now-working lift.

"Glad you did that," piped up one of the old gentlemen, "He's been there for ages!"

At that very moment the lift doors opened and, like a scene from 'Fawlty Towers', the two old girls from upstairs stepped out and walked past us on their way to the bar, pausing only to look down and say, "Oh, the poor man. Has he had too much to drink?"

It turned out that the guy who'd collapsed was the coach driver, who'd suffered a massive stroke while in the lift. Which is why, on our way to the hospital, we referred to his passengers as 'gangster grannies'!

Being an adrenalin-junkie, I loved my medic-on-a-motorbike work. But while it put me at the sharp and serious end of the job, it also introduced and exposed me to sights and situations that no first responder ever wants to experience. And although I should have been enjoying this new high point in my career, after a while I gradually came to feel that I was attracting death and destruction wherever I went, especially where children were involved. This took its obvious toll on me. My sleep patterns became increasingly erratic, and my stress levels were on the rise again. At times I felt like I was in 'The Sixth Sense' movie, in which I kept seeing dead people. So poor were my results at work, that my fellow paramedics were calling me 'Harold Shipman'. And what I still hadn't realised was that the almost daily death toll and trauma I was experiencing on the bike were digging up the graves of buried memories from Belfast, causing my mental boiler to build up another crushing head of pressure.

I woke around two in the morning with a central chest pain that was working its way down my left arm. Not wanting to alarm Cara, I went downstairs to consider the situation. I was a paramedic after all, albeit one displaying clear signs of a heart attack. But instead of calling for an ambulance, I decided to self-medicate. I threw back some paracetamol and codeine for the pain, took 300mg of aspirin to thin my blood, and waited for the tightness in my chest to subside before going quietly upstairs again and back to bed.

The following day I was working from the response car on Portland, so during my lunch break I used the onboard equipment to do a complete 12-lead ECG, which ran a full electrical trace of my heart to detect and display anything abnormal. When it was done, the printed strip revealed exactly what I'd feared. I'd had a suspected 'inferior infarct' – otherwise known as a heart attack. I was distinctly worried now, but again, just like back in the Army, I decided not to tell anyone. Afraid to face the reality of what was happening within me, I simply took another aspirin and carried on with my shift – hoping that it would get better.

The water balloon burst just two weeks later, as I was driving to Swanage ambulance station to start a shift. I knew by now what was going to happen next, and that I needed to pull over before I became a menace on the road. Eventually I found a quiet spot that allowed me to cover my face with my hands as my emotional repression fuse blew causing a massive crying fit that overwhelmed me once more. *Fuck! Not again!* Yet again, I didn't understand what was happening to me – because big, grown men don't cry, do they? I knew I'd been under a ton of pressure, and that I could cope with it, but now the chest pain and other problems in my life had been adding to it. The tragedy was that I'd known about these problems for so many years, but I was too – what? – Proud? Ignorant? Stupid? to do anything about them. I was ex-military, a full-time paramedic, and a part-time firefighter. My role in life was to help, protect, and look after people. Psychology – that ethereal stuff that goes on behind the scenes – wasn't in my job description, so it didn't figure into my worldview. After all, none of my mates had these problems, so why should I?

When I'd finished, I washed my face with my water bottle, dried my eyes, and ensured that I looked normal again before recommencing my journey to the ambulance station, where I enlisted the aid of a fellow medic to do another ECG check. This time we both confirmed the physical and technical symptoms of a suspected heart attack – but just as we were contemplating the next step a 999 call came in and we had to respond. Ironically, it was from a lady with chest pains, and I felt like a bloody hypocrite telling her that she should have reported it straight away, rather than wait for hours.

Our clinical findings dictated the need for a hospital so, after we'd handed her over to the A&E staff, I went to the Emergency Department, showed my ECG to the cardiologist, and was immediately admitted to Dorset County Hospital. I ended up staying there over a week and, after numerous tests, and constant monitoring from that thing that goes 'ping' by my bedside, they gave my ticker a bill of good health and put the cause down to stress. But while I was looking forward to returning to work, as soon as the Dorset Fire and Rescue got wind of the news they pulled me off the job and channelled me straight onto the counselling path.

To this day, I cannot thank them enough.

I started meeting with Jinny, a local TRIM (Trauma Risk Management) counsellor on the Isle of Portland who specialised in EMDR (Eye Movement Desensitization and Reprocessing). To be honest, I initially thought it was a load of rubbish. There was nothing wrong with me and, sitting in front of a stranger, following her hand moving from bottom-left to top-right, plus having to think of this as a safe place, was ridiculous. It didn't help that Rob Grey (Murph), another firefighter, knew when my session was running and, at the pivotal moment of shifting into my safe, peaceful place, he'd drive past the window honking his bloody car horn. Safe, peaceful place, indeed!

But after several weeks of psychotherapy sessions with Jinny, my mental structure had been mapped, and I was diagnosed with complex post-traumatic stress disorder (PTSD). She'd figured out that the trigger point was 15 years ago, seeing and having to treat my mate Jamie after that coffee jar bomb in Belfast. Apparently, this trauma had lodged like a piece of shrapnel in my brainstem, and all the other events afterwards – the mass graves, the children's deaths, the suicides, the cardiac arrests, etc, etc – were piling up behind it, adding to the blockage and increasing the back-pressure.

The human body is a miraculous structure, and the brain even more so. Between them, they're able to protect themselves, repair internal and external injuries, reroute blood flow for the greatest chance of survival, and even regenerate organs – but sometimes they need outside help, like first aid, surgery and drugs to give them a helping hand. However, extreme things can also happen to the body which it cannot fix fast enough, and even the most skilled doctor can't do a thing...

Likewise, just as the body processes and filters food for its best chance of survival, the brain does the same with experiences. Mine had been badly messed up and needed fixing, and this was what Jinny did for a living. She even explained the science to me – how the TRIM procedure was used with newly-traumatised patients to prevent their mental drawbridge from fully closing, and how EMDR effectively loosens and lifts the sewer grille in order to clear out the blockage beneath.

Most of us look back on our lives and imagine how we might have done things differently. Me – I truly and genuinely wish I could. I want to sincerely apologise to everyone I've ever scared by being aggressive – both actively and passively. To anyone I've ever threatened, especially my friends and family, I can only say that I am sorry, and accept that it was me who did that. But I want to let them know that it was a broken me – and broken things often have nasty, sharp, and exposed edges.

Thanks to Jinny, I no longer have the temper I once had, when I was known as 'Punch first, Ask second, Ingram'. I still have bouts of feeling inadequate, but experts say that this is down to how I was discharged and dumped like sewage by the Army. Now, when I have my 'grey days', I know I can always count on Cara and my friends to help me.

The sad thing about being an ambulance professional, a paramedic, is that most of the jobs you attend – the ones where you make things right – are usually forgotten by the end of your shift, so all the good things you do never outweigh the bad. You only remember the serious accidents, the life-changing injuries, the cardiac arrests, the fatalities, the overdoses, the hangings, the child deaths, and so on. Even worse, those memories spring back to life whenever you drive past the house or stretch of road where the incident occurred. If you ask any paramedic, most couldn't tell you how many people they've seen dying or dead, nor how many cardiac arrests they've attended –because they've lost count. It's probably the same for police officers and firefighters too.

Once I was declared fit, instead of returning me straight back to work, the brigade insisted that I took Cara and Freya, our baby girl, to Devon for some convalescing. Harcombe House is the Fire Brigades' home for injured service personnel, giving them the time and opportunity for treatment and recuperation in the natural, nurturing environment of an old stately home, with its own physical and psychological malady treatment areas, fishing lakes, nature walks, and swimming pool. Within the grounds were self-contained bungalows. Cara was pregnant with Lili at the time with only a month to go, so the holiday was especially welcomed by her. For me, however, compared with some of the other, more extreme cases here, I felt like a fraud. We were in the pool and, while Cara sat on the side talking with another lady, I started chatting with her husband, a retired firefighter. We were busily exchanging stories, until he asked at what station I was based. When I told him Portland, he searched his mind before asking where that was, to which I explained that it was a tied island at the southernmost point of Dorset.

"Dorset?" he responded, horrified, "Doesn't Dorset have retained firemen?"

As soon as I answered, "Yep" he reacted as if I'd just offered him DIY surgery on his testicles. Appalled and affronted, he exclaimed that he did not believe in 'retained service', and that in *his* time he'd worked with 'proper' firemen. He then moved away from me as fast as you can in water, got out of the pool, and stormed towards his lodging. His wife apologised profusely to Cara, before leaving to catch him up. Cara immediately asked me what I'd said to him, and if it had been anything aggressive, but I assured her that I'd been on my very best behaviour. The truth is that I was proud of being a retained firefighter, along with the many other men and women who give their personal time to crewing appliances over a period of shifts, to ensure constant and consistent cover 24 hours a day on every day of the year, including public holidays. I used to give 90 hours cover a week, on top of my 37.5 hours as a paramedic, regardless of whether I'd just completed a day or night shift. To show their solidarity, Cara and the girls often left the island to head into town on the mainland, so that I could get enough rest at home, and even accepted me missing our family events when someone was needed to keep a pump running.

Fortunately, it's not all 'London's Burning', with Blue Watch tackling one blaze after another around the city. Knowing that prevention is infinitely better than cure, Dorset Fire and Rescue spent a vast amount of money and resources on fire safety awareness, and one of our tasks was visiting houses and businesses on Portland to ensure they had adequate fire protection, including smoke alarms in every home. I was doing this with Andy and another paramedic officer from my ambulance station. We'd completed our paramedic shift, and were now giving cover to the brigade by visiting homes. One belonged to an old lady in one of the old Portland cottages, with three floors and very steep stairs – though to be fair to her, she seemed to manage them with ease. We introduced ourselves and, after a quick look around, Andy pointed to the ceiling at the top of the first flight of stairs, saying "Go on, boy. Stick one up there." Then, while he stayed downstairs to have a 'hearts, minds, and cuppa' with the lady, I started to fit the alarm at the top of a very narrow and precarious stairway. I was doing a grand job until I started to put my tools away in the cramped space, slipped off the landing and, following the acute gradient of the steps, slid all the way down to the bottom – which left me nursing a badly bruised and battered arse. Andy said

Stefan and me, this was taken when we drove to meet the family for the first time.

Above: This was the military base we stayed in for 6 months in South Armagh. This is the top sanger where Coco fired the burst of machine gun fire from.

Below: Tassagh Road bomb where two RUC officers were blown up and a secondary device exploded when we were patrolling nearby.

Above: One of the many graffiti drawn walls in Belfast.

Below: One of the many briefs given prior to going out on foot patrol in Belfast.

HMS Brazen being towed off the rock by a Chilean Navy, in the foreground can be seen the ships stores which had to be moved to the flight deck in an attempt to reverse the ship from its grounding.

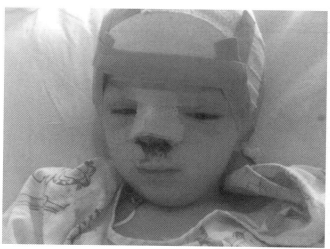

This was taken after Stefan's first operation.

Above: Stefan and the amazing Professor David Dunaway CBE. This was taken after his very last visit.

Below: Foot Patrol in Bosnia

Above: CP Paramedic work in Iraq.

Below: The only toy in the orphanage.

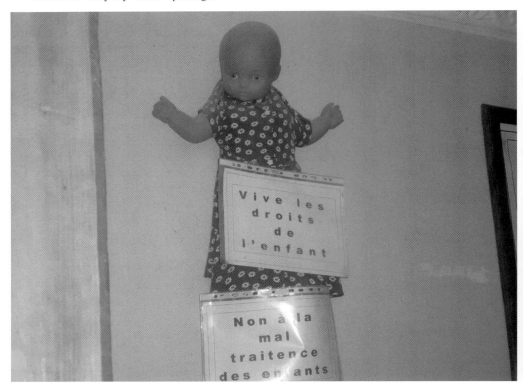

Above: The new orphanage being built.

Below: The Completed new orphanage.

Above: About to be towed out in the life raft for the start of the challenge.

Below: Mungo Jerry and me singing 'In The Summertime'

Above: Covid helicopter flight crew.

Right: Freya the morning after her long Scoliosis reversal operation.

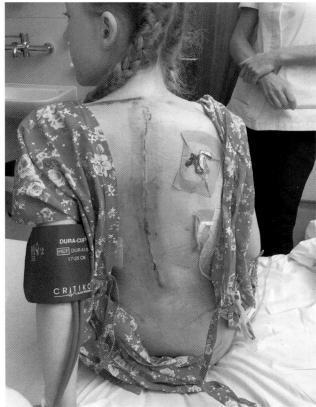

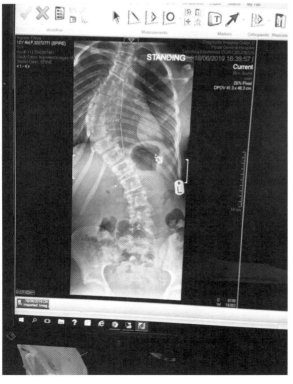

Above: The final photo after the epic 76 mile walk backwards. Freya and me.

Left: Freya's first x-ray showing the extent of her deformity.

Above: Surviving Minds Foundation Bowl where our wellbeing took place.

Right: NHS Paramedic duties during COVID

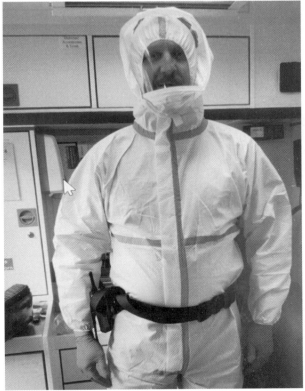

Receiving the Serbian Humanitarian award in Belgrade.

Receiving the MBE from the Lord Lieutenant.

Above: Retained firefighter with Freya.

Opposite: Receiving the Freeman of The City of London.

Offshore Paramedic.

Stefan and his beautiful wife, Milijana, taken March 2025.

nothing, so I attempted to pick myself up and pretend that this was all part of the job. Until the old lady asked me, "What on earth did you do that for? Would you like a cup of tea?"

To which Andy's response was, "Don't worry, madam. He's just a silly boy."

I remember another incident clearly, this time involving Murph – my breathing apparatus (BA) partner on most shouts, as we tended to buddy up regularly. We were the second pump away to a property fire on Portland, and could already see the smoke coming from the front door as we arrived. The crew on the first pump was new and just blundering around, so as soon as Murph and I jumped off the vehicle with our BA on, Andy instructed us to go in first.

Handing our tallies over to the BA controller – the guy who monitors what time you enter, how much air you've got, and when you should be coming out – we entered through the front door into the smoke-filled property. A neighbour had reported people inside, so our primary objective was to find them. We made our way towards the kitchen doing a right-hand search – where you keep close to the wall to your right, moving your right hand up and down it for reference, using your left hand to sweep in front of your face for obstructions, and your leading foot tapping the floor for collapse or weakness. During training, watching firefighters doing this looks idiotic, but the technique was developed, and subsequently proven, to save lives.

In movies like 'Backdraft', where firefighters enter a burning building with flames licking around their feet, they're able to run through a property rescuing people who can be seen from a short distance away. The reality is very different, and near-impossible. A property fire is usually full of thick, black, choking smoke – thicker and blacker than you could ever imagine. It's so dense and gungy that you're constantly wiping your mask with the back of your hand, just to see anything at all in front of you. It's really scary stuff, and anyone who says it isn't has never done it.

We ended up in the kitchen, also full of smoke, where we found a guy lying unconscious on the floor. Whereupon Murph, in his deep, broad

West Belfast accent, called over to me, "Hey, Shag! We've got a fooking casualty!"

I got on the radio to Andy and relayed this information, minus the expletive, before turning back to Murph, who'd just picked up the guy like a rag doll. With Murph supporting the top half of his body, and me the lower half, we got him out of the building – to the bellowing accompaniment of "Casualty!" "Casualty!" "Fooking casualty!" along the entire route.

Once I'd completed my convalescence at Harcombe House, I returned to both the Brigade and my full-time paramedic duties. The only problem was that, unbeknown to me in the meantime, the days of response bikes were coming to an end, and it wasn't long before they were all pulled off the road. The official reason was 'health and safety', even though we had never crashed the bikes! In truth, the service really needed patient-carrying resources and, while ambulances and cars met these criteria with ease, motorcycles definitely did not! So, I found myself back on an ambulance, doing normal jobs and, once again, wanting more excitement!

> "Throughout our time working together we had many incidents that lightened our days and allowed us to see the lighter side of our job which, all too often, was beyond dark with the typical jobs of the day.
>
> Wayne always acted with professionalism alongside me at every job. However, we could see the humour and, when on our own, were able to laugh in the face of adversity – which as paramedics you must be able to do, otherwise your mental health and wellbeing would be in tatters.
>
> We were also retained firefighters in a seaside island station, with retained firefighters from every walk of life, and many seeing trauma and death for the first time. We both used our experiences to support our crews, building and bonding lifelong relationships. When I was in charge of the appliances as an officer, whenever I looked behind me at my crew, I knew that my job was going to be easy due to the brotherhood and bonding that we'd built within the station.

Wayne has always been a supportive colleague and, since we have left the service, a very good friend. When I had a cerebellum stroke, Wayne was there in an instant to support not only me, but my family throughout my recovery. We often catch up for a coffee and share our stories, which we remember fondly.

There are many more memories, both dark and humorous, but some we must keep for a later date…"

Andy Randell

"I first met Wayne after he finished his Technician Training, early in 2005. My first impression of him, seeing this burly 6' 2" chap coming into the crew room, was feeling that this guy might be bit of a handful to mentor! But my first impression was wrong. He is a warm chap, with an easy smile, a big heart, and always willing to go that little extra for people.

The Technician Training he had just finished is a good start to the job, but many find the transition from the classroom theory to the more practical reality quite daunting. Not for Wayne, though. His previous military training and experience stood him in good stead, and he took to it all in his stride. He has to be one of the quickest students I mentored at picking it up, and pushing on to more advanced levels.

The only time I actually saw Wayne get a little stuck, was with a job we got called to at one of the local prisons. An inmate had taken a dislike to his cellmate and (after waiting for him to fall asleep) poured a whole kettle of boiling water, filled with sugar, over him. He finished off by repeatedly hitting him with a wooden table leg.

When we arrived, the patient was in an understandably sorry state – severe burns to his neck, arms, and torso, as well as deep cuts and bruising to his head and face. Wayne was attending and froze a little at the sight, and I could see he was wondering to himself "Where the hell do I start with this?!!!" A quick glance at me, and all I said was "ABC, mate..."

ABC stands for Airway, Breathing, Circulation – something drilled into all emergency staff as a systematic way of approaching every compromised patient, in importance of what's going to kill them the quickest. After this little reminder, his training instantly kicked in, and we breezed through the rest of the job without any further issues.

We worked through his mentoring time with the normal mix of jobs, ranging from minor falls with no injuries, to full-on 'brink of life' emergencies. Dealing with this brings people together, and we become good pals and had more than a few laughs. I can remember driving to emergencies on hot summer days – windows open, music on, and singing (loudly and badly) to Coldplay. Wayne pushed on, breezed through his training, and kept going to becoming a well-respected paramedic. A very special time was when my wife and I were fortunate enough to be invited to his wedding to the lovely Cara, on the shores of Loch Ness. All those times, I look back on with a smile. Our paths have taken different directions, but I know that his big heart keeps on giving to people in need."

Jay Mercer

"On a freezing winter's day in Weymouth, Dorset, I commenced my day shift with Wayne. I remember the ambulance we were working on – it had a dodgy clutch, and we thought it may go at any time. Well, that turned out to be the least of our problems on that shift ...

Early in the morning, we were called to reports of two people in cardiac arrest in the doorway of a local supermarket. A 999 call had been made by a member of the public so – two people not breathing, and no signs of life.

We hopped into the ambulance without hesitation and left Weymouth ambulance station, heading for a stretch of road called 'The Weymouth Way'. I considered myself a good driver at the time and, with my advanced training and experience to date, I was confident in driving quickly as we made our way using our blue lights, sirens, and claiming the exemptions we had to exceed the speed limit, en route quickly to these two people.

I knew it was going to be icy that day, and took it carefully. The road seemed okay, with no visible ice, as we travelled down this treacherous stretch towards a roundabout. As we approached it, I applied the footbrake and the ambulance suddenly lost control – wheels spinning and sliding on a sheet of invisible ice. Despite my frantic attempts to regain control, the ambulance slid perilously towards a looming lamp post, and then – an almighty bang! Time seemed to slow down as I gasped in horror, with Wayne hanging on for his life, and we had no choice but to watch it play out like a movie over which we had no control, and playing the part of the leading characters. There was a deafening crash as the ambulance collided with the unforgiving metal of the lamp post, which teetered for a moment as the ambulance tipped over, the impact having thrown it onto its side, spinning us 180 degrees, and trapping myself and Wayne inside. As quickly as we could, we unbuckled our seatbelts and worked out what had happened. I turned off the sirens – once I'd found the button that had shifted with the crash. Then, together, we kicked the windshield out to make our escape, crawling out of the now-inverted ambulance, before climbing up the embankment up to the road.

Stood on the roadside, we observed another crew whizzing past us, then stopping to make sure we were okay, before carrying on to the double cardiac arrest call. The rear of our vehicle now dipped into Radipole Lake, and bits of ambulance were scattered all over the place but, thankfully, we were okay. Wayne and I brushed off our uniforms, we were picked up by a manager in his car, and it wasn't long before we had collected the sister vehicle of the one we were on, got straight back to work on the same shift, and were responding to calls again.

I gained a reputation for a while and, for a good six months after, the dispatcher in ambulance control would call me on approach to the roundabout to make sure I made it through! Despite me being the lead clinician, and having been longer in the ambulance service, I followed Wayne's lead and his stoic character which, I am sure, comes as part of his time in the military. We just got up and carried on doing our job, without any fuss. And the two dead people? Well, they were two homeless guys who were fast asleep, breathing, and okay."

Jim Ryan

"My name is Andy Crawley and I am an Ambulance Technician with SWAST. One day I was the senior technician on a double tech crew. We were asked to back up the Paramedic Motorbike for a collapsed lady. I remember pulling up outside the harbour masters office and being directed to where Wayne was with the lady. It was as we entered we heard one of the staff trying to talk French in the worst impression ever. I remember we all started laughing which really annoyed him to the point he told us all to f""k off and stormed out. My crew mate and myself laughed all the way back to Dorchester ambulance station."

Andy Crawley

Chapter 15

2010

Back Home

In addition to the ambulance work and the firefighting, I was also providing instruction for a company in Hereford which taught a range of first aid courses to civvies and ex-military guys going on the close-protection, or bodyguarding, circuit. This opened up a whole new world for me, I met fellow professionals, and learned a lot from them – including Andy Purdie, a former SAS paramedic, and now chief instructor for the company. Andy and I struck up a great friendship from the start, and one day he pulled me aside and told me that he was going back to Iraq as a paramedic for G4S, a private security company – and would I like to join him? Straight away, and several times afterwards, I gave him the same response – that I was done with that lifestyle and now wanted it easy. But he must have recognised something in me and persisted. He was right. Who was I trying to kid? I'd always wanted to go to Iraq, my work was becoming mundane, and I longed like hell to be back in my old way of life!

Not long after, back home from work, Cara asked if I was okay. Most wives have a sixth sense for this kind of thing. She knew that everything was not okay, and I was only putting on a brave face for her and our children. I told her about Andy, and that he'd asked me to go to Iraq with him. Cara understood me well. She bit her lip, and closed her eyes to think. Then she nodded and told me, "I want you to be happy. So go, get whatever's inside you out, and come back to us. We'll always be here for you…"

The next day I called Andy with the good news and handed in my notice to the ambulance and fire services. Within two weeks I was in London for a briefing and medical exam, and a week later landed in Basra, surrounded by a cordon of grizzled close-protection (CP) operators. We went through the usual show of Iraqi police officers checking our visas, who finally 'validated' them for just $110 each. After several hours of having been forced to sit and wait, I was finally allowed to collect my kit and went through to the airport's reception area, where I was met by a solidly-built guy named Nick King. I didn't know it then, but he and I would become very close friends, and still are to this day. After confirming my ID, he gave me the usual man-hug by which most soldiers greet one another, before escorting me to the on-site Ops Room.

It felt strange being back in a war zone, especially as a civvy. But it also felt good, and satisfyingly natural to me. Looking around the room, I could see which teams were on the ground in our area of operations (AOR), before being offered a brew and a chat with the ops officer and some of the other lads. Most were ex-British soldiers, including Gurkhas and Fijians, and a few had served with the French Foreign Legion – a real mixture of unique individuals.

One thing I quickly realised, was that regardless of what country you came from, or what background you had, you were treated as a brother here. And as a paramedic – one of their most precious commodities – I was a newly-arrived superhero, here to get them all home safely.

After our brew I collected my weapons, which included an AK47 and a Glock 17 handgun, plus body armour, helmet, spare mags and boxes of ammunition. I'd do my official weapons training over the next few days, but Nick gave me some quick TP (training practice) in stripping down, assembling, and loading, just in case. Fully armed with my bags, kit, and weapons I was finally shown to my room. I wasn't really sure what the arrangement would be, and I was half-expecting to be bunked in a space under a stairway somewhere. What greeted me was better than anything I'd ever imagined – even as a sergeant I'd been used to sharing a room, but here I had my own portacabin, with internet, TV, and a fully-working fridge! Amongst this relative luxury, and sense of normality, the scary thing that I remember wasn't the fact that I'd put myself back in harm's way, nor that I was once again in a different country amongst people who instinctively hated and wanted to kill me. It was that, as soon as I entered my room and closed the door, the first thing I did was to sit on my bed, strip down my weapons, and start cleaning them.

This was a defining moment for me, as I realised that (a) I was back in the working environment I knew best, (b) I felt comfortable about it, and (c) I was still institutionalised. I knew that my true home was with Cara and my girls and boys. Yet here, in an unfamiliar and hostile country, I was in a natural and familiar environment in which, somehow, I felt safe.

For those who served in the recent Iraq war, we were based at the COB, the Contingency Operating Base, at Basra international airport just outside the city centre. This had been the home of the British Army for many years until it was handed over to the US military, which created a totally different environment than when occupied by HM Forces. All along the main drag, right the way through the camp, was one coffee shop after another, including most of the well-known names. They also had their own Pizza Hut, KFC, and an extensive buffet of burger bars. There was also the PX shopping centre but, as I found out pretty damn quickly, private security firms weren't allowed in without a pass – and to get one of those you had to be US service personnel. Still, it didn't stop me trying!

Back in my room, after I'd been sorting out my stuff for about an hour, Nick arrived to give me a guided tactical tour of the camp – especially to the mess hall. The COB is mind-bogglingly huge, and an absolute nightmare for anyone in security logistics. As an example, smack-bang in the centre of the base is the airport's control tower – the natural bullseye for the local militia, who used it as an aiming point for all their inbound missiles.

We drove around for a while, familiarising ourselves with the area, and staying strictly within the 15mph speed limit. It seemed that every junction was manned by an American MP just waiting to 'bust our ass'. It became clear that they hated the private military sector, seeing us as cocksure and overpaid mercenaries. I couldn't disagree with the well-paid part, but I knew that every soldier, no matter where in the world they're stationed, will always view it as their own territory. So as a Brit on their turf, I didn't want to give them an opportunity to hurt my bottom.

After a few coffee-stops we headed to our dining area, which was used by several contract companies and the contractors we were looking after. I must say, the food was incredible, and I learned that this was managed by a succession of Indian lads who spent up to a year in-country. Talking with them later, they said that if they could manage to get a full year's work here, they could earn enough to retire. They also ran our laundry service, and even cut hair. I tried the latter once, but made the mistake of accepting the offer of a head massage, which was one of the most painful experiences of my life. The way he beat the crap out of my scalp, I thought he'd be better suited to interrogation. Adding insult to injury, and having just escaped 'Guantanamo Bay', I bumped into Nick outside, who had heard my cries of pain and was still pissing himself with laughter.

As I said, the food was fantastic and you could have as much as you wanted, just as long as you didn't waste it. I was really enjoying my meal, a large plate of assorted meats, when a female American voice came over the PA system with, "Incoming! Incoming!" followed by a loud 'waa waa waa' tone. This was played over and over, and I learned that this was to be our serenade whenever the local yokels shared their latest batch of 155mm rockets with us, launching them into the camp at random for our delight! Several civilian employees near us jumped straight up and ran out of the mess hall towards the communal concrete shelter. I got up to follow them until I saw Nick, Trev Kirton, and all our other CP guys just sitting where they were, carrying on with their meals. One of them actually reached over and pinched a steak that had been left behind! So I shrugged, continued eating my meal, and waited to see what happened next. A few seconds later, three loud 'crumps' were heard as rockets hit the camp, but I learned later on that the rascals who'd launched them were effectively playing 'Battleships', and rarely hit anything important.

Nick also explained why none of us had moved. This was because the Iraqi contractors had laid gravel all around the shelter and accommodation areas, so if a rocket landed it'd be like an anti-personnel canister round going off. It was definitely better to stay inside because out in the open, you'd be literally sandblasted, and shredded alive. Many believed that the gravel was an intentional act of sabotage by the Iraqis, who wanted every last one of us dead. On the other hand, it was a cheap and plentiful material in this country, so who's to say? Paranoia plays strange tricks with the mind.

We received several attacks like this each week, which justified our handsome salaries, and occasionally one of our two Phalanx anti-missile systems would return fire. These were mesmerising to watch, especially at night, as their computer-controlled radar automatically searched for and tracked enemy rockets in the air, and then engaged them faster than any human operator could. First, you'd see an overarching red stream of 20mm Vulcan cannon tracer rounds heading upwards towards the source, followed by a 4-5 second chainsaw-like 'brrrr' as a one hundred-round burst of armour-piercing penetrator shells was delivered precisely to an inbound aerial target at over a kilometre per second. After these onslaughts, I rarely saw signs of impact from anything headed towards us. But what went up must have come down again, somewhere, and more than likely on the other side of the fence. I did witness the result of one, when a night-time hit was scored on a small fuel depot about 200 yards from us. I couldn't get involved, of course, but that didn't stop me watching, from a short distance away, how the pros here tackled a fuel fire. Another occurred while I was Skyping my boys, Harry and Toby, both now in their teens. I'd do my best to have a serious fatherly talk with them, but I always seemed to be fighting a losing battle against 'Call of Duty' on their Xbox. This time, during our chat, the "Incoming! Incoming!" lady came over the PA, which immediately grabbed my boys' waning attention – not because they assumed I'd be in danger, but because they wanted to hear what it sounded like when the bloody thing hit! I told them I was in my quarters at the centre of the camp, and they probably wouldn't hear much (I didn't want to worry them) to which they asked if I could stick my microphone out of the doorway for them... Heh, boys, eh?

The following day I met the healthcare manager, Eddie Irons, a paramedic who'd spent several years in Hereford with the SAS and, most importantly, a 'no shit' guy to work with. As the role of paramedic was a new and necessary one, he'd been hired to oversee its operation and hire in the team. Other than Andy, I was his first new guy on the ground and I followed him to a 40' x 8' ISO container which held all the medical kit he'd been ordering over the past few weeks. I was expecting a few shelves and lots of spare space but, as soon as I looked inside, my eyes lit up, a huge smile came over my face, and I felt like little Stefan in Hamleys. This was a paramedic's paradise, full of plenty of everything you could possibly need for every conceivable medical situation! Eddie was clearly the right man for the job, and his special forces experience shone through – especially as his budget allowed him to leave absolutely nothing off the list. I was totally in my element – and happy as a pig in the proverbial. This place was better equipped than some hospitals I'd seen! If you had a limb blown off, we could fix it. If you'd sustained such facial trauma that your airway was blocked, we were your guys. If you were in excruciating pain, we could do something about it fast. But let's draw a line here – we're not supermen, and if your toilet's blocked then there's bugger all we can do about it. So please don't ask.

It took us the entire day to painstakingly fill every medical bergen we had with the appropriate kit and drugs. We packed each one exactly the same way, which not only made them interchangeable, but every vehicle was equipped identically. This ensured that a medic could jump into any of them, and instantly access the right item for an emergency.

Chapter 16

2010

Preparation

To ensure the paperwork was in order, medics had to sign a load of PGD's (patient group directions) confirming that we were confident in the use of each drug, plus how, where, and what to do with various medicines. One I was unsure of was a pain-relief inhaler named Penthrox, which required you to break and empty an ampoule of liquid into its foam base, before giving the casualty a mouthpiece to hold between their lips and suck in briefly whenever they needed to reduce the pain. It was very similar to Entonox, a 50/50 mix of nitrous oxide and oxygen (or laughing gas, as it's more commonly known – if you don't use it properly). I informed Eddie that I'd never seen nor used it before, and he explained that it was used by the Australian ambulance service, before giving me one to try.

Experiential learning is often used by ambulance services in Entonox training, and the students learn by taking a few inhalations so they knew what to expect. That evening, in my room, I gave the Penthrox a test. I sat down on my bed, imagined I'd just been injured, then took several deep inhalations, before waking up flat on my back a short time later. It had totally knocked me for six, and I immediately knew how useful this could be – especially when dealing with multiple casualties.

The following day we carried out contact drills while inside a vehicle. Driver training was done on a designated area of waste ground, and we'd drive up and down its dry, sandy surface simulating contact right or left, contact centre, contact rear, casualty here, casualty over there, and so on. We practiced skidding to a halt and immediately exiting the vehicle, learning from the pros the best place to kneel, or get behind – to protect yourself from the next incoming round. We also went through drills on how to cover me, the paramedic, while I went to help the casualty. This was new to the CP guys as, prior to this, they'd simply grab the casualty, bundle them into a truck, and then burn rubber to the nearest medical aid. Now, they had a medic who'd be attempting to stabilise an injury on the cramped rear seat of a 4x4. Whoever said that war was glamorous?

In the afternoon we drove to the ranges to zero my weapon, which was a new experience for me. Of course, I'd been on a firing range before, but not in the relaxed professional atmosphere that prevailed here. On British Army ranges safety is paramount, often to the point of being anal, which is just tolerable. There are times, however, when your small-arms instructor can be a total pain in the arse. The range becomes their classroom, and they make the maximum use of their short-lived period of power.

This session was run by ex-special forces, so they already knew each other as safe. Their drills were shit hot, they trusted us as fellow pros and, just as long as you didn't act like an idiot, they'd reciprocate and treat you like a grown-up. They watched as you took one of your weapons, test fired a few rounds to see if they hit where you'd aimed, and adjust slightly if they didn't. When you were satisfied, you'd do the same with your other one, zeroing this in too. Well, I'd spent 18 years as a recce soldier, and our long-range, long-term weapons were surveillance, stealth, and comms. I'd never been a sharpshooter, even after all the hours Mick spent with us on the ranges. Although he'd tried to teach us SF tactics, he'd always been constrained by the (to him) pedantic rules of Big Brother.

Most of the CP lads would fire a few rounds, adjust, fire a few more, and be satisfied with the result. Me, on the other hand... well, I was slamming round after round into the target, reloading my mag, then doing the same again, over and over. It was on my return to the ammo box to reload that Dave approached me with, "Thank fuck you're our medic!

2010: Preparation

What's the problem?" So, I told him honestly that the AK they'd given me was useless. The sight was out, the stock and foregrip were loose, and I strongly suspected that the barrel had been bent. "Hmm," was his considered response, before taking it from my hands, quickly checking it over, then dropping to the ground to fire five rounds from a prone position, five rounds kneeling, and five more stood up. Other than the first two rounds, each grouping was no bigger than a 50p coin. He then proceeded to teach me how to hold each weapon and fire it optimally. I followed his instructions to the letter and, bugger me, it worked! For the first time ever with a rifle, I actually enjoyed what I was doing. To be fair, they did discuss reissuing me with a Remington shotgun, seeing as I couldn't hit a barn door at ten paces. But, I reminded them, if I had to start shooting then our situation was well and truly fucked, because I was a professional medic and not a hired gun.

I was assigned as 2IC to Trev, who'd served with the Parachute Regiment and spent many years working the CP circuit in Afghanistan and Iraq. Trev was a legend in both the paras and the CP world, and Nick had already told me about working with him in Afghanistan on a covert job. They'd been driving around the country carrying out various tasks and were now on their way to a British Army forward operating base (FOB). Nick was on the back of the vehicle with the GPMG, Trev was commanding, and the GPS wasn't working, so they decided to pull up at a small village and ask the locals where they were. Trev got out of the vehicle, map in hand, rifle slung down his side, and nonchalantly walked up to three local males standing beside a building, overtly looking at his map. From a distance Nick realised that Trev must by now have seen the three AK47's propped up against the wall behind the men, but he didn't miss a step and walked right up to them, asking, "Right, where the fuck are we, then?" These three guys helpfully pointed to the map and, all smiles, Trev thanked them, patted one on the shoulder, and strolled back to the vehicle. When Nick pointed out to Trev that they were Taliban, Trev just said, "Yeah. I know. Let's go, quick. And don't shoot them…"

Big brass ones aside, Trev was a solid as a rock, dependable guy, who taught me loads throughout my time in-country. Although officially employed as a paramedic, or Tier 2 Medic, I also carried the title 'Close Protection Operator'. However, there were those who thought 'operator' was a euphemism for 'mercenary'- someone who'd do anything for the money – especially abroad, where the rules no longer applied.

It was true that we were paid a stupid and stupendous wage, but this was due to the extreme risks involved, and no one who signed up was ever guaranteed to return home alive. But the dirty M-word was never used by anyone I ever worked with – only by those back home who were jealous of what we were earning, but didn't have the B's to apply for the job themselves!

Chapter 17

2010

Remote Healing

We'd all deploy out on jobs in three specially-armoured Toyota Land Cruisers. Trev would be in the lead vehicle with an Iraqi driver, the centre vehicle would have the client plus two local nationals, and I'd be in the rear vehicle along with another Iraqi local. At first, I was surprised that we had three expats accompanied by four locals, all issued with AKs – but you had to learn to trust these guys with your life, just as they needed to trust you with theirs!

Our responsibility was to drive the client from the COB to their designated meeting area – usually at the Rumaila oilfields. We'd pull up at the open sandy area in front of each oil establishment, drop them off safely, wait for them to complete their appointed task (which could take under an hour, or the entire day), and then escort them back safely.

In addition to being medic for the two teams, my role also included keeping eyes on the rear of the convoy. The Iraqis here had no sense of road awareness – driving at speed and overtaking in either lane. I'd warn Trev if there was a fast mover, left or right, in case of vehicle attack. He'd report back on potential choke points, or possible IED's (improvised explosive devices) at the roadside – and these came in many forms, stuffed inside anything you'd normally ignore, from an old tyre to a dead dog. The company had already lost two guys to a device in Majnoon, just after I'd arrived in-country. They'd been practising exactly what we were doing now, but that time a device detonated, taking out the middle callsign. Debriefing the teams afterwards, they concluded that these guys had died instantly, there was absolutely nothing that could have been done to save them, and it could easily happen again. This was a sobering thought on every excursion, and another reason they paid us well to be here!

We were told that the device was a shaped charge supplied by Iran, though personally I didn't give a toss where it came from. Remembering Northern Ireland, I contemplated the mentality and motivation of those who planted them because, once primed, these bloody things are totally impartial as to who they'll claim and maim. Soldiers, office workers, and inquisitive schoolchildren are all fair game to an IED.

As we usually had hours to wait, I set myself two goals for my time here. The first was to complete my NEBOSH diploma in health, safety and environmental management via remote learning. The second was to teach my team first aid. I started by giving them several tests, and was shocked at how little my fellow professionals knew. From experience, I know that once you start this game, medics don't automatically acquire the Holy Jacket of Invincibility. Far from it, and if we were ever attacked, Sod's Law would ensure that the medic got hit first!

It really worried me that these guys didn't have a clue, and I wanted to ensure that, no matter which of us got whacked, they'd all be able to administer proper first aid. I prepared, organised, and conducted lessons while on-site and, eager to learn, they threw themselves fully into every opportunity. We certainly weren't short of equipment, and it was better used for training than left to expire in a container.

Soon, every member of my team was able to treat catastrophic bleeds, close-sucking chest wounds, decompress lungs, and to confidently place airway adjuncts. The next stage was to test them in a live-action scenario. I'd already prepped Darren, our other team leader and, one morning, as our team arrived on site, he immediately got out of his truck and dropped to the ground like a sack of spuds. I shouted that there'd been an explosion from under the car, and that both of Darren's legs had sustained a catastrophic haemorrhage. I watched proudly as every one of them sprang into action. They weren't perfect, but in under three minutes they'd applied bilateral tourniquets to both legs, lifted the casualty onto

2010: Remote Healing

a scoop stretcher, packed him into the back of our makeshift ambulance, and were on their way to the nearest medical facility. Not bad going for rookies, I thought, and I'd filmed the whole thing on my phone for debriefing later.

During one initial training session I noticed one of our Iraqi lads, Karar, listlessly moping around – which was unusual as he'd always be the first to ask questions on medical matters. I took him to one side and asked if anything was wrong. He bit his lip and told me that he'd gone to his doctor the previous evening with a boil on his arse and, instead of giving him antiseptic cream or antibiotics, the doctor had cut it out and it had got really painful. But since I'd asked, would I mind checking it out? Now, it wasn't in my job description to be examining an Iraqi national's arse cheeks, and normally I'd have toed the company line and said no. However, the poor guy was clearly in agony, and I was intrigued at the standards of the local medical practice, so said I'd take a look without promising anything. I picked up my kit and we walked over to the security gate commander's office. After waking him up and asking him if he'd leave the office for a private matter, I asked Karar to drop his trousers and bend over. What I found was nothing short of horrifying. The boil, lump, or whatever it was had been cut deeply out of the inside of his right buttock and was chafing against the other side every time he took a step. The worst of it, though, was that the open hole, measuring a good 4" long, 2" wide and 1" deep, had been left open and untreated. This was shoddy work indeed, as the doctor hadn't even applied a dressing, nor provided painkillers. I started to clean out the wound, which was already showing signs of infection, and at this point Karar was now in extreme pain, so out came the Penthrox (told you I'd use it!) before packing the wound with sterile dressings and sealing them over. I then had to organise a new driver to replace him, as there was simply no way that he'd heal up whilst sitting down on that. He needed to be looked at properly, in a sterile environment, and to get started on a course of antibiotics.

Word soon got around that G4S had brought doctors with them and one day, while we were sat around waiting for our client, a civilian child approached us, accompanied by his mum. She couldn't tell me what was wrong, but the boy was pointing to his belly so, rightly or wrongly, on company time, I treated him as best I could – but this opened the floodgates and, very quickly, his entire family, friends, and neighbours were all arriving for health checks.

What else could I do? This was a hearts and minds opportunity to gain the support and trust of the locals, but instead it escalated into a steep learning curve showing me that, even though I wanted to make the world better, this was not the time and place. Our client could have returned at any moment, any of these Iraqis could have it in for us and I was creating a huge security risk. Reluctantly but inevitably, I had to tell them all to go away, in order to fulfil the reason for which I'd been allowed to come here at all.

One Friday evening we were all called into the Ops Room, to learn that the US Army had halted all ground movements as a precaution. Their intel had picked up that a local Shia militia leader was planning a 'Day of Rage', and that this would create an ideal reason for his Mehdi army to plant more devices along our route to the oilfields. As my team were on 'earlies' the next day, we'd have been among the first to prove the roads. As this was now a military operation, we were confined to base. Saturday produced no strategic news for us, but on Sunday morning their task force encountered a newly-buried IED, along the road of our daily route. One of their soldiers had lost a leg, but kept his life, when his fully-armoured truck was destroyed in the intense blast. For us, in our Land Cruisers, it would have been a massacre.

We also learned that, on Saturday, three car bombs had been detonated in Basra, killing around 20 civilians and injuring many more. What intel didn't know at the time was that this militia leader was so disappointed with the low death toll (he'd hoped for many more!) that he planned a further, upgraded day of more intense rage the following weekend. To make absolutely certain, he ordered his army to detonate multiple devices, one after another, right the way throughout southern Iraq – which succeeded in killing over 50 civilians and seriously injuring over 250 more. Fear, confusion, and destruction were the key components of his game.

The strategy was beyond our comprehension. We'd had no idea that this had been planned and were all out on the ground when the explosions started. As the coordinated devastation spread like wildfire through the country, we were all ordered back into the COB, even though this herded us all into one area. This was clearly part of the plan, and the expression 'fish in a barrel' was in all our minds as, over the next 24 hours, day and night, missile after missile rained down on our camp, each one trying to take as many of our lives as possible.

This leader then went public about what he called the sickening number of civilian martyrs and casualties affected in the nationwide protest against 'US occupation', and the following weekend held a nationwide 'Day of Regret' to express its sorrow and misery. Talk about 'rabble rousing', because these were the conditions we had to work in, and under, during our time here.

Six months into deployment our security contract with the engineering company was up and transferred to protecting British Petroleum. The changeover involved numerous PowerPoint presentations to us from their senior management, and ours to them in the fields of prevention and cure. For their projects to commence, and continue working effectively, the Americans wanted their entire local workforce to be 100% fit, so we organised tests for tuberculosis, syphilis, and other common, undesirable infections. While checking my own team, not only did my driver test positive for TB, but both he and my spare driver had syphilis. We didn't then have the antibiotics for this, so I asked him to get treated by his local doctor, and bring me the empty vials as proof. He smiled and said, "No worries, Mr Wayne", then started to walk out of the door, before I stopped him on impulse. "This means no jiggy-jiggy with your wife, because she needs to have the medicine too, so you'll need to bring her vials as well…" To which he smiled again, nodded understandingly, and left the room, closing the door behind him. A few seconds later the door reopened, and my smiling driver peered around it to ask, "Mr Wayne, do I need to bring them for my girlfriends too?" *Bloody hell!* Apparently, he had two on the go, as well as his good lady wife. Then I recalled a time when, not that long ago, I also thought that this was perfectly normal and acceptable behaviour for a man.

The three ladies I struggle with now are my wonderful wife and my darling daughters, all of whom I love dearly. Thinking of them, I realised that the handover coincided with Cara's forthcoming birthday so, in absentia, I decided to send her a special greetings card via a popular website. Wanting to make it unique and memorable, I put a lot of thought into what should be on the cover. Normally you'd upload a pic of your family, a memorable place, or your favourite pet but, being me, I thought I'd do something completely different. I stripped naked with just my holster and pistol (unloaded!) covering my bits. Then, using a whiteboard marker and mirror, scrawled 'HAPPY BIRTHDAY' across my chest in all-caps. My trusty sidekick Nick was waiting outside to take the picture and, in the middle of Iraq, naked but for my belt and sandals, and looking like an extra from 'Spartacus', I stepped outside onto the gravelly ground with my arms spread apart, as if to embrace my wife. Nothing to it really, except that at the same moment our CEO just happened to walk around the accommodation block to come face to face with my bare, untanned, Great British arse. He stared at me, burst into laughter, and exclaimed, "Oh my God! And you're the guy protecting my execs from terrorists!" before retreating the way he'd come, shaking his head.

Cara received the large envelope while staying at her parents, and proudly opened it in full view of her mother and sister. Now, I love my mother-in-law dearly, though she does have some interesting views on life. Which is why the sight of her near-nude son-in-law prompted her to comment, "Oh! I thought it would be a lot sandier there…"

> "I started working in the south of Iraq in the early 2000's, went on to a diplomatic mission in Afghanistan with the FCO, and returned to Basra on an oil and gas project which is where I met Wayne. We got on great from Day One, and to this day has been like a brother to me.
>
> Iraq, in those early years, was not for the faint-hearted, and definitely those who had other misconceptions were either asked to leave or were sent home – because they weren't of the right calibre for the role.

The wages were good at the time, but started to plummet as companies undercut each other for contracts, and in the end the hard-working guys on the ground took wage cuts. Small at first however, the small cuts became bigger cuts, and the standards and quality of personnel dropped dramatically.

The COB or, if I remember rightly, the Contingency Operating Base next to Basra International airport, was huge. Its amenities were good, and gave many other agencies a relatively safe place to operate from. Working hours were long and the constant threat from militias and roadside IEDs was prevalent. Evenings were the best time to unwind after long days on the roads, visiting different locations, and catching up with the boys to see what their day was like, and we usually met at the coffee shop where the banter and slagging went on – to the delight of many. The best thing about all the banter was there were no holds barred, and no worries about being PC. Everything was just good fun among the lads. Nothing like good humour – dark or light – after a long day.

Sleep was a different thing altogether, as the local militia took much glee in launching rockets and mortars into the COB when you needed to get some restful sleep. While that was happening, the US unit let rip with their rocket or mortar interceptor, which definitely woke everyone up!

Another interesting time for me was the medical scenarios that Wayne and Andy took us through. Great fun, and as realistic as possible. Valuable lessons and experiences all round!"

Nick King

"Iraq in those days were crazy times. Every day you lived with the threat of either being blown up by an IED, or shot whilst out on mission. Another option was being blown up in your bed by a Chinese rocket or mortar sent over from the local militias at night back in camp. On top of that you had the constant battle with the Iraqi police and army, who would take any opportunity to try and arrest you on false allegations so they could make money out of your release. Corruption was rife, especially from the authorities.

But despite these daily threats to our lives, life was made bearable not only by the pop star wages we were rightly earning to put our necks on the line daily, to get Iraq up and running again after the war, but mainly by the trust and confidence you had in your team mates. All ex-military, highly trained, and professionals whom you knew you could trust would be by your side if things went wrong.

The best part of working with this private army was the relentless banter and slagging that anyone who has served in the military is aware of. This made things bearable and was a much-needed source of relief during these crazy days. Some of the banter after work, in the camp coffee shops, will be my fondest memories of working with a fine bunch of men and girls."

Andy Purdie

Chapter 18

2010

Essential Travel

Times were changing. We were now working for a much larger company and the differences in our structure and practice were becoming apparent. The trips out of camp had dried up like a desert well, the frequency of missile attacks had slowed down, and my life had become monotonous. I'd be up each day for the Ops brief at 9am smash the weights until mid-morning, then soak up the sun until the afternoon gym session.

People came and went and, typical of our guys, one of them had acquired a genuine, brown leather sofa. Mucking in together, we eventually got it on top of the air raid shelter, where we'd usually spend our time exchanging pleasantries while waiting for a job, or lying on a towel getting a tan to show off back home. A proper sofa would add a real touch of home to our current surreal existence. Unfortunately, we found out the hard way why nobody else wanted the bloody thing – that a large expanse of leather, exposed to the midday sun of Iraq, transformed rapidly and without warning into a sizzling griddle – and that anyone who sat on it got up pretty damn quickly again with a shriek, leaving behind a personal, permanent bum-print. Inviting friends around, and collecting their autographs like this, was quite funny for a while.

But despite the stellar wages going into my UK bank account each month, I was starting to feel like one of our fire extinguishers – all pumped up and primed, but on permanent standby just waiting to do something useful. This wasn't what I'd signed up for and my eyes lit up one morning when an email from a UK medical company arrived, asking if I'd be interested in working at a gold mine in northwest Africa. I'd always enjoyed being paid to see the world so, as I was due leave in a few days, I responded right away and arranged to meet at their head office in Kingston upon Thames on my return.

Back in the UK, I sat with the director, Alex, and we chatted over my CV to see if I fitted the bill, and when I was available. I needed to finish off in Iraq first, so we mutually agreed to start my new job the following month. The admin staff at G4S were extremely accommodating, saying that if I ever wanted to return, there'd always be a place for me.

I gave myself three weeks with the family and flew Cara, the girls, and my boys to my parents' villa in Spain for some private quality time. This passed all too quickly, and before long I was meeting Alex again in a coffee shop at Waterloo train station. I wasn't sure if this was standard operating procedure, or the dodgiest deal ever, because after chatting for a short while he simply handed me a one-way ticket to Nouakchott, the capital of Mauritania, and left me with, "Good luck, and keep me informed." Still thinking about that parting comment, and concluding that he just needed to confirm that I was actually on my way, I took the Tube to Heathrow, from where I got a connecting flight to Paris, followed by the main flight to Africa – and this became the start of a long, frustrating, love/hate relationship with Air France, because every single take-off from London would be delayed, with me sat either in the departure lounge or, even more annoyingly, inside the bloody plane.

It wouldn't have been so bad had my connecting flight not been right at the other end of Charles de Gaulle airport. Every foreigner who's ever got lost there knows that if you need help, and you don't speak French, then you're screwed. Their attitude is that every civilised person should speak a second language – and it should be French. So, what did I love about them? Well, the company always flew me Business Class, so I learned enough French to become an authority on ordering duck.

Just before I left Iraq, Andy had sat me down and asked if I really wanted to go to Mauritania, because it was a known hotbed for al-Qaeda. In fact, he painted such a poor picture of the place that I visited the gov.uk website to get some intel on the country – but all they said, fundamentally, was 'Do Not Go Here'.

Great…

Despite my last-minute misgivings I hadn't wanted to let Alex down so, after having convinced Cara that it was safe, I was now about to land in the Islamic Republic of Mauritania. Well, the Foreign Office had advised against all but essential travel. And this was essential, because I'd already made a promise. My first impression of the country, as I alighted from the plane, was the heat – the hottest and driest I'd ever experienced in my life – although the word 'Sahara' on the map should have prepared me. I was already sweating like the proverbial pig in a blanket from the long wait after we'd landed and immediately felt the need to down both the spare bottles of water I'd brought with me.

We were all shepherded to the indoor Customs area, locals and expats together, though as soon as I entered the building I was approached by a representative from my new employer. Wearing a traditional white dishdasha, and a welcoming smile which revealed the few remaining teeth to be a darkish brown, he asked me if I was 'Mr Wayne', which I duly confirmed, allowing introductions and handshakes to be exchanged. He then guided me through Customs, where my hand luggage was scanned, before continuing to the conveyor belt to await my luggage. On the way, I noticed numerous piles of suitcases and holdalls already in the corner of the room, and casually asked my new friend whose they were, seeing as my flight hadn't yet unloaded its cargo? Just as casually, he informed me that these bags had gone missing several weeks ago and had only recently turned up at the airport to be claimed. I also learned that, not only was this disappearance the norm here, but many of the contents would have disappeared too, reducing any expectant collection to one of futile disappointment, with no hope of recompense.

After collecting my suitcase and checking that it was more or less as I'd packed it (any valuables travelled on my person), we exited the building and headed towards a parked minibus. As soon as we stepped outside, however, we were greeted by a seething throng of individuals.

These were the city's homeless, poor, and unwanted – easily recognised by their dirt and dishevelment. I was taken aback when a woman presented me with a baby in her arms, telling me that she was without food to feed her child. A glimpse of the baby's face revealed flies drinking the moisture from the corners of her eyes and I instinctively reached into my pocket to pull out a few dollars to give her. Immediately he saw this, my driver shouted and kicked her backside, whereupon the woman quickly moved away to try her luck elsewhere. He then explained that these same beggars were always here for every new flight that landed, intentionally seeking out first-time visitors to their country.

We got into the minibus and started to drive with increasing speed through the city, at which point he explained that the company plane was being serviced, so I'd be going instead to a local hotel, where I'd be housed temporarily. It was then that my senses, which were heightening by the moment, went into overload. I'd just left a country where, due to the elevated threat levels, it would have been suicidal to stay in any hotel. And hadn't my own government already warned me, as clearly as the English language would permit, not to come here? I started to panic. Where the hell was the secure CP detail I'd expected? I had no weapon, there was no first aid kit that I could see, and I was being driven to an unknown destination by a gap-toothed maniac through a West African city at a speed that seemed to be limited only by engine size – dodging cars, donkeys, goats, and civilians, all of whom seemed to be trying to get to the same destination by the same time. Yes, I know that I'm used to the UK which, for a motorist, is the third safest place in the world, and I always try to make allowances for other country's safety rules – but this was just plain bonkers.

The term 'car' here is an ambiguous one, loosely describing anything on 3-4 wheels in a state of motion. The new Mercedes and BMWs were easily recognisable by definition, but at the other end of the mechanical scale were rusted chassis held together by wire, having long parted ways with their 'optional extras' – like bonnets, wings, and doors. I just kept quiet and sat hunched up in the back as far down as my 6' 2" frame would allow with my seat belt on, trying to be the grey man. Fortunately, the windows were tinted, so I could see out and hoped to hell that no one could see in. Gangs of fighting-aged males occupied every street corner, sitting around with bits of wood or ciggies hanging out of their mouths, and just spoiling for any kind of action. I felt myself ageing rapidly. It wasn't that I was on my own, a stranger in an even stranger land without any form of protection other than my good looks and ready wit. My new-found friend kept completely turning around to face me, asking one question after another about London, and if I could get him a visa to come over and stay with my family – all the while holding a speed that, back home, would end you up in court!

After several lifetimes (I thought I'd died once), we ended up at a 4-star hotel which, in the UK, would have barely earned a one. I was escorted to the foyer, signed in, told that I'd be picked up next morning at 5am and then left on my own. The room was pretty basic and the first thing I did, once I was certain the driver had left, was to change it from the first floor to the second. One reason for this was in case I'd been stitched up as a potential hostage. The other was if a car bomb detonated outside the hotel. On the ground and first floors there's a far greater chance of the blast being directed into your room. The second floor gives you the best chance of survival. Anything higher up just increases the time it takes to get out of the building. I closed the curtains to impede any flying glass, then did a recce of my surroundings, especially to find the staircase and the fire extinguishers. Back in my room, I checked that all the windows worked and how I'd get out through each of them to the ground if necessary. I also made sure there were no adjoining rooms. Finally, I took out the cheap wooden doorstop that I always carried with me, and wedged it tightly under the closed door. This small low-priced item can make the difference between someone bursting unexpectedly into your room, or finding the door impeded when they try it. Being very thirsty now, and having spotted a few shops near the front of the building, I decided to go grab a few one-litre bottles of water. But not before hiding my passport in the slit I'd created in the rigid plastic bottom of my bag, and taking two wallets out. The first was my good one, which held my cash and cards. The other was a 'throwaway', containing the equivalent of £20 and a few out-of-date credit cards. This way, if I was going to be robbed, they'd get my second wallet, and a quick look inside usually convinced the mugger or pickpocket to run off with it. The good one was hidden deeper on my person. I even do this in Europe, because losing your main wallet is going to screw you up regardless of the circumstances.

I wanted my stop at the shop to be fleeting, but it's always a good idea to check what you're buying. The first three bottles I picked up had broken seals, and it took a bit of rooting around at the back to find the unopened ones. I suspected the shop owner had used the sealed ones for herself, before refilling them with local tap water for tourists. With gut rot successfully averted, I grabbed a few bags of crisps and chocolate bars before heading back to my room, using the stairs this time. I learned from an Australian Scout leader that, in the estuaries at the far north of the outback, you need to change your route each time you walk from your camp to the toilet area, and again on the way back. This is because the unseen crocodiles watch for patterns in movement because, once they know where you'll be at a given instant…

My wife finds it irritating that I live like this habitually but, I remind her, I'm still alive. Back in my room, with the wedge staunchly in place, I rehydrated myself, downed the snacks and, at around 8pm got myself early to bed to the sounds of the bustling hubbub of Mauritania.

At 5am next morning I was seated at the back of the reception area, nervously watching everyone who came in while waiting for my transport to arrive. 5.05am came. So did 5.10am, and 5.15am. Only then did the multitude of cigarette ends on the floor make me realise that this was SOP. At 5.30 my driver arrived with his cheerful grin and darkened teeth. Exhaling a mix of stale smoke and old coffee into my face, he informed me that a serious sandstorm was on its way, so we'd have to drive all the way to the site, about five hours away *Oh, God, not again…* But my concern, and my rising stress levels, didn't end there. I'd just left a country in which all road travel was life-threatening and any interaction with the local police could turn into a death sentence. I was about to do both, without a trained team of pros, without backup at base, without a radio or contact number, without my weapons, and with a total stranger who thought he was my best friend and wanted to spend Christmas with me!

We left the hotel and headed out of the city, now taking roads with relatively less movement and avoiding only the obligatory donkey, goat, or stray dog. And my new best mate still insisted on turning around to talk to me, asking me about my home, where I used to live in London, and could I help him get a visa? I don't know what he must have thought of me, because all my senses were now turned up to 11. Over every mile we covered, my eyes and brain were trying to calculate, as fast as possible, my chances of survival – scanning every yard, foot, and inch for the tell-tale signs of an IED, and all the while trying to respond encouragingly to a barrage of banter without using the word 'Yes', or anything that might get me dumped by the roadside. At one point, as we passed a pile of threadbare tyres at the side of the road, I realised two things:

(a) I'd just exhaled, closed my eyes, and opened my mouth – waiting for the blast to come...
(b) My sub-conscious mind was trying to send me another series of messages – that my driver had probably never left this country in his entire life. That he must know these roads like the back of his hand. That he was being trusted and paid to drive me. That he wasn't going to risk damaging a company vehicle, and thus lose his job. And that he wasn't going to put his life on the line doing this job – let alone that of the passenger in the back who might just be his passport out of here!

I really needed to chill out and make a conscious effort to relax. Maybe even enjoy the experience. I mean, this wasn't a war zone, was it? But each and every country has its own rules, its own unique personality and customs, and its own means of getting into trouble. I still had a lot to learn...

Chapter 19

2010

First Impressions

◇◇

July. Summer in Sahara. The sun was rising and so was the temperature – which translated here into 'heat' – and I was exceedingly grateful that the air conditioning worked. This was going to be a long drive so I tried to make most of it. With each passing mile, I felt more able to relax, and started to take in the sights, terrain, and personality of the country in which I'd planned to spend the next year of my life.

Now that I'd finally got a grip of myself, I got out my iPod and started playing my favourite rock tracks. There's nothing more relaxing for me, when away from home, than listening to The Clash, or The Jam, at full volume. I say 'away from home' because my artistic tastes differ considerably from those of my wife Cara, who is heavily into techno dance crap – whereas the music I prefer has been carefully composed by consummate professionals, interlayered with deep and meaningful lyrics that can be heard clearly, although not always relinquishing their full depth until you've actively meditated on them. They're also diligently recorded and mastered in dedicated and acoustically-treated studios – not in someone's sodding bedroom!

In my defence, your honour, I'd been indoctrinated. During the first part of my military career, I'd been forced to listen to these bands blaring out of every room in the accommodation block. As an NIG, I was made to stand to attention at the door of our old troop corporal, while he played the Jam's 'English Rose'. What an incredibly patriotic composition, with such heartfelt lyrics. If you want to understand me, or any one of the thousands of British squaddies stationed abroad for their Queen and country at this time, I'd like to submit this track as evidence.

Mr Paul Weller – I salute you, sir.

I woke up.

'Rock the Casbah' was playing in my headphones, the minibus had stopped, and through the driver's window the police officer was staring at me *No! No! No! No!* Call me anal if you like, but I need to be fully aware, and in control, of my surroundings at all times. My brain hit a big red emergency button, opening a large valve deep inside my body and sending a flood of adrenalin to each and every one of my senses, all of which were now on full alert. *Shit, shit, shit! How the hell had I let this happen?* I started to prepare myself mentally and physically for what was to come – the sham arrest, the public exhibition of being dragged from the vehicle, then being cuffed and bundled away to an isolated safe house until the ransom was paid. But the local law enforcement seemed half asleep. Had we woken him? And why was his AK47 still propped up in the doorway, inside his wooden hut, several feet away from him? It had definitely seen better days. Rusted, and covered with road dust, it sure as hell hadn't been looked after by someone whose life depended on it.

The AK47 is an amazing rifle and the world's biggest seller. Not just because it's made of pressed steel and cheap to make, but because it's reputed to fire in any field conditions. As a young soldier in Germany, I heard that they'd buried an AK in the ground for a year and when they dug it up it still fired. I'm not sure I'd bet on that, but I can guarantee that a single 7.62mm round from this rifle, anywhere in your body, would totally ruin your day!

And why was he holding our travel papers, which provided authentication for our route, upside down, while pretending to scrutinise them? With a studious nod he handed them back to my driver and waved us onward. As we pulled away slowly, and I surreptitiously dared to look behind, I watched him slump back into his chair inside the checkpoint and close his eyes once more. Despite his relaxed manner, whatever had just happened here, and whether or not the guy was just a simple jobsworth, my driver had seemed genuinely scared of him.

The long, uncomfortable journey seemed to go on forever, and I'd never seen landscape like this before. On leaving the city, the ground felt as hard as volcanic rock, with vast empty plains that went on for miles in every direction, but gradually the distant sand got closer, encroaching right up to the sides of the road. The same with the dunes, which increased in size the further we travelled until they finally became enormous. Out here, in the desert, caravans of camels stood patiently next to the road, with others to be seen further ahead in the distance. I'd seen these before in Iraq, but rarely more than a dozen at a time. Here was a very different culture, with their numbers approaching fifty to over a hundred. During my time here, I'd learn to use camel milk as medicine – but that's a story for later.

I lost count of the rusting, stripped-down vehicles on both sides of the road, having clearly crashed here. And while they should have been a warning to others, they didn't deter my BFF from driving at breakneck speed, regardless of the camels, while constantly turning his head to keep me informed of everything he could think of. We passed several more checkpoints where the officers barely gave us a glance, before turning off the main road onto a beaten-up track to the mine site. Thinking we'd be arriving soon, I started packing away my iPod, only to learn that we had another hundred miles to go! This was by far the worst part of the journey as, without reducing speed, we weaved our way around every suspension-cracking bump and pothole en route – and I vowed never to use a land ambulance along here to evacuate anyone with a spinal injury.

After an interminable two-hour, stomach-churning, spine-jolting eternity, we finally arrived at the mine site. Nursing my newly-whiplashed neck, I was taken to security to show my passport, visa, and travel documents, and get my all-important ID card. As I entered the building, I was stunned to meet Derek and Dermot, a couple of Irish lads from the Foreign Legion, who asked if I'd just come from CP work in Iraq!

2010: First Impressions

Without giving any details, I told them yes, to which they laughed and said they'd heard I was coming. Blimey, they're not kidding when they say that 'The Circuit' is a closed one! I was escorted to the exploration company who were employing me as their paramedic. The place was a hub of activity, with multiple maps displaying topographical details of the area and coloured infills for ground samples, spread out on boards all around the room. There, I was introduced to Charlie Davies and Joe Fifield, respectively the exploration manager and exploration general manager. After greetings all round, Joe led the way to my portacabin so I could drop off my bag. Harkening back to Iraq, I was quite concerned that our accommodation huts were immediately adjacent to the open desert and separated only by a high, diamond-wire fence. I was then shown the canteen, which included the Sahara Club (more on that later), and the camp's mosque. Joe also pointed out the camp's extensive PA system over which, he warned me, the faithful (and everyone else in the camp) were woken at around 3-4am each morning and summoned to prayer. Finally, we reached the medical centre to meet Mike (not his real name), our on-site paramedic. Mike had received his initial training as a combat medic, and then retrained as an offshore medic after leaving the Army. It soon became apparent that Joe had been badged '22 SAS' and Mike '23 SAS'. Joe was a typical no-nonsense, let's-get-this-job-done type of guy. Mike, on the other hand, was a nice guy but constantly on edge, and I got the impression that some of his internal wiring had shorted out.

Situated just outside the main mining area, where the gold was mined, processed, and turned into bullion, was the medical centre, which consisted of five rooms. There was the emergency room, with a couple of couches inside. The second room was shared by the two doctors working alternate shifts. The paramedic had a smaller room, the male Mauritanian nurses (there were no female ones) had their own consultation room, and there was a small pharmacy. However, the whole place was a shit tip. The emergency room was caked in a fine talc-like dust. Medical kit lay around everywhere – often open, and non-sterile. In fact, there wasn't a single sterile area in the entire place. Later, I came to learn that the air-con filters were clogged, there was sand in everything, and there was no accountability – in or out – for dispensary drugs.

Mike then introduced me to the 4x4 which doubled as our ambulance, and this too was in a shocking state, with medical equipment lying loose in the back and a heavy 90kg oxygen bottle rolling around on the floor with an open mask still attached. This really surprised me, as all the Special Forces guys I'd known made sure to keep their medical kit in tip-top condition, because lives and limbs literally depended on it – but there was no evidence of this attitude here.

Arriving next at Mike's hut, I noticed a recently-washed pair of khaki trousers, a pair of boxer shorts, a T-shirt, and a single pair of socks poked into the fence to dry. Surprised, I followed him to his room, which turned out to be as minimalistic as you could get. Inside his wardrobe there was just one pair of socks, a pair of boxers, a pair of trousers and a T-shirt. I couldn't believe this so, jokingly, I asked where the rest of his stuff was. With a straight face, he pointed to outside and replied, "On the fence…"

Now, I really needed to know; he'd been on-site for six weeks with just three of everything? Why, I asked him? He looked around furtively, before showing me a map of our part of Africa and said that if he ever had to get out quickly and head west to the coast, he could do it in under a minute. There was a backup map in the vehicle, which he always kept fully-fuelled, and a jerrycan full of water in the back.

Oh…

Unthinkingly, and wanting to change the subject, I asked if he was putting the kettle on. He responded with a yes, he could, but there was only one mug! My room was adjacent to his, so I retreated to unload all my clothing and personal belongings and attempt to make my place, at least, as homely as possible. An hour after I'd unpacked, and Skyped Cara and the girls, Joe came over to take me to dinner. On entering the dining area, he smiled and hinted that it might not be the most hygienic of places. He was right. Here, the cockroaches were king, and could already be seen running around everywhere, along the floor, up the walls, and across the ceiling, from where they dropped tactically onto our tables as we ate. Hell, I wouldn't have been surprised to see a group of the little blighters sat around a tiny table in the corner – smoking, drinking, and playing cards.

Fast forwarding to a few days later, and just when I thought I was getting used to the place, I was eating a salad when I felt an unusually hard crunch in my mouth. Quickly spitting out the contents into a napkin, I realised that I'd just chewed on the carapace of one of these bloody things. Even worse, it wasn't all there! The rest was about to sustain me with some unforeseen live protein. But tummy bugs aside, my first real morning at work was accepting the handover from Mike. Once he'd finished bringing me up to scratch, we had lunch, then he grabbed his small daysack, headed over to the airstrip adjacent to the mine, and left on the company plane. That was the last I ever saw or heard of him and, reading between the lines, it was probably a mutually-agreed decision between the company and his agency, which was why Alex had wanted me here ASAP.

There was no further orientation nor training for me. I was now the official on-site paramedic, so theoretically I could change everything that was fundamentally wrong in the company's healthcare system, including our response vehicle. I walked around the premises, making a list, before respectfully informing the doctor of what I would like to do. Without even looking up from his computer screen, he just said, "You can do whatever you want."

I started by introducing myself to the nurses, told them what needed to be done, then put them to work tidying up the place. This was to include themselves from here on because, for established health professionals, most of them looked like scruffy vagrants. They, and the entire working area, needed an intensive deep clean, and we spent all day doing just that. Many of them took a dislike to what 'the new guy' was doing and, though I couldn't communicate well in French, their sullen tones, and the scowls I received from them, were a universal language, making their thoughts quite clear. But if this was to be done properly, then I needed to start as I meant to continue. My inner staff sergeant came to the fore and, with the occasional stern look and moderately-raised voice, the groundwork was completed. Giving me his full support, Joe had got hold of the maintenance guys and, while we were blitzing the rooms, he instructed them to repair the windows to stop dust coming in and secure the heavy oxygen bottles to the walls with lockable chains. Not ideal, but at least it would stop them from toppling over and causing injury. He even organised an independent cleaning party, which was now busily stripping everything out of the emergency room, and scrubbing every square inch of the place, prior to thoroughly cleaning all the equipment and putting it back according to my directions.

A unique part of our setup here was the Sahara Club – a solitary room set aside for expats to have a quiet alcoholic drink. Now, Mauritania was a strict Muslim country where alcohol was banned, but somehow the company had managed to obtain this permission, on the condition that there was absolutely no drinking outside of it. To complete the job, our South African contingent cooked their barbeques here every Friday evening, we always looked forward to these, especially as they spent all afternoon burning wood in a pit to create the coals, ready for later that day.

That night, at the club, Joe told me that he liked the way I worked and wanted to discuss plans for improving our emergency response. He'd wanted to do this for ages, but Mike just hadn't been interested. We talked for the entire evening, eagerly and cheerfully feeding off each other's ideas, and it was clear that a great friendship was blossoming.

Chapter 20

2010

Incarcerated

On the Friday morning after the big clean-up, I was going through the pharmacy inventory when a nurse burst in to tell me that one of the male expats had collapsed. We rushed to the 4x4 and, following his directions, headed off to the site. Once there, I grabbed the response bag and oxygen kit from the back, and quickly followed the nurse to where the casualty lay. The first thing that surprised me was the shocked faces of the staff gathered around the casualty. They'd never actually seen a medic attending an incident – because doctors and other medical staff were only ever seen at the medical centre. It was like saying that you only ever saw firefighters at a fire station! Well, this was going to change. The initial translations I was getting about the casualty was that he was already dead, but even with my limited training as to what happens to a human body after it dies, these conditions do not include a pulse, steady breathing, and intermittent mumbling. A second opinion was definitely needed!

He was an Australian employee who'd reported feeling unwell for the past three days, and though he felt worse today he'd still come in to work. He'd collapsed while chatting to one of the local nationals, and all he could remember, after coming to on the floor, was people running around him like headless chickens. I started with basic observations and found his blood pressure much higher than normal – dangerously high, in fact. Asking about his medical history, there was nothing about high blood pressure in him or his family. He wasn't experiencing chest discomfort or pains and, other than the high BP, he seemed okay. So, I asked if I could take him back to the site's clinic for an ECG and further tests. Back at the centre I had him lie on the couch, removed his shirt, and attempted to apply the ECG electrodes to his chest. I say 'attempted', not because I'd never used one before, but this particular model must have been made in the 17th century! The only way to attach these ten electrodes to his body was with the permanently-attached suction cups, which made them difficult to sterilise, near-impossible to keep in place, and fully impossible to replace when damaged. I was sticking them down with surgical tape when the doctor came in, accompanied by the mine manager. The doctor immediately asked what I was doing, so I gave him a breakdown of my initial observations, then the ones I'd done here, and would give him the rest once I'd captured the ECG readings. He then asked why I was using the ECG? Taken aback by the question, I explained that I wanted to rule out any underlying cardiac conditions. He then stated that there was no need, as he already knew why the guy's BP was so high

"Oh, thank goodness!" I exclaimed, "So you know his history? *Why isn't it on his record?*" To which the doctor replied that he'd never seen this patient before, but he himself had the same problem. Surprised, I asked him if he was okay, and his reply was simply, "It's the air conditioning." Now even more confused, I told him, "Sorry, doc, but I'm not sure if made myself clear. His BP is already off the scale and I'm worried. He's got no history of this condition, and I believe that it needs further investigation at a receiving hospital." But the doctor refused to accept what I'd told him and repeated that the problem was due to the air conditioning. He then went on to explain that he himself had a bad knee and that it always started to hurt the moment he entered an air-conditioned room! I couldn't believe this, not just for the sake of the patient, but because this crap was coming directly from the mine's doctor, putting me in an exceedingly difficult position.

I have never in my professional life gone behind the back of any doctor, but I now found myself losing the trust of the senior clinician on site. Much as I thought it wrong, I discharged the patient and asked the mine manager, a big American guy, for a quick chat. I explained my concerns and that I believed it dangerous to leave the patient on-site, in case he had a cardiac condition and suffered a heart attack or stroke. The manager asked me what the doctor had said, before telling me that, as far as the mine's medical procedures were concerned, the doctor always had the final say. There was nothing more I could do so, feeling totally pissed off with the standards here, I went back to tracing the origin of the drugs being supplied to us and finally identified a supply depot in Nouakchott. I then decided to visit this place next week and, at the same time, conduct a recce of the local hospitals in case we needed to use them. This wasn't just me trying to assert myself, but because neither of these critical tasks had ever been done since the company had set up business here.

Sunday morning, I was just arriving at the clinic when I learned that the same expat was in his bed and difficult to wake. Cardiac arrest was foremost in my mind as I switched on the 'blues-and-twos' and sped through the site on my way to him. I already knew where his room was, pulled up outside, and was greeted by the usual rent-a-crowd at the entrance. Thankfully, he wasn't arresting, though he certainly needed urgent hospital admission. His BP was off the scale again, and this time it'd be even more dangerous. How far can you blow up a balloon before it bursts at its weakest point? What does the skin of a balloon look like after it's been inflated and deflated several times? How many warnings does a person need? And how often are the words 'internal bleeding' preceded by the words 'died of'?

While he was being assisted in walking carefully to my vehicle, I got on the phone to Joe. I'd already made the command decision that, whatever happened to me as a result, this guy would be medically evacuated to a hospital. I gave Joe a full rundown of the events from Friday to now, told him that the guy needed an urgent casevac and could he arrange the flight out? Leaving this in his very capable hands, I drove the guy back to the medical centre. And this is where the problems started.

On arrival, I was confronted by an extremely irate doctor demanding why I'd asked for a medical evacuation. Standing alongside him were the camp manager and several other senior staff from the mine, including the casualty's own line manager. I ignored them all and focused on getting the patient, who was now being supported by two nurses, onto the couch. We then started to hook him up to the monitoring equipment, including oxygen saturation (sats), BP cuff, and ECG, but while we were doing this the doctor demanded, now in a raised authoritative voice, that I stop immediately and leave the building. It was at this point that the infamous Ingram wrath was invoked, and I turned to him. Trying my best to remain respectful, I told him, "You. Shut the fuck up and help, otherwise this man could die...". I then turned to the site manager, "Sir. This man is seriously ill. We need an immediate medical evacuation. Now. And it should have happened last Friday...". The doctor shouted this was unacceptable, and that he was the senior medic, before storming out of the building. I apologised to the site manager, but again stated the importance of the situation and my initial concerns, which had turned into serious worries, before reminding him that we needed an urgent aeromedical casevac – and not an overland one. Sensing I was right, and without questioning my reasons, he turned to another employee and verified that a plane was on its way. Then he turned back to me and, to my surprise, apologised, saying that he should have listened to me last Friday.

I found the doctor in his usual place, behind his desk, looking at the internet. Keeping myself calm, I informed him of the situation, my findings so far, and told him that I needed his help to reduce the patient's blood pressure. I said that we had IV access, and asked what medicines we could give him.

To my dismay, he said nothing. He didn't even look up from his screen. Shaking my head in frustration, I returned to the emergency room and gave the patient (whose name was also Wayne) two squirts of GTN, which I knew would reduce his systolic pressure (top reading), though I wasn't sure if it'd do anything for his diastolic pressure, which was still far too high. At this point Joe arrived and threw a spanner in the works, telling us that a sandstorm was on its way and the plane wouldn't be able to fly to our site. However, if we could drive the casualty to Nouadhibou, roughly three hours north of us, then the plane could meet us there instead. The camp manager said he'd arrange for all the documentation to be done and, once Joe had taken over, I grabbed my overnight bag, passport, and response bag, and joined my patient in the back of a 4x4 to be driven to a part of the country I'd never seen. We were told to expect the usual police roadblocks, but that our medical emergency paperwork should get us through.

All seemed to be going well. We'd already passed through three checkpoints without hindrance, and I started to trust in the country's administration and organisation. With my patient comfortable I began to relax, with no idea of what was to befall us. So far, we'd encountered the usual type of police officer, in their roadside patrol box, accompanied by an ill-maintained means of deterrent and law-enforcement. The next checkpoint, however, was substantially different. With just 10 miles to go before our destination, we stopped at a barrier lowered across the road, but this officer seemed much more alert. On the left of the road, about 40 metres away, was a low red-bricked building with a corrugated steel roof, from where another officer sat behind a window, carefully observing our vehicle. To the left of the building was a police car, the first I'd seen here. A verbal exchange took place between the barrier guard and our driver, who then turned and told me that he had to take all our passports over to this building. I obediently handed them over and then sat impatiently waiting for him to return and for us to be let through. Several times our driver looked back over his shoulder from the office to our car, and I saw the officer point his finger towards the car and myself, so I explained to my patient that this was probably due to the numerous Iraqi visas stamped in my passport. However, our now-worried driver returned to us without our passports, saying that the chief wanted to speak with me. Edgily, I asked if the chief was aware of the importance of our journey but, clearly-scared, the driver insisted that I must go. Annoyed at this bureaucratic affrontery, I exited the vehicle and strode purposefully towards the building.

It was only when I got close that I noticed the terrible state of the place. Not only was it built with poor quality bricks, but what mortar lay between them all must have been in really short supply at the time. I was amazed that it was still standing upright. The window through which the officer observed the barrier was half open space, half steel bars, and the thin sheet of roof appeared to have been simply laid on top of the bricks, with no sign of any fixtures. I'd built better camps as a child in the local woods. On my approach I started to assess him as we watched each other through the window, building up a mental picture of how best to deal with him. His uniform was a sandy dirt colour that hadn't felt an iron since it had been issued, and on his head was the largest peaked hat I'd ever seen in my life. I imagined scaling this monstrosity, with ropes and carabiners, to discover a large white 'H' painted on top!

He reminded me of a despotic official from a Harold Lloyd film, who'd given himself a name like 'El Presidente' – and I made up my mind to take no shit from him. Reclining in his chair, waving my passport around as if he controlled my destiny in his hand, he looked at me for several minutes, occasionally smiling, before talking to his colleagues behind him which generated some forced laughter. Now fuming, and pissed off with his attitude, I said, "Look mate, I've got a seriously ill patient in my ambulance, and I really need to meet the plane at the airport so we can fly him to a hospital." Smiling again, and sounding to all the world like a Bond villain, he replied, "You have outstayed your welcome, Mr Wayne..." *Oh...* . "Sir," I replied, changing my tack slightly," I've only been here a few days, I'm a medic at the mine, and I really need to get my patient to a hospital. Please, can we go?" Still smiling, he repeated that I had outstayed my welcome – and that my visa had run out... *Oh no. No. No, No, No, this can't be...* That cold shiver, the moment all travellers dread, now ran down my spine as he showed me my visa. It had been issued for three days, and not three weeks as I'd thought. As his delighted words echoed around my head, still waiting to be processed, I knew I hadn't got a leg to stand on.

"Mr Wayne. You are under arrest..."

At this, two officers came forward and took hold of my arms, forcing me towards their car. They were soon followed by their chief, who'd now finished packing the paperwork into his briefcase. Despite my situation, I did a double-take, and almost smiled, as I saw that El Presidente can't have been more than five feet tall, and this reminded me of one of my best mates from the regiment back in the UK.

Even though Tom Kelly was a highly experienced firearms officer, we always gave him grief about being vertically-challenged. At 5' 7" he was considered short compared with the rest of us big, strapping blokes. On leaving the Army he'd joined the police force, after they'd removed their archaic minimum 5' 8" height restriction in 1990. However, the ruling didn't apply to us, and our hilarious ribbing even followed us abroad. Shortly after 9/11, we were in New York for Alex Mallin's stag weekend and were stood on the subway when an attractive lady asked if we were Brits. Proudly, we said we were, and all of us soldiers, too – except for Tom, who deftly commandeered the conversation with, "No, I'm not. Not any more…" So when, of course, she asked him what he did now, he told her that he was a police officer. "Oh," she responded, quite seriously, "I didn't know they had such small policemen in England!"

My thoughts then turned to the 'police force' in Iraq who, when they couldn't extort a ransom from kidnapping a foreign national, would score points with Al Qaeda by handing over the hostage. I'd heard a true story of two SAS guys, dressed as Arabs, who were arrested at a roadblock while driving in Iraq. Fortunately for them, their team understood the gravity of the situation and mounted a major operation to raid the police HQ and get their mates out just before they were due to be smuggled out to Al Qaeda for certain torture and beheading.

Foreign companies were finally and financially forced into adopting a zero-tolerance, no-negotiation-with-terrorists policy, which became a win-win for the police. The companies still did their best to get their staff back through backdoor negotiation, but this didn't stop some poor bugger being beheaded or burned alive. It did a bloody good job of keeping the 'infidel' out of the country, I can tell you.

My mind went through every permutation of every scenario I'd ever known, and each one ended with me wearing an orange jumpsuit, seated in a dingy room in front of a cheap video camera, about to have my head hacked and severed from my body. Desperate now, I started to plead with them that I was a medic with a sick patient who needed to be in hospital – but within seconds I'd been bundled into the rear of the police car followed by one of my arresting officers, while the other got into the driver's seat. My size hadn't gone unnoticed and, to ensure I that was out-manned, another officer got in on the other side of me. Finally, completing the picture, the chief took his place in the front passenger seat, and we set off to a destination known to everyone but me. I was well and truly fucked, I knew, and honestly believed that I was never going to see Cara and my children again. I was already on my way to an off-the-grid location, to become a fleeting story on BBC News.

As the car gathered speed I took stock of my situation, trying to formulate a plan before it was too late. Referencing all the action movies I've ever watched, I'd use my body mass to take out the two goons either side of me with an elbow smash to each face, strangle the chief, then shoot the driver twice in the back of the head with the gun I'd pulled from one of the guys beside me. Then, after the car had crashed and turned over several times, I'd climb out, safely cushioned from the impact by my two 'bodyguards', set the vehicle alight to cover my tracks, and then make my escape to freedom, following my predecessor's carefully laid-out plan to flee the country. But this wasn't a movie, and these things just don't happen – let alone work – in real life. I looked around at the four guys surrounding me, just doing their job. They were certainly untidy, smelling of old sweat and tobacco, with white stains under the arms of their uniforms. Their chief was just as bad. The two in the back were constantly smiling at me, displaying their blackened teeth, and the chief would occasionally look over his shoulder, just to check I was still there and under control. Their entire demeanour was undisciplined, unprofessional, and unpredictable, which meant that anything could go wrong if I wasn't careful. My mate Tom had told us that there's nothing as sad and miserable as someone who's just been arrested, so I decided to play the game by their rules. Although I'd been cocky earlier, I'd now play the cowed grey man, becoming a model prisoner until my chance presented itself.

The drive to the city was bleak and uneventful, and I spent most of it looking down at the floor with a thousand things running through my mind. The most stupid idea I had, while keeping my head down, was to count the seconds and remember each turn the car took. Well, it worked for Liam Neeson in 'Taken', and everything had ended well for him, but it doesn't work on a straight road that goes on for longer than the bloody movie! As soon we entered the city, all my ideas went out of the window and I had to start thinking anew. I was truly shocked at what I saw, and the only way I can describe it is, if you've ever watched the movie 'Black Hawk Down', it was like that. From the outskirts the first thing that caught my attention was a group of 20-30 men of fighting age gathered at the side of the road, followed by a donkey crossing the road, then a goat. Down a side street, belching out thick black clouds of smoke, was a pile of burning tyres. I actually considered informing my escort, as a paramedic, that not only was this environmentally unethical, but it could also damage their health.

By now I was certain that I was being kidnapped and, the further in we progressed, the more I believed that I was en route to a clandestine safe house – a single room hidden within a white concrete forest – to start my prolonged period of captivity. Though I tried to put a brave face on the situation, what could I do? Why the hell hadn't I checked my visa – the fundamental, #1 rule of Travelling for Dummies like me? I knew it had been organised quickly, and that the company would have been working on extending it. They'd probably thought that, once at the mine, I wouldn't be needing it for a long while until it was sorted. It didn't matter that someone, somewhere, had dropped me right in it by not informing me. I'd remembered my door wedge and my second wallet, but my crucial travel visa? I'd just given it a cursory glance, and thought it had said three weeks.

By now the opportunity to remember each turn we'd taken had long gone, but even in this desperate situation my mind was still trying to make light of it. As we passed a fruit stall by the side of the road, my limbic brain thought 'Mmm, nice melons…' which, being the boy I am, immediately made me think of breasts, which then made me think of a 'Carry On' movie. To this day I can't think why, in the back of that car, my life and future highly uncertain, I whispered under my breath, "Ooh, Matron…"

The police car took a sharp left and drove down a slight hill to a large building. We stopped at the entrance and the chief got out, followed by the driver and one of the officers, who snapped something to me in Arabic and pushed me out of the side, where the third officer was waiting to grab my arm and follow the chief into the building. We carried on through another door into a totally bare corridor, but for a single seat onto which I was forced down, still handcuffed, before being left alone with my thoughts. These guys must have watched a lot of movies on intimidation techniques.

I knew that the main door hadn't latched, and the one we'd just entered wasn't locked either, so for a brief moment I considered taking my chance and racing back out the way I'd just come into the street, where I'd quickly mingle with the crowds. But even though I had an awesome suntan after several months in Basra, and with the Saharan sun already taking its toll, my limited knowledge of the language meant there was no way I was going to fit in as a local.

Many more unbidden thoughts like this crossed my mind, like camels in a desert, while I sat and awaited my fate. One notably daft one was that, when they started to interrogate me, I'd give them nothing but the big three – name, rank and number. Until I played it out in my mind, that is. I mean, they already knew my name, my rank was now 'Mister', and the only number I had was on my bloody passport, which was what got me here in the first place! Having said that, it was only out of date by a day or two. So, really, how bad could it be?

After what seemed like forever, the chief walked out with his boss, who looked considerably more professional and better presented. Finally – someone who would see sense and allow me to return to looking after my patient. He walked languidly up to me, holding my passport in one hand, before greeting me in perfect English with, "Mr Ingram. You appear to be extremely well-travelled." Sensing that the famous Ingram charm was working I replied, "Yes sir, though I must tell you that Mauritania is, by far, one of the most beautiful countries I have ever visited!" This compliment was followed by the irresistible Ingram smile and, had it been a movie, the sunlight would have glinted charismatically off my teeth, accompanied by an audible 'ting'. However, it was the boss who stole the scene with his next remark, punching me straight between the eyes, "That's really pleasing to know, Mr Ingram. Especially as you'll be spending a good deal of time here in confinement", before bestowing his own gratuitous smile upon me, and walking away. My mouth dropped open, and flies could have laid eggs in it and hatched them out before I'd finished processing all the possibilities of what was coming next. On the chief's word, two officers grabbed my arms and escorted me further down the corridor, to a pair of large steel doors. Beside them sat another officer who stood up quickly to attention and unlocked it. My escorts then removed my handcuffs, shoved me through the gate, and quickly locked it behind me. This is when I realised that I wasn't being kidnapped at all. Instead, I was now an honoured guest of Nouadhibou prison.

I looked around and my heart sank into my boots. Okay, I've probably watched too many cowboy movies, but I felt like an outlaw walking into a bar, silhouetted by the noonday sun behind him, and everyone inside (even the piano player) stops what they're doing to stare at him. Well, this bar was a huge, square, bare, open sandy compound, about 500 yards a side, with a 20-foot-high wall around it. Protecting it from the baking sun was a corrugated tin roof, which provided shade to over a hundred inmates – and I really hate the implications of that word.

This wasn't a prison. This was an arena – and I was the only white combatant. I looked up at the single guard tower, and felt the blood drain from my face as I realised that not only was it unmanned, but there wasn't a single guard inside the compound. Well, on the plus side, I was no longer afraid.

I was bloody terrified...

I knew I could use my fists in a fair fight, but this wasn't the movies where they come at you one at a time – I mean, who ever does this in any brawl? Here, my size was an advantage, so I pulled myself up fully, breathed in as deeply as I could – puffing out my chest like a bullfrog – put on as mean and hard an expression as I could muster under the circumstances, and swung my arms away from my chest to look bigger as I moved purposefully to the rear, left corner of the shaded area of the compound. Once there, I found a relatively quiet place to sit, blend in and think about how the hell I'd ended up in this situation. More importantly, what the hell was I going to do about it? I knew I had another, massive advantage, but had kept it quiet until now. Why they hadn't done a full-body search, at any stage, was beyond me, because I could have been carrying any kind of concealed weapon. What I had, in fact, was even better – my slimline mobile phone. But I'd wait until later, after I'd settled in, to avoid drawing any immediate and unwanted attention to myself at this stage. Avoiding all eye-contact, and doing my best to look nonchalant and bored, I soon ceased to be of any interest, and the other prisoners went back to their dice games in the sand, or their group discussions. They all looked used to the unbearable heat, whereas I'd not had a drink since inside the car. About 20 feet away to my left was a half-empty bottle of water in the sand, which meant that it had either leaked, or someone had already taken a long swallow before dropping it. I'd encountered enough tropical illnesses to know what nasties could already be breeding inside, but what alternative did I have? How long before we were all fed and watered again? Why was it even there, and why had nobody else touched it? Who'd already drunk from it, and was it even water? But, shit, I was incredibly thirsty so, walking indifferently over to the bottle, I picked it up, carried it back, opened it up, and took a sniff, before gingerly putting it to my lips to check if it really was water. After a few minutes, with no reaction from my mouth, I took a very small sip and waited again. No complaints from my gut this time, so I took a full gulp and kept the rest for later.

    I stayed in the same sitting position for about an hour, trying to keep cool, save energy and blend in with my surroundings, before deciding to remove the phone from my pocket. I knew this was a potential death sentence, because this device would be in particularly high demand here, and only the strongest would prevail. I drew my knees right up to my chest, my fingers interlocked at the front, gathering in my resources, and letting my head hang as I pretended to be asleep. Then, after a while of this, and when no one was looking, I let my hands drop

2010: Incarcerated

naturally, slid my left hand into my pocket, palmed the phone, and moved it into my groin area. I waited a little longer for any movement around me. Satisfied there was none, I raised my head and looked around impassively, before lowering it again and checking if I had a signal I almost gave the game away as I couldn't believe my luck. I shifted position as I moved the phone and pressed the speed-dial number for camp security, before raising it to my ear as I moved both hands to behind my head, seemingly trying to get comfortable. To my sheer and utter relief, not only was the call answered, but by the broad Irish tones of Derek Fergus, the mine security manager. There then followed the most desperate and clandestine telephone conversation I'd ever had in my life.

"Derek, its Wayne..."

"What the fook?"

"Mate. Listen carefully. I've been arrested. I'm in the prison in Nouadhibou. If I go missing, this is the last place I was..."

"...What the fook are ya talking about, ya fooking numpty?"

"Mate, I've been fucking arrested, and I'm stuck in the jail with a shitload of prisoners. They might kidnap me. They might even bumfuck me..."

"Yeah, you wish... Look, don't go anywhere. I'll make some calls, and get the fixer to find you. Okay?"

"Mate, I'm in a fucking prison! Where do you think I'm going?" I asked hysterically, while trying to keep my voice down.

"You sure it's not the immigration centre"? asked Derek, the signal so clear he could have been sat right next to me.

"I don't fucking know! It's bloody huge, there are high walls, there's a guard tower, and there's a hundred locals here who don't look like they volunteer with the Salvation Army!"

"Ah! Right. I know where you are. I'm on it. Stay there..."

The call ended. Still panicking inside, and hoping to heaven and hell that no one had heard me, I quickly switched it to silent and moved it carefully back to my pocket, before huddling myself up with my head down, becoming the grey man once more. Several hours went by, during which the locals appeared to be moving in closer – or was this my imagination? With nothing else to do, my brain started thinking about this fixer whom Derek had on call. Would he do a James Bond, parachute into the jail, discard the black 'chute and then, wearing a dinner jacket and bow tie, calmly infiltrate the prison while eliminating everyone who got in his way, before grabbing my arm to lead us both out to safety along the way he'd prepared? On his way out, he'd stop only to surprise El P, the chief who, on recognising me, would try to back away, aghast, as I moved in fast, close, and personal, to deliver an almighty, size 10 boot to his crown jewels.

Oh! Would the fixer even be a 'he'? Now that would really be something! And this was probably the reason why Mr Akers would often shout "Ingram! Are we keeping you awake, you somnambulant little toad?"

I waited a further three hours without incident and was just thinking about calling Derek again when I heard a loud commotion outside the iron gate. I didn't have a clue as to what was going on, but the other prisoners started to move away. This did not feel good…

The gate was pulled noisily open and El P, his boss, and another local man I didn't recognise were standing in the entrance, their eyes scanning the compound until they collectively settled on me. Then the new guy looked directly at me, smiled, and said, "Come on, Wayne! I'm here to take you to the airport!" *Bloody hell!* Quick as a flash I was up and, with one last glance around me for safety, made a hasty dash over to him. The guy offered me his hand, and introduced himself as Cheikh *(pron. Shake)*, the local 'fixer' for the company. Though he looked nothing like any of the James Bonds, never had I seen a more welcoming sight! As we were both about to leave, the chief stepped forward to assert himself. Grabbing my arm, he told me to sort out my visa, and that I was not welcome here again.

I never got to deliver that kick, which I'd have genuinely regretted later, but the pissed expression on his face would do instead. I was soon in the back of another company car, driven to the local airport to board the company plane, and was finally reunited with my patient, who *thank*

God! was still alive. After a quick set of observations, I okayed it with the pilot to start our journey, and buckled myself up next to my casualty to monitor him throughout the flight.

After a few hours we landed at Las Palmas airport and, as soon as the plane had finished taxiing to its holding area, we were met by a civilian ambulance, which was staffed by a doctor and two female nurses. I kid you not that, as soon as I saw them, my brain took me straight back to another 'Carry On' movie. The doctor was wearing the usual starched white coat, but both his nurses wore short, white dresses cut just above the knee, those white tights with the accentuating white line down the back, white high heels, and a small white hat. I couldn't stop smiling as I gave a full verbal handover to the doctor, before suddenly realising what effect this could have on the patient – because I certainly knew what it was doing to me! These nurses were extremely pleasing to the eye, their outfits were skimpy – to say the least – and I was bringing him here to help lower his blood pressure! I have to say that mine was already up.

I travelled with them up front in the ambulance, and he was admitted to the receiving hospital for further tests while we waited and watched. At one point the doctor told one of the nurses that he wanted to conduct another ECG, and as she bent over in front of me to retrieve the ECG dots from the bottom drawer, I couldn't help but notice that her prim little uniform came complete with a tiny white thong! My recumbent patient didn't seem to mind, though. He'd seen it too, had clocked me gaping, and promptly burst into laughter. I smiled back at him, told him that he was now in good hands, and left to find my local accommodation.

After checking in, I thought I should call Cara to bring her up to date – though the conversation didn't quite go as I'd expected. As soon as she picked up the phone, I tried to explain quickly what had occurred that day, in order to let her know that I was now okay – but she interrupted me with, "Where are you now?"

"I'm in Las Palmas," I replied, "With a patient."

"Oh, great. Well, I'm at home, running round like a bloody blue-arsed fly looking after our two young daughters, and you're on bloody holiday. I'll call you back later..." *SLAM!* And that was it – the end of a perfect day. As I left my room, gutted, to console myself with a massage in my all expenses paid, 5-star hotel, I didn't think I'd ever understand women.

"Wayne's arrival on site was a breath of fresh air, considering the security department had enough trouble rounding up exploration mavericks without the antics of his predecessor. Dermot and I took stock of him and, after the usual banter to sound a new arrival out, we agreed that he was a solid operator, and would fit into the crowd nicely.

I recall my phone ringing that day, seeing a UK number pop up on the screen, and wondering if it was another cold call. Fortunately, it was Wayne, delivering his good news with a healthy dose of humour. When I had finished wishing him good luck in his new surroundings, I assured him that we would get someone onto the case immediately.

Mauritania is a peculiar place, the people warm and friendly in general, with many educated and capable entrepreneurs. Unfortunately, civil engineering and construction does not appear to be high on the curriculum, and the place is stuck in the early 20th century. Similarly, the attitudes of government officials are also stuck there, meaning that sometimes you require a good local contact to fix problems as they (often) arise.

Luckily for Wayne, we had a very good relationship with one such gentleman, a successful businessman and considered a close friend. Upon hearing of the situation, his voice relaxed slightly and he said it wasn't as bad as it sounded (probably to him), and that he'd make a few phone calls. I came away from the call satisfied that things were in hand, and that Wayne wouldn't have to endure such pleasurable surroundings for long. True to his word, our friend called and said that someone was on the way to the police station in Nouadhibou to collect Wayne, and that he'd spoken with a senior officer in the police to get clearance. A few hours later, as is usually the case, Wayne called to say he was tasting the sweet air of freedom and on his way to the airport. After wishing him well, and reminding him of the forfeit for a schoolboy error, he confirmed his arrival at the plane and we left it at that.

Following on from this escapade, Wayne returned to site and got stuck back into his work, delivering a professional service to the company and providing reassurance to all the staff living there. Obviously, neither Dermot nor I missed the chance to call him on his forfeit, usually on a Saturday evening in the Sahara..."

Derek Fergus

Chapter 21

2011

Destiny

Several days later I returned to Mauritania, where I learned that the reason I'd been arrested was that I'd been included in the thousands of people from the Sahel region of Africa who tried to reach the west coast of neighbouring Morocco, in order to cross the Strait of Gibraltar in a small boat to Spain. That's why all those roadblocks existed, and why I'd managed to pass through all but the last. By overstaying my visa by one day, I'd officially become an 'illegal'. I'd not been arrested by police, but immigration officers – hence Derek's question. The place where I was held was not a prison, as I'd thought, but a detention centre for those travelling without the correct documents, which is why I'd not been searched. Fortunately for me, Cheikh had explained my situation to them, stressing why I was there and the emergency situation in hand, and they'd cooperated in releasing me.

With my lesson duly learned (sorry, Mr Akers!), and now fully armed with a six-month visa, I determined to immerse myself into my work as exploration paramedic and clinic manager, eradicate my Iraqi thinking and make up for any trouble I'd caused to the company, before heading back to the UK for my three weeks of R&R.

However, on my return I found many changes. As a result of my incident in Nouadhibou, and the subsequent survival of my patient, the problematic doctor's contract had been terminated, and I was now free of him. He'd been replaced by the other Syrian doctor whom I'd always found extremely helpful and was now earning twice as much working both shifts! Most importantly, Joe had accepted each and every one of my proposals that we'd discussed, and was in the process of implementing them all – including giving me autonomy over most fields medical and paramedical.

This included a long-overdue audit of everything in our drugs cupboard. It took me several days, but I finally had a complete record of everything we had. I also implemented a sign-out sheet for all medicines – and you'd think that this would be common sense – but I was shocked at the resistance I initially encountered, with nurses either ignoring the new ruling, or openly refusing to comply.

The weeks that followed were spent between diagnosing minor injuries and ailments in the clinic during the morning sick parade, and offering advice to the Bedouin – the nomadic Arab tribes who inhabit the desert – if and whenever we came across them. As the exploration paramedic, I'd often accompany Zeidane *(pron. Zidann)*, our exploration HSE (health, safety, and environment) representative, on his drives into the desert to visit the drilling rigs, and it was on one of these excursions that we stopped near a Bedouin encampment. Circular tents were spread out over a small area, with camels tethered in between. This I had to see, knowing how rare it was to see a genuine Bedouin camel close up – though I'd heard you had to be careful near them so I approached the camp somewhat, er, tentatively. On hearing our approach, an elderly gentleman appeared and asked what we wanted. Zeidane wasn't with us today, but I had another Mauritanian with me as translator. We exchanged the usual pleasantries, and he learned that I was a medic visiting the drilling sites. That always does the trick, and very soon I had the usual queue of locals sporting the usual array of ailments, which here included eczema, ingrown toenails, and missing teeth. I did my usual "Ummmm. Now let's see…" routine and, after a quick check of their blood pressure and temperatures, all but one of them seemed okay.

A small girl about two years old had a raging temperature and needed paracetamol to reduce this. Calpol for children would have been ideal, and I made a mental note to get some. I discussed the situation with her parents, about how she was going to take the tablet, and learned that she only drank camel's milk! However, this gave me an idea. Knowing how careful you have to be with children's doses, and that here 'age' was only a concept, I compared her with my own girls to gauge how old she was, balanced it against her weight, and broke up a tablet before crushing it up between two spoons, front to back. With every last lump removed from the white powder, I added a small amount of milk from a cup they'd scooped from a metal pot and – hey presto – Camel Milk Calpol! She drank the mixture straight from the spoon, and immediately pulled the most scrunched-up face I'd ever seen. Clearly, she'd never been medicated before, and would never trust another medic again, but her parents were happy, so we wished them well and headed off into the desert again like Lone Rangers.

Later on, back at the office, I asked Zeidane why the Bedouin always left behind an unsightly pile of rubbish – including plastic waste – at their campsites. Surely this must be against their respect for the desert? He explained that it was because of their nomadic heritage and, in days of old, whenever they returned to a former campsite, the rubbish would have always rotted down to nothing, having returned to nature.

I was astonished at this and asked if they knew that modern plastic was the long-term scourge of the planet, and whatever they dropped now would still be here hundreds of years later! For a few seconds he stared wistfully into the distance, before replying, "They are nomads..." and throwing his own empty bottle out of the window!

Most people think of Sahara as a vast, arid sandpit, and there are certainly parts of it like this, but where we worked was a mix of sand dunes and rocky outcrops. Atop some of these you could find several-hundred-year-old pieces of pottery, and even stone arrowheads. Interestingly, although they were just lying here, out in the middle of nowhere, and often sticking up from just beneath the surface sand, it was totally illegal to remove them from where they lay – and you could get yourself a lengthy prison term for trying it. However, once you learned to appreciate this parched, desolate environment, and to cope with the heat, it was a truly incredible place. Just like Paul Atreides on Arrakis, I felt that I was only just starting to understand what Zeidane had meant.

As part of our education on local hazards, we'd also look under the occasional rock for camel spiders and scorpions. I was already familiar with the latter, but the former I really hated, especially when they made a rattling or clicking noise as a defence mechanism. These things were large, very fast, and seemed to be a cross between a spider – complete with ten 'legs' at the front and a pointed face which opened wide to reveal four pincers – and the long body of a scorpion at the back, though without the stinger. Interestingly, these creatures have a bad rep for running after humans at up to a frightening 10mph, but the most valuable thing in the desert for them is shadow, and all they're doing is chasing yours – so they can keep cool in it! Also, contrary to popular belief, they're not venomous – though they can still give you a nasty bite if taken by surprise.

When visiting the drilling sites, I'd often give first aid training and advice on, and against, snake and scorpion stings – hypocritical though this might be. I'd also conduct health and safety inspections, passing my reports on to Zalan, the HSE Superintendent for the exploration department. This allowed me to put my NEBOSH health and safety qualifications into practice, and for anything I didn't know I'd ask my mate Jason Snow, another ex-soldier now working as a Project Manager for Exploration, who was always happy to advise me on local affairs.

And that was life working as an on-site medic, either treating minor illnesses and injuries, or doing HSE inspections on the rigs and kitchen areas, over a 'six weeks on – three weeks off' routine. One thing fast becoming a concern was that the mine population was growing exponentially. When I'd first started, we had around 1,800 staff – a mix of expats and local nationals, but over the past six months the workforce had expanded to over 9,000. Not only that, but the site itself was expanding, now with two mosques, a fire station, and a new accommodation block built on what used to be open desert beyond the fence line.

Each week I attended the mine managers' meetings, and sent reports back to Alex in the UK, because it was becoming increasingly clear that our medical response setup could no longer meet our current needs. I was asked if my company could provide full and extensive clinical facilities of our own, so I dutifully contacted Alex, aware that this would be a huge, lucrative contract for him. Alex responded with professionalism, saying although he could supply the X-ray equipment, and everything else we'd need for a hospital, morally it wouldn't be right. For the size of the company we were currently caring for, they really needed an equally large, world-level medical company to look after them. I reported this back to the mine managers, dutifully representing the ethics and attitude of Alex's company – which is why they're still one of the leading medical suppliers in the UK today.

The task was put out to consultation, with International SOS (ISOS) winning the contract. They brought in South African doctor Leon du Toit, and planning manager Andy Meany, both of whom were professionals in their field and superb ambassadors for their company, and straight away they changed how the place needed to be run on a larger scale – especially addressing my concerns with medicine supplies. They showed us a layout diagram of their standard 'pop-up hospital', which would be built here over the next few weeks. They also brought in one of their own paramedics, another South African named Oki, a huge figure of a man who'd been with ISOS for many years and knew how they operated worldwide. By this stage Steve had moved on to another project, so I remained onsite to oversee the handover and ensure that all the kit supplied by my company got returned home safely.

The exploration department was having a hard time with safety, and far too many careless occurrences. They were now running over forty rigs and worked an incident record system that started with a Near Miss at the bottom, followed by a First Aid Incident (FAI) where the employee needed first aid either at the scene or in the clinic – even for a sticking plaster or paracetamol. A Restricted Work Activity Case (RWAC) was more serious, and usually resulted in the employee being given limited activity duties, instead of their usual job. At the top of the list was a Lost Time Injury (LTI), where a workplace injury required either a stay in hospital, or extended time away from work. The department was sitting on eleven LTI's for the latest reporting period, which was alarming even for 9,000 staff. Zalan was doing his utmost to reduce these but, as he repeatedly told me in exasperation, this was not his main line of work, and he didn't have HSE training. Not only that, but his attempts to implement HSE in extreme fields of work like here, in the desert, was like pulling teeth. But his contract was due to end soon, and he was looking forward to his new role in Central America as a geologist – his passion. Unbeknown to me, my appeals for help hadn't gone unnoticed, and Charlie, the exploration manager, called me into his office to find out what my plans were after my contract was up. To be honest I hadn't really thought about it. My philosophy was that if you were good enough at your job, the work will always find you! I replied casually that I'd probably just find another medical job somewhere and, just as casually, he asked if I fancied taking over from Zalan as the new exploration HSE manager. I said I'd think about it and left it at that. I was about to return home for Christmas and decided to discuss it with Cara. But before I left, Charlie told me that the company's HSE Director for western Africa, who was currently at our site, wanted to see me for a chat. We went over my qualifications and experience, followed by a definite job offer if I was interested, and okay with the terms of the contract. I returned to my department to collect my bag, wondering why Charlie had such a big grin on his face and, as I left to catch the plane, he shouted that he'd send me the contract while I was away. Jason drove me to the airfield and I told him what Charlie had just offered me. He said that if I decided to take on the job, he'd give me as much help and backup as I needed. I was grateful for this, and said I'd think about it. It was a lot to take on and I still wasn't sure, but at least I had one more rotation to go before my contract expired.

Two days before Christmas I received the contract, along with the job description *(thanks, Charlie! Happy Christmas to you too)* which I read through several times, then telephoned Andy Meany from ISOS, who was also back in the UK, to ask his advice in case I was missing anything. He heard me out, before telling me that he couldn't believe it either. I then showed Cara, who read and re-read the same paragraphs which I'd already been over several times. Slowly shaking our heads in sheer astonishment, the reality of the Christmas gift we'd just been given, quite matter-of-factly by the company, was only just starting to sink in.

This cheeky young lad, whom Mr Akers had said would never make anything of his life, was now being offered a long-term contract with one of the world's largest mining companies, for celebrity wages, a business-class travel package, and an incredible private health plan for the entire family, including my boys. Even better, everything was tax-free, as the company would pay this! We realised that, by accepting this offer, we could pay off our mortgage in two years – and for someone who was used to moving, nomad-like, from job to job, this was the Holy Grail of contract work. It was also a no-brainer for me in terms of career advancement, even though I knew I'd be jumping the ship on which Alex had got me free passage – but this is the contractor's world, where almost every job is short-term, without the guarantee of another one afterwards, and you usually take whatever turns up next.

But there was something else too – an innate, difficult-to-put-your-finger-on feeling – that I was following a path that was slowly unfolding before me, and leading to my destiny – should I choose to accept it. I didn't know what it was, but I felt strongly that if I continued to do my best in everything I did, and as ethically as I knew how, then new opportunities would continue to arise along the way and guide me towards it.

That Christmas Eve I made a long-distance call to Charlie, telling him that I'd always been a big fan of HSE, before signing and emailing the contract to him. And that was it. After Christmas, and my final rotation, I'd become a highly-paid and valued full-time employee of one of the largest companies in the world, doing a job I felt born to – that of saving and protecting lives.

Chapter 22

2012

God's Will

⬦⬦

On returning to Africa, I found that ISOS had well and truly taken over, and had their own paramedic covering the site. Both Leon and Andy were also in-country, and gave me their full permission to spend the last part of my contract as an exploration paramedic. This was wonderful, as it would allow me a natural, all-inclusive handover from Zalan. I got to know Zalan a lot better during this time. Now in his mid-50s, he was a geologist by trade and heart – and an incredibly good one, too, as I learned from his team. He'd never once mentioned having HSE qualifications, and I got the feeling that, in the absence of anyone who did, his competent attitude and transferable abilities had got him pushed into doing the job.

As we crossed the desert in our trusty 4x4, he started telling me openly of the problems he regularly encountered – not so much from the expat drilling companies themselves, but the local nationals employed by them. One example occurred when we arrived at a Mauritanian drilling site, manned solely by local national personnel. After informing them that PPE (personal protective equipment) must always be worn on site – even by ourselves – we walked over to the rig. Beside each rig a large, 10ft x 6 ft rectangular hole had been excavated 5-6 feet deep into the rock below the sand and then filled with water for the drilling equipment. I couldn't imagine how water could survive in a blisteringly hot desert without draining or evaporating away, though I later learned that the area was a mix of sand and bedrock.

At our site inspection I saw that this hole had no protective barrier around it, nor any other means of identifying it as a danger at night, especially as the rigs worked a 24-hour pattern with alternate day and night crews. I informed the drill lead who immediately ordered his crew to put hazard tape around it, but while chatting to him I noticed an extensive black stain in the sand, where the rig received its fuel from the supply lorries. I picked up a little of this sand to smell, and yes, it was contaminated with diesel fuel. The lead quickly placed the blame on the fuel truck, saying that it was all fine when he'd started to fuel the rig, before heading to the rest tent for tea with his men. When he returned several minutes later, however, he'd found the fuel pouring onto and into the ground. I pointed out the obvious fire hazard, and that all fuelling processes needed to be supervised. Now, the contaminated sand needed to be dug out, then bagged and disposed of properly. Before leaving, I told him I'd return next day to check the area and complete my report. Zalan and I returned to camp, did the necessary paperwork, and I informed Charlie of my findings.

The following day we drove back to the site, which on first impression looked immaculate – until I checked the area where the leak had occurred. The stain was gone, but there was still a strong smell of diesel in the air. I scraped my boot across the surface, and of course all they'd done was shovel a fresh layer of sand on top. I now realised that, as the new boy on the rock, I was in a head-on predicament. My job was to ensure that H, S, and E were taken seriously, and they'd deliberately undermined my request. So, should I turn a blind eye to what I didn't see, or do I act decisively and create enemies?

An old Sergeant Major taught me to always choose your battles wisely. You're going to win some and lose others, so focus hard on the ones you need to win, and yield those which aren't as vital to your long-term goals. This shows that you're flexible, and they'll take your absolutes more seriously. I noticed Zeidane watching for my reaction so, aware that he was one of the few here who took HSE seriously, I asked the drill lead to switch off the rig, and told him that we needed to have a staff meeting in their tent.

With everyone assembled, and the rig safely off, I introduced myself and informed them of my job title, what it entailed, and how seriously I took HSE and the safety of everyone here. I went into the details of my previous inspection, and the requests I'd made to correct them. I then told them that, due to the serious nature of the diesel leak, the fire risk that the fuel/sand mix created, and the contamination of their beautiful country, we'd now have to shut down the rig until I was certain that the spill had been removed correctly, and I could report the satisfactory clean-up to the mine managers. Wanting to leave them on a high note, I made it clear that their rig was not to start up again until after my inspection later that afternoon, but that this was the only fault I could find, and everything else had been maintained to a high standard of safety. Zeidane translated every word, and probably added a few of his own, judging by the many drooped heads and muttered words as we left. However, he was over the moon throughout our journey back, telling me how really pleased he was to be working with me, and how seriously he took his position. I nodded and smiled in response, but was inwardly dreading having to tell Charlie that I'd just shut down one of his production rigs.

He was bent over several maps from the area we'd just inspected, in deep discussion with his senior geologist about their goals and timelines. I hung back until we were on our own, then told him what I'd done and the reasons why *I'm damned if I don't, and damned if I do...* but to my surprise he was 100% behind me, and even accompanied me that afternoon for the reinspection, to emphasise how serious this was.

Well, now I had backup, though it proved unnecessary because, greeting us on our arrival, there were over a hundred large, heavy-duty plastic bags, dutifully filled with contaminate. I signed the site off as safe, the rig was reopened, and I'd won my first battle. With that success under our belts, Zalan departed happily a few days later, and I was now officially the site's Exploration HSE Superintendent.

Although HSE was just one department at the mine, it had six subdivisions: Exploration, Mining, Transport, Production, Fire & Rescue, and Environmental – each of which had its own superintendent and workforce. I now had four staff, of whom Zeidane was my #1. On the day I officially took over, I introduced myself to each of the individual drilling companies at their evening briefings, which were held each night prior to the crews going out on their evening shift. It was while I was talking that I observed Zeidane at the side of the gathering, jumping up and down and waving his arms about frantically. I knew that he wasn't prone to epileptic fits, so I quickly made my excuses and my way over to him. One of the drillers had just lost two of his fingers at a rig. This was my first day on the job and I was already responsible for a serious – *how the hell did this happen?* I asked who'd been involved and if everyone else was okay, then asked him to meet me and the drilling manager at the medical clinic, where the employee had been taken.

My first surprise was that, as HSE Superintendent, I wasn't allowed to enter the emergency room, whereas not long ago I'd been in charge there! This was due to the nurses stamping their newly-found authority on the area (*oh, come on!*) until Oki came out and saw me waiting in the corridor. Just as surprised, he asked me why I was here and not there. After a brief, eye-rolling explanation, he brought me in to look at the injured guy and take pictures for my report. The casualty was a Mauritanian national, who had severed the tops of two fingers on his left hand, just beyond the first knuckle. Later reports confirmed that his missing fingertips couldn't be saved, and that he'd lost them after putting his hand in an area where a shearing action took place between two metal components. The most alarming parts of the report were that he was on his break, he shouldn't have been there, and he wasn't wearing any protective gear. When I asked him, later on, why he didn't have his protective leather gloves on, he just shrugged and said that they wouldn't have made any difference, because it was Allah's will that he'd lost his fingers.

Discussing the situation with Zeidane one evening over dinner, he suggested I talk with the camp's imam, which I did the next day. We had a long discussion about our potentially divergent viewpoints and, when I finally asked for his help, he said that he'd tell everyone who attended afternoon prayers about the importance of wearing PPE at all times. The following morning, I couldn't believe what I saw. As if the desert fairies had passed through overnight, it was almost a different site – every single Mauritanian national was in full PPE! Wow, from here on I'd include the imam as part of my team! Before we set out into the desert for our daily inspection, I observed Zeidane in serious conversation with a worker. As he climbed into our vehicle, he looked very concerned and told me that one of his friends was ill in bed with malaria. I still carried my own medical bag, so I said that we'd check on him as our first priority.

It was mid-summer, the heat was intense, and being out in direct sunlight was like opening a pre-warmed oven door. We stopped outside his friend's cabin, got out quickly, and went inside – into a room that was even hotter than outside. His friend lay shivering in bed, with the quilt pulled up to his chin. Zeidane told him that he desperately needed to cool off, switched on his air-con, and started to pull down his quilt. And that was when we saw that the poor guy, dressed in only his underwear, was still wearing his safety gloves! Zeidane snapped out of his shock and asked why he wearing them when he was ill? And I was gobsmacked when the reason was translated back to me – because the imam had said that they must wear PPE *at all times*.

Needless to say, we took him back to the medical centre for immediate treatment, and then paid a quick visit to the imam to clarify one or two issues...

During the rest of my tenure, HSE statistics in Exploration gradually improved with no further LTI's. Zeidane and the rest of my team were really enthusiastic with the changes, and I even managed to arrange a distance-learning NEBOSH course for them all. Charlie also allocated every other Saturday for training, and the drilling companies set up a rig in our car park so that our team could train on them. They also learned about HSE requirements, conducting good safety audits, and why reporting near-misses was vital – for example, when you're driving, the theoretical difference between a Near Miss and a trauma (followed by an insurance claim, by or against you) is less than a millimetre.

This practical arrangement worked both ways and, just as in Iraq, I gave my staff and the drillers lessons in wound management, breaks and strains, and how to deal with scorpion stings and snake bites. One team had reported an increase in snakes at their rigs during the night. The local species in their area was the horned viper – identifiable by two short hornlike scales above each eye. They didn't usually kill humans, but their hemotoxic venom – wherever you found it – could still be lethal, even in small doses. Drillers were killing the snakes that entered their site, and then bringing them back to show their mates. One actually brought back a live specimen, which he kept as a pet in a plastic bottle! I took this off him, with the intention of releasing it back in the desert, because snakes can still administer toxins when dead. I promised to visit them again at night to find out what was going on. On my first night visit, I could see the problem straight away, and why it was endemic across all the other four sites. Before heading into the desert, each team collected their evening meal which they'd eat during their shift. However, instead of putting the leftovers in the bins provided, they'd leave half-empty food cartons on the floor of their tents – not realising that, even in the desert, this created an unhealthy vermin problem. Here, it took the form of little desert-hopping mice, which would flock to the tents each evening for the regular meal that these kind giants had been leaving for them ever since their arrival. However, further up the food chain, the snakes, who only ate meat, soon learned that they didn't have to roam the desert any more for live prey, because they were all gathered here, at the same time each day, in one place!

A swift lesson in food hygiene resolved the H&S problem, and also the E issue by explaining how snakes are beneficial to the environment by keeping the rodent and tick populations in check. This simple solution prevented future injuries, and kept the balance of nature intact, for all the organic lifeforms involved.

> "I don't know where to start, as a story needs a person to gather his imagination to realize what was happening during that time. For me, it began when Mr. Wayne Ingram was a paramedic, but after only a few months it became clear that he was the right person in the right place, and was eventually appointed health and safety superintendent in the

exploration department. I had worked with him before in the exploration department as a safety supervisor and, even then, I realized his values as a manager and as a person. He was the best manager I ever worked with, and even more than that he is my friend. He has always supported my decisions and let me learn from my mistakes.

On a personal level, he was a man who was loved by everyone who knew him. In addition to what he provided to the exploration department in terms of protecting lives and property, he also took on a role in charitable work outside the department, which contributed to the success of the orphanage in Nouadhibou".

Zeidane

Chapter 23

2012-2013

The Orphanage

As I became more deeply involved in my work, it wasn't long before other aspects of general safety started to blip on my radar. The company had its own airfield and this necessitated having their own fire service which came under Fire & Rescue. Though we already had a fire-fighting appliance on site, it didn't have a full-time crew – the idea being that, should a fire break out, then allocated expats would crew the truck and put out the fire. But, as any firefighter knows (the clue is in the name), the work is extremely dangerous and requires intensive training with plenty of practice. I attended a fire which started here when locals were cutting holes for windows into steel shipping containers to make them habitable. To create a fire and keep it going, all you need are heat, oxygen, and fuel – and we certainly had plenty of the first two. The third was provided by the flammable materials and oily residue inside the container – which hadn't been removed before the sparks started to fly. Jase and I started to tackle the blaze, but pretty soon we had around fifty Mauritanians joining in and doing everything they could do to help. However, without training, experience, and coordination, they weren't just putting themselves in danger, and creating a worsening situation that we couldn't control, but they were actually putting our own lives at risk. I discussed the experience with Ken, our Fire Superintendent, who asked if I knew of any trained firefighters who might like to man a fire appliance in sunnier climes. As a result, three lads I knew from Dorset Fire & Rescue flew out into new careers, crewing the truck and training the locals in manning a full-time fire station.

Soon after, I was asked by the company's public relations office if I could accompany Fabiana, a delightful and gregarious Peruvian lady, to visit an orphanage in Nouadhibou. I accepted and, now that I had a proper visa, and was allowed out by myself, I agreed to do a safety audit of the place while she did her PR thing.

The following day we set off north, this time on a thankfully uneventful journey, though I couldn't suppress a giggle as we passed without hindrance through El Presidente's roadblock – an involuntary reaction that didn't go unnoticed by Fabiana. During the journey she told me we'd been invited to a Mauritanian wedding – a cousin of the company's local fixer.

Surprised, I said that I hadn't brought any smart clothing, although I'd already met the fixer. At this her face lit up with realisation, and she burst out with, "Oh! You're him! The only expat in Mauritanian history to be arrested as an illegal immigrant!" I blushed, but she continued, unable to stop herself laughing, "Your story's even reached the capital! You're famous!" With nowhere in the car to hide, I was now at her mercy, and eventually succumbed to her untreatably infectious laughter. I was already planning a new career in stand-up comedy when she calmed herself down and, still gasping, told me that there wasn't a problem as the fixer had already organised the proper attire for me. Impressed by this efficiency, I guessed that the clue was in the job title.

Not long after we'd arrived for our meeting, a Mauritanian gentleman walked in and greeted me with a huge smile and a "Mr Wayne…". Embarrassed, it took me a while to realise that this was Cheikh, my favourite James Bond! I immediately stood up and shook his hand vigorously, thanking him profusely for his previous help. We then had a long laugh – Fabiana included – over the former situation I'd witlessly got myself into. As the long version of the story unfolded – Fabiana was loving this! – I was shaken (but not too visibly stirred) to discover that there hadn't even been a ransom payment involved – I thought the company had forked out thousands for my freedom! Even worse, I now learned that, once they'd made a few enquiries, I'd have been kicked out after a few hours anyway! Feeling totally gutted by this let-down, Fabiana's hysterics were doing nothing whatsoever for my self-esteem.

As though piloting a battleship through the battering gales of laughter, I managed to steer the conversation around to the wedding the following night, to which Cheikh said that he'd collect us and go to his home first, where my garments had been prepared. I was surprised to learn that the wedding didn't start until 11pm and, as we'd only been invited to the reception, we didn't need to get there until midnight. He then left us, leaving Fabiana and I to continue our schedule for the day. A Kinross driver took us to the orphanage, where we were greeted at the entrance by a group of six female staff. The main building was located in the back streets of the city, and my initial reaction to it was 'thoroughly decrepit'. While potentially usable as a temporary troop house, it was totally unsuited to house, let alone raise, small children!

On entering through the main door, I saw a child's doll in a blue dress hanging up on the wall. On it were pinned two sheets of A4 paper on which were home-printed 'Vive les droits de l'enfant' (Long live the rights of children) and 'Non a la mal traitence des enfants' (Say no to child abuse). A shiver ran through me. Why would anyone even need to write this?

I asked, carefully, why the doll was so high up on the wall, out of a child's reach, and was told that it was the only toy in the premises. It was only there to show them what a toy was, but it wouldn't be fair to let just one child play with it. I'd been there less than thirty seconds, I'd not yet seen the children, and my concerns were already escalating. We walked through each room, each as bare and depressing as the last, until we reached the kitchen, which was equipped with a small 2-ring gas cooker and a wooden table. There was no sink. At this point I asked how many children were actually here at any one time? The answer was 'Up to a hundred and twenty…'

The 'medical room' barely had enough supplies to make up a portable first aid kit, and the two largest rooms were filled with children busy with their lessons. I asked why the young boys were sitting at small desks while the young girls sat on the floor. It was explained that there wasn't enough money for more tables and chairs so, in Mauritanian tradition, girls would always use the floor. The second classroom had no furniture at all, and even the teacher sat on the floor.

I learned that the fourteen all-female staff (men wouldn't do the job) were volunteers, though there were rarely more than six present at a time. As I continued with the audit, they gave me as much information as they could about the site. Thirty of the children were full-time orphans whose parents had either died, or didn't want them. The rest were dropped off daily by parents who lived in such extreme poverty that they couldn't afford to feed nor educate them.

A local landlord rented the run-down premises to them. The funds to run it came from charitable donations, though these were severely limited and only covered the rent and, if they were very, very lucky, the absolute basics for the children. The accommodation block was a short walk away across a sandy road though, while trying to keep a straight face, my heart was already breaking before we reached it. A quick glance told me that Fabiana, now uncharacteristically silent, felt the same way. As they unlocked the door, the first thing that hit me was the stench – and this was the last straw for me, because on military operations I'd dossed in more prestigious slums. The only toilet in the premises, a squat affair situated in a squalid, dingy, unventilated room, had an open broken hole in the ground next to it, through which you could not only see the sewage moving along, but also smell the gases coming back from where it amassed, further down the line. Other holes in the floor around the premises gave access to not only the foundations, I was told, but also to rats and scorpions. Electricity was connected to just one area of the building and, even then, only two of the lights worked. In each bedroom, none of which contained a bed, slept ten children, with the little boys huddled together on the floor with a single blanket above and below them to keep them warm, while the girls were given a blanket each to wrap around themselves.

The bedrooms had no windows, either, so I had to use a torch to look around each airless, pitch-black room, and I jumped when a massive camel spider, skulking in the corner of a ceiling, appeared in my vision.

That did it for me. I strode outside, grabbed a length of wood I'd seen on my tour, and returned to batter the thing to a pulp. I didn't exit for a while. I couldn't. Not with my fist still clenched tightly around the wood, and trying to control my breathing while I just stood there, physically shaking with anger. I wasn't just angry. I was absolutely, bloody furious. It wasn't about the unfortunate spider – which was in the wrong place at the wrong time. It was about everything that it represented. Everything that was so utterly and horribly wrong about this place – this care home for displaced 5 to 11-year-olds who, under different circumstances, might have been having a wonderful time in Beavers, Cubs, or Scouts. And I was still trying to process the facts that, overnight, there was no adult supervision on the premises, and the front doors were locked from the outside for safety.

It was the most damning report I'd ever written, advising that both buildings be shut down with immediate effect, and the children moved elsewhere – anywhere but here – to somewhere that was physically, hygienically, and emotionally safe for children. However, Fabiana said this would be impossible because it was a local problem, there was no budget to solve it, and we couldn't get involved. Well, fuck that. I'd spent a previous lifetime in the Army, where getting involved was part of our job description. Somebody needed to do something about this, and soon. Later that day, with the memory of those children deeply embedded in our minds, we were collected from the hotel to prepare for the wedding. Putting on brave faces, we entered Cheikh's home where he graciously presented me with my formal attire for the event – a very fashionable and distinguished-looking dishdasha. Fabiana, of course, had brought her own. Now clad in suitable raiment, we were asked to take seats on benches at the rear of a large tent, from where we could watch the procession of guests now entering. First came all the men, who sat themselves on chairs around the many tables. When they were suitably seated, the ladies then followed, seating themselves comfortably and communally on the floor together. Finally, once everyone had found their places, the married couple arrived, and sat on two chairs before all the guests.

Food, soft drinks, and tea were served throughout the night, while a local band, also seated on the floor, strummed a selection of stringed instruments accompanied by an eclectic selection of exotic percussion. I have to say that, even in my conflicted emotional state, this was a special occasion for me. I felt honoured to be amongst so many happy people in traditional national dress celebrating the newly-married couple, and it was a blessed relief from the troubling and heart-breaking scenes from earlier that day.

Although we'd have liked to stay longer, however, at around 3am we were really feeling the previous day's exhaustion, so we excused ourselves and took a taxi back to the hotel. Little did I know that, while my conscious mind had been taking a relaxing break at the party, my subconscious had already started planning another fundraising event.

Back at the camp next day I told Charlie of my findings, and how genuinely concerned I was for the safety of these local children. Then I suggested that, if the company couldn't get involved, would I be allowed independently to conduct a sponsored event to raise money for their situation? His interest piqued, he asked what I proposed. I said that I intended to cycle between Mauritania's two coastal cities, Noaukchott and Nouadhibou – a one-way trip of roughly 480 kilometres, or 300 miles. After a quick think he said he could certainly grant me the time off to accomplish the task, but would need to check on any other issues that could be involved. Now inspired that something was actually being done, I went off to start organising it. The first item on the agenda was to find a bike.

Several days later I was called to see Derek in the security office, where he was waiting for me with Khalifa, the mine's security representative for Mauritania. Khalifa wasted no time in putting a halt to my plans, due to the ever-present Al Qaeda kidnapping threat. Apparently, word was already out about a thick-witted expat planning a solo road trip out in the open, and making it really easy for them! To be honest, I really hadn't thought through the security implications. All I'd learned so far is that bicycles are neither a popular nor reliable means of transport in the desert, which is why nobody had one!

After a few more days of brain-bashing I came up with the idea of spending a full 24-hour period cycling on a static gym bike, but instead of doing it alone I'd invite 24 people to each cycle for one hour, at their own speed. Each would start five minutes before the previous one finished, to get warmed up properly and to create a constant and consistent activity. The event would be called 'Cross a Mile n' Bring a Smile!' and I asked not just ex-pats, but for local national personnel to be involved too because, like my first fundraising event for Stefan, this was for a local cause.

On the morning of 9th Feb 2013, we all gathered in the gym and, just before 9am with a Mauritanian national proudly representing his country on the first exercise bike, everyone counted down loudly to his start time before he was off and racing! Well, that was the idea, and with hindsight I should have run a practice session with him beforehand, because he was clearly new to the machine and looked like he was enjoying a Sunday morning meander around Regents Park. But everyone was having a great time, I'd ensured that the locals were only given periods that didn't clash with their prayer times, and that people like Gary, Charlie, Wayne, Pete, and myself ensured that the activity continued to run through the quiet night-time hours.

The entire event, begun by a Mauritanian, and ended by another in front of a large crowd and their imam, had been a complete success. The gym bikes had been ridden continually for 24 hours, covering a distance of 860 kilometres (over 534 miles!), and in doing so raised a total of £67,000! This was a huge amount – far more than I'd expected – but then we were surrounded by the generous and well-paid personnel of several drilling companies who were – quite literally – sitting on a gold mine! Also, I'm not ashamed to say that I can be persuasive at times, especially where children are concerned, and I have no qualms about using people's heartstrings as lifelines.

For their generous cooperation and donations, I would like to thank the following:

Capital Drilling, SGS, Tom Browne International, CCC, Azlma, TMLSA, Hatch, NCTP, and Kinross.

Fabiana found out who, in local government, was responsible for the children's home, but when I suggested to her that – now that we could afford it – as well as renovating and refurbishing the building, we could add a large extension to house everyone properly, have a bigger kitchen, medical room, and so on, she advised strongly against it. Because if we did, the guy renting out the building would have then cancelled the agreement, forced the children out, and moved his own family in. Instead, her team worked with the Nouadhibou city council to identify a suitable undeveloped piece of land. Using the money raised, we'd build a brand-new orphanage, complete with a safe play area, a bed for every child, provision for temporary guests, a hygienic and fully-equipped kitchen with a sink and running water, classrooms with enough desks for every child to sit down, paper, pens and – the icing on the cake – lots of toys!!!

I did manage to visit the site while it was being built, but had to limit my time there as the HSE was far from adequate, and I wasn't responsible for the contractors. I saw a bricklayer carrying breeze blocks wearing a hard hat and flipflops. Another was working on the exterior of the building, at least 20 feet off the ground, by standing on a single scaffold plank sticking out of the window space. Worse still – the only thing keeping the plank steady and level were the two guys inside sitting on the other end!

From the initial planning to the grand opening, the project took just under a year to complete, with the company coordinating with the council. I had very little involvement after that – but it didn't matter. Like the creation of the universe, my job was simply to get it started with enough energy, resources and guidance to keep it going in the right direction.

Life in the desert continued as normal until a fateful day changed the course of my life. Everyone was aware that the showers in our accommodation had been poorly designed, with glazed wall tiles fitted to the floor. While these had plenty of grip when dry, as soon as they got wet the floor transformed into a tropical ice rink. And of course, it's only when the shower floor's wet that you're not wearing boots, nor any other form of PPE. I'd learned to wedge my feet against the shower walls which, if I was careful, usually prevented me from slipping. One day, however, I was in a rush – turning the shower on, stepping straight in, and ending up in a tangled, pain-ridden heap on the hard and slippery tiled floor, in the certain knowledge that I'd just buggered up my ankle again. This happened a couple of days before I was due leave. There was no way I could be treated here in time for this injury, so a quick visit to the onsite doctor for painkillers got me back home. On the company's medical insurance, I was able to get a consultation at a local private hospital, where they tried a cortisone injection without success, followed by an arthroscopy, also to no avail. Several months later, while back on leave again, they were finally forced to fuse my right ankle, to which I'd added further insult to injury by breaking it in a whole new area, and needing to confine myself, once more, to a lengthy period of rehabilitation. This meant that, just like in the Army, I was forced to terminate my contract, a year before it was due to end, on the grounds of poor health. Which is why I never got to see the grand opening of the orphanage, though I was sent a certificate from the company and many pictures from the HSE staff, all of whom wished me well. It was a superb PR coup for Fabiana and her team but, far more importantly to me, those children were now safer, healthier, and much, much happier.

> "I first met Wayne when he joined Portland fire station as a retained firefighter, and I must say we got on well from the start. He was diligent, liked rugby enjoyed a pint/whisky or two, and was professional throughout.
>
> After Wayne had been out in Mauritania for a while, he sent an email to me which I must say was out of the blue. He asked if I would be interested in joining him in Mauritania to help develop an Emergency Response Team (ERT) with a mutual colleague and friend Pete Kelly, another firefighter from Portland. Pete and I readily agreed. However, on our arrival at the mine site our thoughts were "What have we let ourselves in for?" as our 'fire truck' and

'equipment' was an old Unimog, with even older houses and branches!

But with our professional knowledge and skillsets, Wayne's infectious positivity and enthusiasm, and Ken's knowledge and contacts, we gained more equipment and developed the ERT's capability over time.

Wayne has the default setting of wanting to help others who are in need, or not as fortunate as perhaps they should be. So, it wasn't a surprise when he told us about his newest challenge, of wanting to raise money for the orphanage, with a 24-hour static cycle. It wasn't long until Wayne's plans were falling into place, although he did have an issue with filling some of the 'silly o'clock' time slots during the silent hours. To correct this, Wayne approached the ERT, and Ken, Pete, myself, and I believe a few others were press-ganged into ensuring the full 24 hours were covered

We successfully completed the full 24 hours with the goodwill of the Tasiast mine staff, which all grew from Wayne's idea that was planted and grew into reality.

A great time was had out in Tasiast, Mauritania – working hard, playing harder, facing new challenges, and overcoming them. But chiefly, having the privilege of meeting good people from all over the world, and being able to call them my friends

Would I do it again? Yes, 100%, and I would be on the next plane out there…"

Gary Watton

Chapter 24

2014

The Next Operation

While laid up at home recovering from the ankle fusion, having to use crutches while wearing a surgical support boot, and generally feeling extremely sorry for myself, I thought I'd use the opportunity to contact Slava to arrange for Stefan returning to the UK, eleven years after his last operation. The family actually came back to the UK two years after the big event in 2003, for David Dunaway to do minor follow-up surgery on Stefan's nose – but it was only for a short time, there was no media involvement, and I never saw them as my ambulance training had started.

Since then, I'd lost contact, but that's what tends to happen when you're separated by time, distance, and your individual lives. I'd been a mess after leaving the Army, had finally got my act together with a gold-plated career, then got myself into exactly the same mess again. So, having come full circle, it seemed like a good time to put right a wrong.

Luckily, Slava hadn't changed her number, and responded to my text that everything was okay, Stefan was doing really well, and granting me permission to organise the next operation.

David still had his practice in Harley Street, and was much easier to contact. On a cold, wet February morning I called his office and spoke with Niamh, his practice manager, who actually remembered me from 2003, and put me straight through. Now, only if you're ever lucky enough to meet David will you truly understand what I'm writing now, because my words alone cannot convey the sheer humanity of the man, and how he makes you feel – as if to wonder, "Why can't everyone be like this?" or even better, "How can I be like this?"

As soon as he picked up the phone, I felt like I was chatting with a dear friend, who was genuinely and enthusiastically interested in everything I had to say. Long before we got to the reason I'd called, he'd asked me about my medical discharge, my ambulance and firefighting careers, my time abroad, and my family. He even remembered the names of my children. David was amazed that I was still fundraising for Stefan and, without a second thought, volunteered to complete another operation at no charge – though he'd need to see current CT scans as always. He then advised me, under the circumstances, to contact another organisation he knew, which had been set up specifically to deal with the logistics of such challenging events across the globe. Facing the World (FTW) is a London-based charity conceived and implemented by two renowned doctors in this field. To quote them, *"We are a UK-registered medical charity creating sustainable solutions for children in developing countries who have severe craniofacial defects. We do this by training local surgical teams, providing multidisciplinary surgical treatment, and donating necessary equipment"*.

As part of accomplishing this task, and to share the load, they ask professionals like David to give their time freely to perform these critical surgeries in London clinics and hospitals, and cover the logistical costs through the charity and not the NHS. Their work has been such a huge success that they've recently branched into Vietnam and trained over 75 local doctors to perform such surgeries there. In just five years, this incredible charity has trained over 200 doctors and facilitated over 40,000 such operations to be performed throughout the world.

He gave me the number of FTW's Graham Banton, who'd been briefed about my history with Stefan. I didn't really know what to expect from an executive director, but was pleased to find him extremely approachable. To take things further, he invited me to their office on London's Fulham Road to grab a coffee, and offered me an apartment to stay in, just two minutes' walk away.

Fresh from luxury accommodation in Mauritania, and knowing that I was headed for affluent Chelsea, I took the train from Weymouth to Waterloo, thinking about my next 24 hours in the most exquisite accommodation money could buy. However, such thoughts were dashed on arriving at their address and making my way up the stairs. The executive director's office was a single drab room shared by him and the secretary, which was certainly efficient. There was a small kitchen and a room with a TV, settee, and a few toys *Oh, wow!* A smile of joy came over my face – probably the most heartening in a long time – as the reality of this situation hit me. Here was a charity attempting to raise funds so that facially-disfigured children from all corners of the Earth could have life-changing operations. They may well have been making thousands in donations, but they were willing to accept a bare minimum for themselves to keep things running, while preserving as much as possible for the actual purpose of the charity. The Scouts, a paramilitary organisation in the UK which I support wholeheartedly, have a similar ethos and won the 'Charity of the Year' award in 2022. Despite having fewer than 400 full-time, enthusiastic staff – mainly in one central HQ – they manage 143,000 adult and 20,000 teenage volunteers to inspire and train over 424,000 young people aged 6-25 each week with skills for life (Jan 2023 census figures, rounded to the nearest thousand).

Graham was a great guy, a lot younger than me, and extremely good at his job. I'm sure he could have got a far higher-paying one elsewhere, maybe in corporate management, but he was happy to do something that was infinitely more satisfying. I mean – imagine, in your retirement, looking back at what you'd achieved with your one life!

Over a brew we talked about how they could help with the logistics in bringing the family back to the UK, including their visas, though they weren't able to help with the costs as all their available funds were tied up in other projects. I fully expected this, and assured him that I was extremely grateful for their assistance, and I'd continue raising the money to allow Stefan back. He did, however, give me keys to the self-contained flat he'd promised, which I gratefully accepted as it would constitute a considerable cost-saving during Stefan's stay.

We exchanged contact numbers and, as I had other meetings in London the same day, he walked with me to the flat, conveniently located opposite the Chelsea and Westminster Hospital. I learned that it had been donated by the Frenchman who ran the 'Tray Gourmet' delicatessen on the ground floor below, and that his shop also offered generous discounts to NHS staff.

The fully-functional flat was perfect for everything I'd need – bed, kitchen, dining area and bathroom – without a shred of extravagance, and I looked forward to using it as my base when the family arrived from Bosnia. With two major problems already solved, knowing that all the logistics would be handled by pros, and that the operation was definitely going ahead, all I needed now was another CT scan, and to start raising funds once more!

I contacted Stefan's aunt Dzejna about the scan, then started the usual job of calling the local newspapers, radio and TV stations to get the media on board. While I'd have greatly preferred to keep this private, or at least low key, I knew that without public support we'd never raise the money. Thankfully, the interest from them all was extremely promising, though I hadn't considered the fact that, the last time Stefan had been in the news, he was an adorable little 4-year-old boy, and not a teenager.

Just as in 2003, everyone was unbelievably generous with their donations although, this time, the results were slower and the news didn't have the same impact. Other things had changed too – we weren't a registered charity, and the bank account we'd used previously had belonged to the Army! Calvin was still running his taxi firm, and again started pulling in favours from every direction to help raise awareness and funds. With the help of HSBC in Weymouth, he and I set up an account in the name of 'The Stefan Savic Appeal', which required both our signatures to safeguard every financial decision. During the first few weeks I commuted to London regularly to see David and Graham, to keep things going and build up the relationship with FTW. I also had to keep reminding Dzejna about the overdue CT scan, without which nothing could move forward. This wasn't easy, as the only place it could be done was in Sarajevo, several hours drive from Laktasi. I imagined that the scanner in Banja Luka must have had a meltdown by now, and my imagination 3D-modelled the entire city being drawn inexorably into the gaping, glowing maw beneath it.

Dzejna and Stefan made the journey and sent David the scan, which inspired me to continue. We were still raising money, but far too slowly to meet any kind of deadline, so in order to kickstart the process I called the Dorset Echo and told them I was prepared to sell my beloved Sachs 800cc motorbike to help raise the urgently-needed funds – and they could turn it into a story if they wanted. I'd bought it two years ago, second-hand, partly because it looked like a cool cross between a roadster, sports bike, and cruiser, and because it was all I could afford at the time! This gave them a new angle, and another local article for the paper. As soon as it was published, I received a call from the Echo with the contact details of a local grandmother, who wished to remain anonymous, but wanted to talk to me. Intrigued, I called and introduced myself, before having a lovely conversation with a lady who explained that she and her husband had followed my campaign from the start, and had been extremely moved that I'd kept my promise in continuing to help this young boy. I thanked her for this, but she continued. Her husband had died a few years earlier, and his insurance had provided well for her. She'd since spoken to her family, who had all given their blessing for her to help, so she wanted to know how much money I needed to reach the target.

Embarrassed, and also shocked by this – because there was no way I was going to deprive a retired lady of her savings – I told her that we were okay and only needed, maybe, a few hundred pounds. She told me not to be silly, and that this clearly wasn't the truth otherwise why would I be selling my motorbike? How much did I really need? She had me there, so I sheepishly told her around ten thousand pounds, fully expecting the line to go silent. To my absolute amazement, she responded with, "Well, that's more like it! Who do I make the cheque out to?"

The only condition she put on our agreement was I didn't mention her name and, when I eventually informed the Echo, I was to refer to her simply as 'a kind granny'. Still knocked out by this act of selfless generosity, I completely forgot that my bike was still on offer, until I got a call that afternoon – the only response I received – from a guy wanting take it for a ride. To be honest, I was gutted, but what could I do? I'd already mentally parted company with her, and knew that we'd likely need a lot more than ten thousand by the time this was all over, so I reluctantly gave him my address and arranged a time.

As soon as I opened the front door and saw the size of the guy (he made me look like my friend Tom) I knew it wasn't for him and secretly hoped he'd feel the same. Thankfully, ten minutes later, he returned telling me sorry, but he really needed something more powerful... Mate, if you're reading this, thank you!

After several more weeks of drumming up funds, which kept my mind off my personal mobility issues, we finally reached the target we'd set to cover not only the operation, but the logistics to get us all there and back. We then informed David and set a date for the operation – again at GOSH's facilities. FTW arranged visas and flights for Stefan, Slava and Dzejna, and accommodation at an hotel they already knew. This was better than the old B&B at Kings Cross, but came at a higher cost. Far from the 50 quid a night I remembered, I received a £2,300 bill in advance to cover their stay. The only potential problem was that the hotel was directly behind Stamford Bridge, home to Chelsea Football Club, and on the day of arrival the Blues would be at home in the Champions League. On 28th April 2014, our arrival outside the hotel coincided with thousands of Chelsea fans parading past, singing and shouting their support for their team. Then a few hours later, after the match, the Atlético Madrid fans did exactly the same in reverse, having just won 3-1.

The free accommodation provided by FTW was very practical, not just because it saved us money, but because a fresh pastry from the cafe below appeared outside my bedroom door each morning, as a kind gift from the owner! It was especially welcome this morning, I considered, munching away on my walk to the hotel, because we were being admitted into GOSH for the operation.

Based on our previous experience, I'd already topped up their phones with £50 credit – though not from the funds we'd raised. All the pre-med checks had been done, and David met us at the ward to calmly explain what he'd be doing as he started the readjustment for Stefan's final nasal appearance. All going well, he should just need one more operation, in two years' time, to finish off.

We were all were used to this from almost a decade ago and, while much had changed in the coffee shops around London, and one of us was now on crutches, Slava still got through the day by chain-smoking and phoning the hospital every 30 minutes. Finally, the operation was

2014: The Next Operation

over, and Stefan returned to his room, unsurprisingly drowsy after the anaesthetic. I was quite impressed, when I knew it had worn off, that Stefan didn't moan, nor even mention the pain in his nose. I know I'd have done… Hell, even though he was on a discretional syringe driver for morphine, he never pushed it, and the nursing staff removed it, unused, the next day. The following day he was discharged from hospital, and his mum and aunt took him back to their hotel to recuperate.

A week later, after his final checks, David gave permission for Stefan to return home, which pleased me as it left us over £9,000 in the account for next time. However, on the morning before they were due to leave, 'Good Morning Britain' asked if we could do a final interview. As we waited in a hospitality room, I saw David Cameron, surrounded by his close-protection police, exiting a studio. At that moment I thought about introducing him to Stefan but, amusingly, Stefan couldn't have been less impressed if he'd tried, so our PM lost his chance.

The interview went well, as David brought everyone up to date on the original problem, what had been achieved since then, and with just one last operation to complete the journey. Stefan was in-camera most of the time, and I was suddenly aware that he was no longer the same trusting little 4-year-old, unafraid of anything, as when he first appeared on national TV. This time was different; at 15 he was a self-aware, self-conscious young adult, effectively being forced to exhibit his facial disfiguration on live television to the whole of the UK – as if this was the most important thing about him. How could I have been so stupid?

I'd had teenage boys of my own, so I had no excuse whatsoever. I should have checked with the family. I should have been aware of Dzejna's attitude as we entered the studios. Why hadn't I even asked Stefan how he felt about all this? I'd been on bloody autopilot, going through all the motions again, and feeling good about myself. All I'd been interested in was promoting the story *my story!* and raising more money. At no point had I ever considered the most crucial aspect of this campaign – Stefan himself – and I realised that, had it been up to him, he'd have probably been happier to have stayed home in Bosnia with his friends, who knew and loved him for who he was as a human being.

Bosnia is a country, different from ours, where a little means a lot. You grow or raise your own food on the land you have, and people accept you for what you are. Although it may not be much, their hard, war-torn lives make them grateful for what they have. This is how Stefan and his friends are – happy, living each day after the next, knowing that there may not be another. History has taught them that situations can change, most often violently, and shatter that happiness at any time... In other words, it may have been the right thing to do, but not in the way I did it. Watching Stefan sitting haplessly in front of Ben Shephard and Susanna Reid, like a faultless flower that's been plucked and pressed, I suddenly hated myself.

And that was when the self-recriminations kicked in *isn't this what I always do? Have I always been such an insensitive arse? Is this how my marriage to Tracy ended, leaving our boys without a father? Is this what I do with Cara, every time I leave her and our family for months on end?*

I felt terrible as Dzejna told me, over coffee later, how dismayed she was at the way Stefan was taking this, seeing as he'd been made devastatingly aware of how he looked to an entire, developed country whose languages and customs were alien to him – especially at the age where a child is most conscious of their body image by internalising and emulating those of celebrities, social media tropes, and their peers – and I'd been totally and callously oblivious to this. I didn't know what to do, nor say. I told her that the press releases and TV interviews created massive contributions towards the money we needed, and that we were reliant on these promotions to raise awareness. I told her how much we had in the bank for the next time, and that this TV appearance would raise even more. So, with any luck, we shouldn't need to do another one – ever. She saw the point of this – and the unfortunate reality of the situation – and said that she'd do her best to discuss this with Stefan.

We said our goodbyes the following day, and they departed back to Bosnia. To my relief, Stefan had seemed a lot better today, and Dzejna had clearly had a good heart-to-heart with him. I settled all the hotel, transport, and hospital bills, and with the extra cash we'd raised from the GMB interview we were left with just over £9,600 for next time. Graham and I discussed the final operation, now planned for 2016, and he promised his charity's logistical aid for their return, along with a letter of confirmation for Calvin and me.

It turned out that, after the TV appearance, and what I'd said about them, FTW themselves had received over £5,000 in donations, and it was clear to us both that our attitude and goals were inseparably connected. At this point, I suggested something I'd been mulling over since Stefan's departure: I'd come to the conclusion that FTW had far more experience, and would always be better prepared, in looking after children than I could ever do as an individual. With Calvin's permission, I would transfer our remaining funds into FTW's account, which they could use towards Stefan's future operation, especially if anything were to happen to Calvin or myself. If the operation didn't go ahead, for any reason, they could use these funds to help other children instead. If the final operation was a success, and any money left over, then Stefan's legacy and sacrifice could help another child facing a similar situation.

I showed Graham's letter of confirmation to Calvin, who fully agreed to my suggestion and, two days later at the bank, we transferred the balance of funds together.

Graham had also been considering something on behalf of Facing the World charity – which is why I am enormously proud to have since become one of its ambassadors.

> "At FTW we used to receive referrals for children from around the world on a weekly basis. They typically suffered from a range of conditions including facial clefts (like Stefan), facial tumours, conflict injuries, and acid attacks, and were often living in the most desperate circumstances. They were referred to us by family members, aid workers, and even passing tourists who had encountered them on their travels. However, due to the many logistical challenges that Wayne explains, it was nearly impossible to get them to London for treatment.
>
> Getting a basic scan or diagnosis is a crucial first step but, without having boots on the ground, getting past that hurdle becomes an overwhelming obstacle. Even if you manage

to get that, and establish that you can help, you then have to earn the family's trust and convince them to make the huge leap of faith to commit to coming to the UK – which involves whole new bureaucratic headaches, like getting visas for people without passports, and often no recorded date of birth. For these reasons, it meant that, despite the best will in the world, planned surgeries for children whom we could help would often, frustratingly, fall through.

When I first met Wayne (hobbling with his ankle boot!) I knew from his handshake alone that none of that was going to be a problem. Here was a man of purpose, who had made a commitment to get something done, and was going to make damn sure that it was going to happen (that's ex-military for you) no matter what the personal cost.

It turned out to be one of the easiest cases we'd ever managed because, whatever we needed to get set up (documents, scans, consent forms, etc) Wayne just got it done – even though we were all too aware that it was often no easy feat. It was clear that he had the family's complete trust in looking after their interests, and he made sure they were supported every step of the way.

It is never easy supporting kids with facial differences, especially through the twin challenges of complex medical surgery and the often-accompanying glare of publicity. The circumstances that Wayne explained after the TV interview happened in nearly every case I worked on. The sad thing is that the surgery wouldn't happen without the media exposure, but it naturally causes you to question the whole process, and whether it's right for who you're helping. However, seeing the confident young man Stefan has become is testament to all of Wayne's tenacity, bloody-mindedness, and commitment to helping those who need it most – and for that he should be incredibly proud."

Graham Banton

Chapter 25

2014

A New Directive

The last few weeks had been a wake-up call for me, and now I knew where I belonged. My local ambulance service joyfully welcomed the return of their prodigal, and I was soon back on the response car. It felt good to be at the sharp end of life again, though it wasn't long before my run of bad-luck jobs reared its hideous head once more.

The serious incidents – the ones that young paramedics look forward to attending – were becoming far too regular. You ultimately realise that they take their toll on you as a human being and, as a result, you start taking your work home with you.

At around 6pm the last call of my twelve-hour shift was to a 5-year-old male who, I was told, was feeling quite unwell. The house was a typical detached property within a small cul-de-sac, a smart des-res surrounded by well-groomed gardens and a smart, clean car on each driveway. As I pressed the doorbell, I was already expecting a similar standard of presentation on the inside. I noticed that only the kitchen light was on, which was unusual for this time of the evening, but the lady responded within seconds and, from her haggard appearance, I knew that this was going to be a 'working job' – one of a serious nature – and I was going to be here for a considerable time.

I produced my ID and started to introduce myself, but she quickly ushered me through the front door into a dark corridor, urgently telling me that her little boy wasn't well. The whole place was dark, save for a narrow chink of light coming from the slightly-open kitchen door. What with my size and well-busted foot, I tend to be clumsy in confined quarters – especially when fully laden with response bag, paediatric bag, and oxygen – so I asked if she wouldn't mind switching the light on. But when she said she couldn't, because her boy started crying each time she turned on a light near him, I had a pretty good idea of what was wrong. Following her into the front room, I saw a small child lying on the sofa with a blanket on top of him. My eyes were adjusting to the low light and, kneeling close to him, I could tell from his eyes that he wasn't well. Ask any paramedic who's ever treated a seriously ill child, and they'll always tell you that 'the eyes have it' – and this little guy's eyes had it big time.

I heard that he hadn't been feeling well at school, and had been sent home earlier that afternoon, so she'd given him some Calpol and let him watch his favourite TV channel. His condition worsened, however, and it wasn't long before he was crying in a painfully high-pitched tone. I reached down to hold his hand to comfort him, explain who I was, and tell him about my daughters, but found his fingers icy cold. I moved to his toes and they were the same, which was enough to confirm my fears. I got up carefully and made an excuse to the mum, saying that I needed something from my car, before going outside and radioing for P1 backup for suspected meningitis. This would trigger a requirement for immediate help, and they'd either dispatch the nearest crew to the incident, or put out a broadcast asking any crew to help. This allows crews on their meal break to sacrifice it to help a colleague, which we've all done, many times. The sad reality is that, in the past, you very rarely received this request on the air from Control. Nowadays, we hear it on almost every shift, due to the sheer amount of calls we get against the dearth of front-line crews on the ground.

Back inside the house, and out of earshot of the little chap, I explained to mum what was happening. The very mention of 'hospital' can frighten a child, and this wasn't part of my plan! I then started a secondary survey of the young lad, and found some alarming signs. His respiratory rate was over 40 per minute – exceedingly fast for a child of his age.

Normally it's around 22-34, but this tied in with an abnormally high temperature of 40.2°C.

For a child of his age, it should be 36.4, with 38 considered high! With a temperature this elevated you'd expect an increase in breathing rate, as the body tries to cope and lower the temperature. But, in many cases, it's pumping blood around as fast as possible in an attempt to fight an infection, and this is what I believed was happening here. I asked his mum if it was okay to strip him down to bring his temperature under control, and also look for the dreaded, non-blanching rash! When people talk of meningitis the rash is always mentioned, and how you should run a glass over the bumps to see if they disappear. In truth I've never seen this, and probably because the rash doesn't usually appear until later.

As I finished my inspection I could hear the sirens, so I informed his mum to prepare quickly, because we'd be leaving as soon as it arrived. I then called Control to inform the ambulance that I'd bring the child out to them, so have the back ready!

When the truck arrived, and the side door opened, I was palpably relieved to see the face of Jimmy Ryan, my former mentor. You'll remember that he and I had worked countless shifts together – and even rolling the ambulance on one occasion! Most importantly in this case, we both knew how the other worked. He'd prepared everything, down to pre-empting the meningitis treatment protocol, switching off the main lights, and leaving only the muted blue light to illuminate the interior.

After doing the handover we confirmed with mum that he had no known allergies, before gaining intravenous access into his tiny arm while Jimmy drew up the drugs. Anyone who's ever cannulated a child knows how difficult this can be, especially if they're scared of being away from home, in an ambulance, with a huge grinning giant looming over them with a massive needle! I took out a £2 coin and let him see it, before handing it to his mother, letting him know that he could have it after I'd put the medicine needle in his arm, okay? Then while he was listening to his mum, who was finalising the deal with him, I slid the needle into the little vein on the inside of his left arm, before withdrawing it and leaving the plastic cannula inside. This was then secured, flushed with sodium chloride to stop any congealed blood blacking it up, and left to Jimmy to inject the medication – which he'd prepared while I was doing my bit. Medicine name, expiry date, and correct dosage were checked, and checked again before it was injected, and finally saying goodbye to the mother and her nouveau-riche offspring as Jimmy blue-lighted them to the hospital.

A few weeks later I found myself in this same area, though thankfully with an easier treat-at-scene job. As I climbed back into the vehicle, my thoughts turned to the child and the outcome. We rarely find out what happened to our patients, which can often be a good thing, but on this occasion my curiosity got the better of me. I pulled up outside the door, rang the bell, and prepared to disappear – never to return – if there was no answer. Then I heard a movement behind the door, and it was opened by a man I'd never seen before.

Flustered, I opened with, "Oh, hello, er, my name's…" And that's when an enormous smile came over his face, he grasped my hand and shook it vigorously, while drawing me into a well-lit front room that I remembered well. They were holding a large family gathering, and I was suddenly the cherry on top of the celebratory cake! His wife sprang to her feet as soon as she saw me, and gave me a big hug and a kiss on the cheek. I was then introduced to grandads and nans, uncles and aunts, as the one responsible for saving their child's life. I then clapped eyes on the little man, who was happily playing cars with several other small boys and didn't even notice me, let alone recognise me as the BFG. Dad then explained that yes, it had been confirmed as bacterial meningitis, but because we'd acted so quickly on scene, transferred him so expediently, and treated him en route to the hospital, he was able to make a full and rapid recovery. Woohoo! One up to the ambulance service! I was asked if I'd like a cup of tea and a slice of cake, but told them I was on duty, before leaving the happy gathering. Wow, that had certainly been a feel-good moment, and I suddenly realised that I wanted to do more in my life for children. *Boom!* Just like the car bomb incident in Northern Ireland, this was the defining moment that changed my life course once more. And like a satnav, my subconscious mind started to

2014: A New Directive

work feverishly in the background to adapt to the change in destination, and figure out the best route there.

The next day I was at home on the sofa with my girls, watching an Indiana Jones movie – the one where he jumps out of a rapidly descending plane on an inflatable life raft and floats smoothly down to earth – when suddenly I stood up and cried, "That's it!!!" Cara and the girls looked at me, dumbstruck, as if I'd lost the plot. And then even more so once I'd explained myself... I told them that all my fundraising events had been for children abroad, outside the UK, so this time I was going to raise funds for Great Ormond Street, and I'd do it in a life raft. Cara stared at me, open-mouthed in disbelief, before asking, "You're going to jump out of a plane in a life raft?"

I refrained from mansplaining why this would be an incredibly foolish thing to do, due to the simple reasoning that, if you were asked to name as many types of aerial people-carrier as you could, which were designed and renowned for their aerodynamic stability and safe landing, not one of them would be a flipping, flapping, flopping life raft!

Instead, I told them of my simpler plan to spend an entire week in one, out in the open sea, without food nor water, in order to raise money for GOSH.

Chapter 26

2014-2015

The Life Raft Challenge

A good way to get something done is to tell people close to you that you're going to do it. Now, needing to make good on my statement, I started to put my plan into action on Monday morning. Oh, and it may sound like an easy thing to do, but without the right people, companies, and organisations on board, you could complete an incredible achievement – something that nobody has ever done before – and no one else would ever know. Even then, it's not straightforward, because for every positive response to a phone call there are many, many more who simply aren't interested. It could be argued that bulk emailing is much easier and more far-reaching, but just think of the number of emails you delete each day without reading, and then multiply this by everyone. As a hardened veteran of fundraising events, I was fully aware of the terrain, and my skin had thickened to military spec, inuring and shoring up my psyche against the imminent incoming barrage of rejection.

I've grown used to the fact that not everyone has a naturally giving nature, and even those who do may not be in a position to help. By definition, the most generous people in the world are already fully committed – with no time, money, nor energy left for any other causes. So, the reality is that you're looking for people who aren't – and that takes a lot of effort to sway them. My naïve, halcyon days of sitting at the base in Bosnia, waiting for the money to come rolling in on the basis of a need, had well and truly passed into oblivion.

The objective was to spend a full week in a life raft, moored to a buoy within Portland Harbour, with just three days' worth of food and water – which would force me to catch fish, collect rain, and manage with whatever turned up naturally. Simple. So, the first thing was to talk with two people I knew very well – Russ Levett, the marina manager, and his assistant manager Paul Swain. When I first met Paul his name took me by surprise, because a very good friend of mine with the same name was injured by an IED in Afghanistan a few years earlier, which resulted in numerous injuries including the loss of an arm. Paul and his brother Lee were both from the regiment, and excelled at any sport to which they applied themselves. Both of them boxed and played football for the Army, their wives (along with all the other wives!) found them extremely attractive and, even more annoyingly, they were really great guys, too!

It was a massive shock to those who knew Paul when they heard of his hospitalisation, but in true British form it didn't set him back, and he just got on with what he had left. He's now a successful DJ around Leicestershire, and represented the Army at golf when our disabled veterans played against the Americans in the equivalent of the Ryder Cup. He even sunk the putt for the UK to win. Top man...

The three of us sat around a table as I explained my intention. In my naivety, I originally thought it'd be an easy task to achieve – after all, the harbour was massive, providing an extensive expanse of water for me to happily sit in, playing Robinson Crusoe. But, like most people, I wasn't aware of the rules, and the harbour master – who did – couldn't allow it as the harbour was open to ships much bigger than me to lay anchor at any time.

However, they might let me moor my raft to one of the buoys inside the inner harbour, 800 metres from the shore. This wasn't part of my plan so, with no possible overlap in a Venn diagram of 'beggars' and 'choosers', the next stage was to bring the harbour master on board. We scheduled another meeting in two weeks to include him, and during this time I'd need to come up with a presentation on why this was such a great idea, coupled with comprehensive risk assessments for the entire event, from preparation to after it was all over.

Fortunately, my previous experience in H&S had given me plenty of practice, and I had many templates from which to choose, while referencing my previous fundraising campaigns. I'd already approached GOSH and asked if they'd allow any funds raised to be donated to them.

They were thrilled by this and, and after several discussions, we decided that the money would go to their Family Accommodation Dept, which they confirmed in writing. This in-house facility accommodated families whose children had been admitted to the hospital, but who didn't live in London, to save them paying exorbitant hotel bills. It also allowed them to be by their child's side whenever they were needed.

The harbour master listened to me carefully – with Russ and Paul adding further contributions regarding safety arrangements – and finally agreed to it, promising us his full support, to the extent of monitoring the port's CCTV system in case I got into distress. With the meeting over and everyone in accordance, he then suggested that I contact an authority who could use my time in the raft to gather data on how the human body coped in such an extreme situation. Apparently, there was very little recorded information on the subject – largely due to the fact that, whenever someone really, really needed to use a life raft, there was rarely a scientific research team close by.

Overjoyed with the day's results, I returned home and reported to Cara over our evening meal with the girls. It was just as I was devouring a delicious roast beef dinner, that she offhandedly said "It's too easy, I think…"

"What is?" I slurred, with my mouth full.

"Spending seven nights on a raft with three days' food and water. You were in the Army living on ration packs, and anyone can go seven days without food, so why not go in with just one day's food and water?"

Now, it must be said that I'm a man who likes his food, and I'll eat anything served in front of me. You're told in the Army that you never know when your next meal will be, but in practice this is complete crap as there wasn't a single day during my eighteen years that I ever went hungry. But not wanting her to think I couldn't do it, I agreed with her wholeheartedly, even stating that I was already thinking along the same lines. As she removed the near-sterile plate from me, which I was still mopping down with bread, she smiled sweetly and said, "Of course you were, darling!"

Over the next few weeks, I contacted the companies who'd offered to help me with the event. My local Currys PC World equipped me with the means to record my experience audibly, and upload it via telephone network to Duncan, of Pipefish Digital Marketing, my IT friend who would convert it into daily podcasts of the campaign.

Hot Cans supplied me with 24 hours' worth of boil-in-the-bag rations, plus a few more for promotion.

Power Traveller provided water-resistant yellow 'bricks' containing rechargeable batteries coupled with solar panels.

And most importantly, Ocean Safety in Southampton contributed the life raft and survival equipment that would allow the event to take place.

Everything was finally heading in the right direction, so it was time to contact Portsmouth University and Professor Mike Tipton MBE, their go-to authority on anything to do with sea survival. He was a great guy to chat with, and he confirmed the harbour master's lament that there was truly too little empirical data on how the human body adapts or compensates in a real survival situation at sea. However, before he could agree to anything, he'd need to see me face-to-face for an assessment.

Two weeks later I arrived for our meeting at the Royal National Lifeboat Institution in Poole, Dorset, and explained that my prime goal was to make as much money as I could to help GOSH's Family Accommodation Dept, but if we could further sea survival science at the same time, then that'd be an appreciable bonus. Mike listened intently to my plan, and especially how it had changed from three days of food and water to just one. As the time approached for me to travel home, he shook my hand and told me that this would undoubtedly help their research. We also arranged an appointment with one of his staff, who would now be responsible for overseeing all the medical aspects of this event.

A few days later I met Dr Joe Costello at the university, where he showed me their extensive premises and all the expensive magical equipment installed there, including a 'cold weather' room and a deep-water tank. He then explained about the various measurements and experiments they'd conduct on me throughout my time 'at sea'. These included my urine output against my water intake, my ongoing blood glucose, how much sleep I managed to get, how much work I needed to do – and therefore the energy I expended – throughout each day, and how much food I actually managed to eat. I was to record these data every three hours between 09.00 – 21.00, and it would all be collated on completion. Before entering the raft, I'd be required to complete a muscle strength test, measure my body weight in my underwear, my body mass index, and have bloods taken by my doctor before and afterwards.

To be honest, I'd not taken any of this into account when I first came up with the idea – especially the bit about 'very little research into what happens to the human body...' But no one had tried to talk me out of it yet so, with the reality of what I was about to undertake getting nearer, I thought it expedient to conduct a professional recce of my intended week-long holiday home within the second largest man-made harbour in the world. The website stated that 'Portland Port offers a safe, sheltered and deep harbour, which makes it a superb choice for all vessels, from small yachts to some of the largest cruise ships in the world. ' It sounded idyllic, though there's no mention of some of the smallest life rafts in the world. If you ever walk the shores of this port, or check out the many fishing or diving grounds around Weymouth and Portland, you'll see several leviathans lodging within the Deepwater expanse, which is why having a tiny life raft moored smack in the middle of them all could have created a somewhat sensitive issue – especially if these behemoths needed to back in, or turn around, in the middle of the night, to slot into their allotted parking space. Like setting up a one-man tent overnight on the M25 carriageway, putting a little flashing light on it wouldn't help you in the slightest!

As the challenge became more imminent, and the butterflies in my stomach started to emerge, one by one, from their cocoons, I attended several meetings to raise public awareness. One of these was at 'Fish and Ships', the local gastronomic event held within the harbour each year, and which had evolved to celebrate not just seafood, but all things seafaring.

Coincidentally, this was the day I first met Ray Dorset – or 'Mungo Jerry' as he's more globally known. Ray's hit 'In the Summertime' stayed at #1 in the UK charts for seven weeks in 1970, and has become a perennial for British DJs ever since. Ray was one of those kind souls who contacted me after I'd asked for celebrities to join me on this special day, to help raise funds for a hospital dedicated to children. I'd already informed ITV West Country, the local news station, about who was coming. I was good friends with Duncan Sleightholm, the reporter from my previous campaigns, and we were already in deep conversation when Ray arrived. This was the first time I'd ever seen the great man in person, but as he strolled towards us both, guitar in hand, smiling, and sporting his well-known mass of hair, it was like stepping back into the 70's. Ray happily discussed the event with us, and how I was planning to achieve it, before asking how he could help – which probably led to the biggest mistake in his musical career. Accompanying me in the raft in front of the cameras, with a group of enthusiastic fans gathered at the side, we sang 'In the Summertime' together. The problem was that I'd only ever heard the track a few times, in the background, on the truck radio, so I didn't really know the words. Or the music. Thinking back now, when he asked me if I knew the song, I should have been more honest. I think I nailed the bit about 'having women on your mind', and I probably overdid the di-di-di di-di'ing, but the rest was a total blank to me. That day I learned the importance of rehearsals, and that night Cara mocked me mercilessly during the newsfeed, which captured me jamming along with this stellar performer, humming hopelessly out of tune and rhythm, and trying to pretend that we did this all the time.

Undeterred by this, and the worst televised recording of his song ever, Ray and I have remained staunch friends, and meet up again regularly for similar causes. He also recommended me to an agent named Jonathon Brosnan, with whom he'd been associated over many years in the music industry. Going by the stage name of Navor Brok, Jonathon was a well-known country and western singer/songwriter from Ireland, who'd had a highly successful career in America during his early years. With this experience he'd ventured into entertainment management, and represented stars in the States and the UK. I duly called Jonathon that night and, for over thirty minutes, discussed my situation with an extremely well-spoken gentleman, with the softest of Irish-American twangs in his accent, and who happily agreed to put wheels in motion for me. The following day he called back to tell me that he'd arranged coverage for me on a London news station. Wow! That week I'd made not just one, but two new and wonderful friends. I've also learned since that, behind his soft Irish lilt growls a tenacious Irish rottweiler masquerading as a terrier.

The rest of my day was spent with children climbing in and out of the raft, showing them how I'd cook my 24hr food rations – adding sea water to activate the chemicals in the outer bag to heat them up – before finally demonstrating to an increasingly restless audience the monotonous task of using a reverse-osmosis pump.

Later on, I visited schools with the raft, explaining what I was trying to achieve and how. I always try to make things entertaining for children, and one of their most popular questions – especially from boys – was 'Would I eat a fish's eyeballs when I caught one?' My answer, yes, would always raise a fresh chorus of "Euughhh's!" Mercifully for them, I'd learned from the 'Fish and Ships' event to leave out the slow-motion RO pump demo!

For my more mature and technically-minded readers, this ingenious piece of life-saving equipment uses multiple layers of fine-mesh filters to extract drinking water from sea water. Its only problem is that, in order to remove the salt and numerous other impurities dissolved in the water, it needs to work at molecular level, separating the pure water from everything else – so the filters need to allow nothing larger than a water molecule to pass through them. Half a litre of drinking water contains 10,000 drops, the first of which you'll see reluctantly oozing from the nozzle after 5-10 minutes of vigorous pumping. Once that happens, don't stop! Because, after that, continuous pumping will gain you an extra drop every 1.5 seconds. This means that it'll take up to three hours, as your strength and resolve run out, to finally fill your 500ml bottle. Think about that, next time you take one to the gym.

As you can imagine, this is an extremely slow and laborious process, which may sound like a waste of time and energy. But if you're ever caught, like the Ancient Mariner, with 'water, water, everywhere, with not a drop to drink' then you'll be eternally grateful for this gift from the gods to quench your raging thirst, fill your endless time, and keep up your diminishing hopes, out in the vast, grey, isolated expanse of the sea.

Just before the event I received an email from a Steven Callahan, wishing me luck and offering advice. Puzzled, I looked up his name, and was astonished to read that he was the sailor and author who, in 1986, sailing the Atlantic, had his boat sink and was forced to spend two and a half months in a life raft before he was found. His book, *Adrift: Seventy-six Days Lost at Sea* is still one of the great sea adventures of all time.

Chapter 27

2015

The Challenge

18 May, 2015. The day, as all days do, finally arrived, and my time had come. Joe turned up on time, and we had a quick cuppa before he drove me to my local GP surgery where Dr Peter Hill took measurements and blood. Joe then brought me to the Osprey Leisure Centre in Portland to measure my grip test and strength, before we both presented ourselves in our respective roles at the press gathering in the upper room of the Sailing Academy.

Freya and Lili's entire classes from St George's Primary School were here, attending the Q&A session with Prof. Mike Tipton and Dr Joe Costello – and while all this was going on, I kept drinking copious amounts of water in an unconscious (but ultimately futile) attempt to stock up, prior to my self-inflicted period of drought.

The weather conditions couldn't have been much worse as I got into the raft, and I tried to avoid seeing this as a portent of things to come. The wind was blowing a real hooley, driving the rain in from the side – just what I needed! Don't get me wrong here – I'm a big fan of rain, as it does a great job of keeping our land so green and pleasant! However, in the Army, when you start your first day of exercise and the weather's chucking it down, you learn that, if you've not prepared, you're going to spend a long time thoroughly soaked and miserable. That's where personal admin comes in – you need to waterproof all your kit, and ensure you've got a spare, dry set of clothes to change into. But since nobody ever has these in a real-life survival situation, I'd decided to wear the same clothes all week.

I'm not ashamed, now, to say that I was... let's say, apprehensive. I already knew that, if I was ever to do this again, I'd do it very differently. When I originally decided to use a 4-man life raft, I was still thinking 'Indiana Jones'. I thought it was going to be one of those massive affairs where four 6 foot-plus guys could lounge around comfortably, doing all their macho 'survival at sea' stuff – but my concerns started when it arrived in a stowaway case measuring just 65 x 43 x 28cm. Yes, that's centimetres. Not inches...

Anyone who's ever camped the night in a 4-man tent knows that it's just big enough for one small person to move, access your gear, and sleep semi-comfortably without touching the walls. Who'd have thought that life rafts were similarly specified?

The principle behind a life raft, I soon discovered, was more like a mountain rescue tent, in which a sheet of waterproof fabric covers a group of people sat huddled together in a circle, facing each other, with the edges of the sheet tucked underneath each of them for protection against cold, wind, and rain. In a raft, four people sitting in close proximity like this provides better stability on the sea – along with the drag of a water-filled 'parachute' which, when dropped fully, can also act as an anchor. So, when you think of a life raft, clear any images from your mind of coastguards in large motorised dinghies, or those brightly-coloured 7-man inflatables used by tourist groups for river-rafting over weirs and waterfalls. A life raft is essentially, to a boat, what a fire extinguisher is to a house. Small and unobtrusive, it's there to save your life should the worst happen, but you hope you'll never need to use it.

Despite living in Portland I'm not a nautical man, and I even get seasick. Now, far from the four-bedroomed, ocean-going holiday home I'd expected to have to myself, my entire living room, kitchen, bedroom, bathroom, and storage area were restricted to a single covered space 164cm (5' 5") square, 112.5cm (3' 8") high, with a small flashing lamp on top.

I was met by several people waiting to see me off at the pontoon. Samantha Leonard from Ocean Safety, Chris Jeffries from 'Motorboat and Yachting', Mike and Joe from the uni, our local ITV news crew, and

2015: The Challenge

my family – all of whom were getting soaked to the skin. My raft was already inflated, with the throw-line tied to a Rigid Raider to tow me to the buoy. After a quick goodbye to everyone I threw my small rucksack into the raft and quickly followed it in, waving to everyone as I began the slow journey to my allotted slot in the harbour – my new homestead for the next week. Although only 800 metres away, the journey took over 20 minutes, because Paul explained that a square raft would always present a resistant flat side to the direction of travel, and any faster would cause water to slosh in over the side so there wasn't much else I could do other than keep still, enjoy the ride, and appreciate the last vestige of human company I'd have for a good while.

Paul tethered the raft securely to the buoy, before instructing me to use Channel 1 on the ship-to-shore radio, and to send daily comms checks at 09.00 and 21.00 to confirm that everything was still okay. Then we shook hands, said our goodbyes, and the Raider soon became another distant sound in the harbour. The challenge had begun.

I knew from my OP experiences that boredom leads to contemplation, which can lead in turn to self-pity, disillusionment, and then despair. I wanted none of this and, now I was here, started by writing down a list of tasks I needed to accomplish each day, categorising each job in order of importance, and saving the less important ones for those times when you want to do something, but don't know what it is. This, hopefully, should break up the day and keep boredom at bay. I have to say that Cara had her reservations about this part, because I'm a human nightmare if I ever have to stay indoors throughout the day. I start feeling claustrophobic, restricted, and tend to eat for two at every opportunity – just to do something! Out here, there would be no escape for, or from, me. Just a tiny, cramped, covered space, with plenty of room outdoors but nowhere to go.

Water, water, everywhere, with lots of time to think...

My primary thought needed to be of the children I was here to help. Those I'd met whilst visiting GOSH, and the bravery they showed daily away from the familiarity, security, and comfort of their homes. If they could do it, then bloody well so could I!

One of my tasks was to create daily podcasts, which I'd record and send to Duncan for uploading to my website and YouTube. This turned out to be not just good PR, but a source of inspiration as the week wore on, because children would often respond and ask questions. With no internet coverage, I wouldn't hear these questions until Duncan and I had our daily 6pm call, he'd record our conversation, and then post my answers to the questions.

One of my ground rules for this campaign, was that I couldn't go in with all the top-end survival gear which the average person doesn't have – and certainly not in an emergency. So, no famous brand names, no designer clothing, and absolutely no military gear. I'd allowed myself the luxury of a cheap pocket knife – the kind every schoolboy used to carry back in the day – which I bought online for £10. Due to the scientific nature of the exercise, I was allowed to use solar power to charge the range of equipment I needed, and the yellow bricks with their range of attachments did a brilliant job for my daily admin. But it only took a few days for the sea air to start corroding the connectors, and my pocket knife really came in useful. This is the kind of feedback I'd be giving to the companies who'd supplied the gear, to help them to help others in future.

Next, the basics…

The human body is built for speed, agility, and grace. Numerous sensors tell it how much water it needs and, once it's used what it wants, the rest is flushed out. It doesn't hang on to water like a camel does for survival, otherwise we'd all have huge, pendulous guts which, like my raft's water anchor, would have its own momentum and slow down every physical activity. Which is why, before taking a caravan on the road, you always empty the onboard water tank. I'm aware of this now, though I wasn't at the time. I'd already decided to limit myself to 500ml of water a day but, as I'd just filled my body to bursting, sneakily thought that I'd not need any more for at least a couple of days. Also, the weather wasn't too hot to begin with, so I wouldn't be losing too much through perspiration either. Out at sea, the life expectancy for someone without fresh water is about 6-7 days. Had I been back in the Sahara, that time would plummet to just three days. But I'd made sure to bring enough with me, plus the means to make more, hadn't I?

Who'd have known that the human body exudes around 400ml of water a day through 'insensible perspiration' – where you don't even know you're sweating, and which you can prove by wearing a pair of PPE gloves for a few minutes? That another 500ml is lost each day just by peeing. And a further 400ml a day simply by breathing out – and that's without doing anything! This is why the recommended daily water intake is 1.5 litres, and this amount increases the bigger you are. Well, I didn't – and you can see where I'm going here...

Initially, as can be expected from my watery binge, my urine was respectably clear when I measured it for Joe's records. So clear, in fact, that just before my first night's sleep I actually gulped down a couple of mouthfuls before dumping the rest overboard. I've been told that, although it's not recommended, drinking your own pee is still preferable to drinking seawater. This is because the human body keeps a tight control of the amount of salt in its fluids, holding it rigidly at around 0.9%. Seawater, however, contains up to 4% salt, and drinking it will force your body to get rid of the excess salt through peeing.

Unfortunately, the maximum concentration of salt in pee is 2%, requiring even more water to get rid of the difference, and dehydrating you even further. Once you get stuck in this cycle, your body will eventually draw water from its own cells to flush out the toxic salt, and keep itself alive – and if you think this sounds somewhat extreme, you'd be right. This is why, after hypothermia, seawater poisoning is the most common cause of death for shipwrecked sailors – and that amongst sea-going folk throughout the centuries, there's been such a long-standing superstition, or no-no, against drinking the stuff. Basically, just because it's wet, doesn't mean that it's good for you.

Well, I was already starting to feel thirsty. I had a fresh bottle of home-brewed pee ready, and I knew I'd drunk my own urine before while being concurrently drunk, myself, at the rugby club. So, how was it? Well, it was warm, it wet my lips, whet my appetite and, like the preceding pun, slightly tasteless. I did the same the following night, before finishing off the bottle of water I'd brought with me, and feeling like a true survivor. However, on the third morning I raised the plastic measuring jug to my mouth once more, and was almost knocked out by the smell! Although fresh, it was now the colour of concentrated orangeade with a sweet, rank, sickly stink – so over the side it went. That defining moment ended my brief affair with excretory substances, and not a drop has passed my lips since.

It was clear – because it wasn't – that I was already starting to dehydrate, so I got out the RO pump to generate my daily requirement. With hindsight I should have started doing this earlier to create a reserve supply – especially once I'd learned how long the bloody thing takes! However, after getting used to it I have to say that, though expensive, it should be mandatory equipment for any crew preparing for a long voyage on the open sea. I know that life rafts can be supplied with rations, including long-life biscuits and water but, believe me, your water won't last long, even when carefully rationed.

Other than the time needed to produce clean water from whatever you put in, the only downside to the pump I found was that it was just 10 inches long so, like using a compact bicycle pump to inflate a tyre, instead of the standard arm's length version, you have to pump harder and longer to get the same amount of air into your wheel. I suggested, post-event, to either fit it with a telescoping handle, or include an extension piece. The only other frustration is that by using it in an unsteady life raft, for which it was intended, stopping some of the precious fluid from spilling and escaping is a nigh-impossible task. This wastage is agonising to experience, though it's a small price to pay for the amount you collect.

Joe had warned me about the constituent ingredients of my tranquil harbour, the delights of which included diesel fuel, kitchen slops, and human waste. He wasn't certain that the RO filter would remove every last trace of these, and a single bacterium infiltrating a weakened immune system is all it takes for some serious hospitalisation. This is why he'd insisted that I take 50ml sachets of survival water into the raft as a substitute, and it became part of our risk assessment. In addition, although this was overtly a survival challenge, providing much-needed data for scientific research, it was also a publicity stunt aimed at raising as much money as possible for children. It really wasn't worth contracting anything nasty, nor generating negative publicity for the harbour. My original goal was to have been out in the open sea anyway, where there'd be far less pollution, so I reluctantly agreed. Having said that, I continued to work the pump as if in a genuine survival situation – otherwise, to me, it would have defeated the entire purpose of the exercise. Sticking religiously to this paradigm, by the end of the week I'd not only become an expert on the pump, but to my surprise the muscles in my right arm were becoming huge. How the heck was I going to explain that one to my wife?

Another way of gaining liquid sustenance was to secure plastic bags to the water traps built into the rear of the raft's hood, which would probably have worked had I been floating freely in the ocean. Tethered to the buoy as I was, it was always the front of the raft – the entrance – which faced the rain, and so only a small amount was gathered. But the nights were usually cold, so on waking each day I found a gift of precious water in the form of condensation inside the cover from my breath during the night. The raft came with two sponges – one to mop up sea water that got in, and the other to keep clean for such rare occasions. There wasn't a lot, and you could certainly taste the raft in it. And the sponge. But it was still a welcome bonus each morning – especially when you have to count your available water in droplets.

I wasn't the only one taken aback, whenever people saw the modest size of my raft – and they'd often ask me why I hadn't chosen something larger, or brought more survival gear. My answer was always that the ethos of the exercise and fundraiser was to simulate a quick escape from a sinking boat – so I'd always keep a 'grab bag' close by, containing the bare essentials to survive such a scenario. This is a common plotline for those serving on land, sea, and air, and the same mentality is drummed into all personnel from Day #1. **Always have a bag that you can grab quickly, and carry easily, which will help you to survive once you've escaped your current situation.** *Don't include anything that you*

wouldn't want to lose permanently, and especially not sentimental or personal items that could be found by the enemy and used against you...

So, I visualised a sailing trip across an ocean, and took this approach with packing my grab bag. Nothing too bulky, but enough to help keep me warm, catch food, and attract attention if I needed it. The smoke and flares were mandatory for the safety of the exercise and, had I been allowed, I'd have brought a lot more water. Permitted items included my woolly hat, a pair of gloves, and a small roll mat the size of my torso – which created a thermal and waterproof barrier between my back – from shoulders to hips – and the cold water beneath the strong but flexile fabric which constituted the entire floor of the raft.

Mike had informed me that, at this time of year, these waters were around 7°C, low enough to be severely detrimental to my organs and health. My trusty roll mat had accompanied me throughout my career in the military, and always kept my vitals warm when sleeping rough. It had started life as a rugged fishing mat to put carp on after they'd been caught, but it was perfect for my needs and, as we often said in the regiment, "It'll do the job..."

One of the questions repeatedly asked during the podcasts was about my sleeping arrangements, seeing as even the diagonal of the raft was shorter than I was. Well, I'd need to rest my head up against a corner of the raft, and lie diagonally to get the most leg room. My roll mat would go under my torso, and my coat over my upper body. My woolly hat and gloves completed the ensemble, and I managed to grab a little sleep before the restricted blood flow to my legs and thighs woke me again. A semi-conscious change of direction then allowed me to slumber again before the next bout of cramp in my neck or legs set in.

Along with the nocturnal sounds of metal lines smacking against masts, the wind whistling through and around everything in its path, and the regular slap of water against the sides of the raft, it all contributed towards a poor sleeping regimen. I knew it was never going to be easy, but at least I had the raft to myself, and wasn't sharing it with those three other guys!

Boredom became a constant companion, and I had to keep doing something. I segmented the days. Fishing. Writing up medical records. Priming and operating the RO filter. Maintaining the raft. Pumping up the air compartments. Charging the batteries. Tidying everything away so I could find it in the dark. Thinking of the children I couldn't let down. And desperately trying to avoid focusing on how much hungrier and tired I was feeling each day.

Cara had been right, as always. Many people regularly fast for three days, solely for health reasons. Others go without food for seven days to enter an elevated spiritual state, or to simply offer themselves to the universe as an instrument. I know of those who've voluntarily gone for forty days without food – just water – in order to receive a definitive answer to a pressing question. Their goal is often to reach an internal point where you don't think of food every waking second and, even at the end, to sustain the attitude that you could go on for longer if needed. This is usually done under controlled conditions, usually by forewarning a friend to keep an eye on them just in case. However, others insist on simply getting on with their lives, their work, and their appointments as usual, without making a fuss about it.

The experience is always useful, in that you learn more about yourself and what you're capable of. It's also different for everyone, depending on your age, your genetics, and your reason for doing it. It's certainly not grounds for beating yourself up if you fall short of your goal. A well-built person may complete the challenge and simply lose weight, whereas an active individual with a fast metabolism may find themselves without energy after just a few days, and spend the rest of the week in a lethargic stupor. But in a life-or-death situation, or if you're responsible for others, this can present an unnecessary risk. I'd also heard that if you're hungry, and there's no food, then you can drink water to alleviate the pangs – but this option wasn't open to me due to the nature of the research involved. Hunger became a constant issue for me towards the end of the event, and probably because I knew I'd be out of here soon. But I needed to think like someone who didn't know if – not when – they'd be rescued, otherwise

I'd look back at myself later as having totally wasted the experience and opportunity.

    I'd started the challenge on Monday and cooked my first boil-in-the-bag meal on Wednesday afternoon, the second on Friday afternoon, and kept the last for Sunday. From my first day I'd attempted to catch fish, ritually dipping my survival line and lure into the water after the sun had set. It was on Tuesday night, while shining my headtorch into the water to draw any fish towards me, that at the periphery of my beam, something big and black swam underneath the raft...

    Snap! Off went the light, in came the line, and I scuttled inside to sit very, very still indeed, believing that anytime soon something huge would rip through the underside of the raft and drag me helplessly into its jaws. Afraid to sleep and snore, I spent most of that night on standby.

    It was only on the Friday night, three days later, that I managed to hook a very small fish using a jig technique. I was hungry and this was an instant meal but, if I speculated to accumulate, I could bait two hooks with the flesh and double my chances of catching something bigger. I cut the fish into strips and hooked them onto the same line I'd been using with the lure. Then, after checking the small weight I'd attached, lowered it into the dark water. Within seconds the line started to jiggle and *woohoo!* on pulling it in I was greeted by a 4-inch-long pouting. Wow! I was over the moon, and gave it a big kiss before putting it out of its misery, then dropping it into a waterproof bag. Quickly I baited the hook again and dropped it in the same spot as before, hoping for the same thing to happen again. But after a long wait I started feeling tired and, leaving the hook in the water, shuffled away to get some sleep. As soon as I started getting comfortable, though, I heard the line rub against the side of the raft, so I got up again and started to pull it in. This one was clearly much bigger and, once it had surfaced, I could see it was about 6 inches long. This was dispatched quickly as before, and also put in the bag. Not needing any more for now, nor wanting to warn off other fish, I drew in the line. Fish, like all other sources of protein, require additional water to digest, so I resisted the urge to eat it there and then. But now, at least, I had food if I needed it.

On Saturday morning, two long days before the campaign was due to end, I felt really exhausted, extremely hungry, and very grateful indeed that I had a piscine ready-meal. It was already a hot day, so I cut them both into strips and laid them on the side of the raft to dry and bake in the sun – my take on fish jerky. I then filmed myself eating the eyeballs for the water, because all the kids wanted to see me do it! Then, with my admin now squared away, I made my 9am call to shore, then decided to sit and relax for ten minutes before my next scheduled task.

I knew I had to do something. It wasn't clear what I had to do, and I wasn't sure if I could do it, but I knew it was important. What was it? Oh, yes. I need to wake up. But you're thinking, so you must be awake. Oh, yes, I must be, and so I got up and started to move about, but my body didn't follow me. It just carried on lying there. Oh, this can't be right. What time is it? And why isn't the sun where I'd left it? It's too bright anyway. Just close your eyes and go back to sleep...

With a great deal of effort, I forced my right hand over the side and brought it back to splash sea water onto my face. At least I think I did. I felt the water on my face, but nothing happened. Why wouldn't my eyes open? I raised my left hand to my face and forced myself to look at my watch. Just for a moment. No, that can't be right. This can't be right! More alert now, I needed to figure out where the last five bloody hours had gone. Is it still Saturday? Oh, thank goodness, yes, but I'd missed my noon appointment for urine, blood sugars, and all my other admin. *What the fuck is wrong with me?* I unfastened my watch and used both hands now to splash more water onto my head and face, trying to get my act together.

Normal blood sugar readings are between 4.0 and 5.8 millimoles per litre of blood, though levels can go up to 7.8 after eating. Joe had specifically insisted that, should my reading ever fall below 3.8, then I was to call it in, end the exercise urgently, and get back to shore for treatment. I'd wholeheartedly agreed, because I couldn't have the university taking the can for my stupidity, aftercare, or death, in addition to dealing with my family, the media, and the insurance companies. I took out my equipment and started the standard procedures. After pricking my finger and taking a sample, the result came back as 1.1. That couldn't possibly be right, so I checked the equipment, made sure my hands were clean, and inserted a new BM stick. Another prick of blood, and another reading of 1.1. Well, that would explain the hypoglycaemic episode, and why I was feeling so tired. Joe's words flashed through my mind, but there was no way I was tapping out at this late stage so I had to make a choice – the raw fish, or the remaining boil-in-the-bag.

Deciding to leave the meal for a real emergency, I checked out the fish, which had only partially turned to jerky. The outer flesh had hardened, but the inner part was still raw and moist. To hell with it, I thought, as I ate the lot – including the remaining eyes. An hour later, another test, and my reading was up to 4.0, so it had worked. Finally feeling more normal now, I was able to stay awake for the rest of the day.

Hey, remember my mate Murph? The firefighter from Belfast with a heart of gold, but whose normal speaking voice was just a dB or two short of a PA system? Well, my daughter Freya was about 18 months old when she first encountered him. Her favourite book at the time was 'Peepo Teddy!' wherein a teddy bear would hide maybe under the stairs, in a cupboard, under the bed, and so on from his mummy and daddy, and it was the child's job to find him from behind a series of interactive hinged flaps in the book. Each night, at bedtime, Cara and I would take it in turns to quietly read to her whilst sitting on the sofa, while excitedly joining in her 'Pee-po!' moment as she apprehensively opened each aperture. It was my turn one night, and we were just getting started when there was a knock on the front door, and I heard Murph's broad, "Oright, Shag?" as he greeted Cara. As he entered the living room to see me, I immediately hushed him as it was Freya's calming time for bed, to which he whispered "Oh. Oright, Shag," as he accepted a cup of tea from Cara. He then brightened with an idea, and asked if he could read to Freya, as all his own children were now grown up. Trusting him totally as a loyal friend, I sat Freya on his knee and went to the kitchen to help Cara.

Children are born with just two natural fears – the fear of heights, and the fear of loud noises. All the others, we learn as we go along...

With Freya nestling on his lap ready for her sleepy sojourn to Peepo Land, Murph started reading in an unusually (for him) subdued voice. However, as he gradually got into character, he soon reverted to his sonorous, stentorian boom and, even from the kitchen, we heard a deafening, "Peeee-Po!!! Teddyyy is under the BED!"

Freya shrieked in fright, and we rushed into the living room to see a look of absolute terror on her face. Cara scooped up our distraught daughter, carried her up to her familiar and peaceful bedroom, and stayed with her while I had a quiet word with Murph. Ever since then – despite the fact that he hasn't asked again, our little girl hasn't forgotten the trauma, and she never again wanted to hear that story. Murph remains one of my truest and most stalwart friends.

Which is why I was so overjoyed to see him that Sunday afternoon in the harbour. When I'd started the challenge earlier that week, a few local bass fishing boats were moored to the pontoon, and I'd recognised one as belonging to my indomitable friend. One day before the event was over, with my stomach grumbling, I was just lying down to have forty winks when I felt the raft start swaying from side to side, as it does when a boat passes by and you get caught in its wash. Only this time, it didn't carry on but stopped alongside me, and I knew I had visitors. Before I'd manoeuvred myself around to the door of my bachelor pad, a white plastic bag was tossed inside.

Looking outside, I saw that it was Murph and his wife Debs; "Oright, Shag?" he shouted, without really needing to.

"Alright, pal. Good to see you! What's in the bag?"

"Well, ah knew youze bee 'ungry, so I brought ya a fooking roast dinner sandwich, with Mars bars and Coke for afters!"

Shocked and in disbelief, I immediately threw it back to him, and said that as much as I was starving, I couldn't eat anything other than what I'd caught or brought on board with me, because Portsmouth Uni was doing experiments, and I couldn't let the children down.

"Oh. Right. Okay, then," he boomed despondently. In return I thanked him, told him I loved him, and that we'd all go for a meal together soon, before ordering him to "Now fuck off, mate!" In response, and right in front of me, he then opened the bag, unwrapped a Mars bar, shoved the entire thing into his mouth, and then laughed and tried to say something as he motored away. That's the sort of guy Murph is. The kind who'd do anything for you, and was always looking for ways to help anyone if he could. A true rough diamond.

I'd like to be able to write that I had plenty of time to think – even meditate – that week, alone with the sea, the sun, and the stars; the revelations I'd received, and the spiritual experiences I encountered. Unfortunately, my prime and constant thoughts were of thirst and hunger, and I had to keep replacing them with thoughts of the kids I'd never met, and those real survivors out at sea, who'd ultimately benefit from my efforts. The ensuing, deepening lethargy didn't help either, but I had other ongoing, more difficult situations to deal with, which wouldn't normally affect a sole survivor on the open sea.

First, I knew, almost to the minute, when I was going to be 'rescued'. I was just playing at being lost at sea, which effectively made me an imposter – a disgrace and insult to those who'd done this for real.

Second, I had the luxury of a fully working mobile phone and, although I was sorely tempted otherwise, I was only allowed to use it for my daily updates from Duncan.

Third, I was only four-fifths of a klick away from the coast. Just under half a mile, or twice the length of an outdoor running track. If it had been, I could have made it to the shore in a few minutes. This proximity meant that I could see people on it. I could even see them waving to me, though I couldn't tell who they were – which made it even harder to bear.

I'd arranged for Cara to 'visit' me every day after school. If everything was okay for her, and it wasn't raining, then she'd walk along the promenade until she was opposite my raft, then stop and wave to me. This turned out to be a terrible idea, because I ended up looking out for her every afternoon – even if it was raining – and no matter what, she was always there.

2015: The Challenge

When you go away on deployment, CP work, or just a regular shift abroad, you know you're going to be away for several weeks. It's part of the job, and you just get on with it. But being away, and yet being so close, was far worse. Each day I'd see people waving and shouting their support to me. I couldn't be certain who they were, nor what they were saying, but this comfort was a sword that cut two ways. When you've lost someone you love, your brain dulls the pain by diminishing the memory. But when you can still see them, and hear them calling to you – I imagined that this must be how a departed spirit feels.

Portland Fire Station sent both their appliances down on our Thursday night drill session, sounding their sirens and flashing their lights to get my attention. Another time I was doing my daily chores when I heard a buzzing noise outside, from above the roof of all places. I opened the flap and there was a drone hovering over my raft! This was the sense of humour and comradeship of Lee Smith, another veteran who lived in my area, and who got some great footage which can be seen on YouTube.

My campaign finally ended with the arrival of Monday morning, and all that was left to do now was complete my admin, tidy up, and wait until 12 noon – the official end of my 168 hours in the raft. During my final podcast I became quite emotional during recording. I tried to say that it was dust, but in truth I was physically and psychologically exhausted, hungry, thirsty and relieved that I'd accomplished my goal, and the mission had been a success. And while it's always hard to be objective at the endpoint, and at least nobody had taken a shot at me, it still felt like the most difficult thing I'd ever done with my life.

At midday I released the smoke canister, and even from across the harbour I heard the roar from the huge gathering of family, friends, media, and spectators waiting to greet me when I finally stepped onto dry land once more. Paul came over on the Raider to greet me, shake my hand, and tow me slowly back to shore.

The first things I encountered at the pontoon were Cara, the girls, my boys, lots of hugs and kisses, and a double Mars bar which I attempted to eat but, surprisingly, couldn't. People who fast, especially for long periods, and for the first time, often prepare themselves for before and during the period, but rarely for after it's over. Your body tries to adapt during this time, your stomach shrinks, its biome changes, and your digestive enzymes are depleted – though this is a perfect time for a hard reset of your diet if you're thinking of eating more healthily afterwards. Thinking about all the food you miss during the event, and what you'll eat afterwards, will do you no favours, as your stomach will start preparing itself for the expected treat – hence the rumbling. But it won't be prepared for you wolfing down a full meal once it's all over. Some people go for white rice – the simplest of meals – but being boiled it contains no enzymes, and you'll have problems digesting it. Your best bet is to start with live, raw fruit – like a banana, which conveniently comes with its own digestive enzymes. Not only will your stomach appreciate this consideration, but it will also taste incredible!

Interestingly, a close, reliable friend later told me of his experience after he'd completed seven days on only water. He'd made the same mistakes as I've just described, but when he tried to eat a Mars bar that he'd saved specially, it tasted so vile to him that he threw it away, vowing never to buy one again. And as he did a clear 'voice/message/thought' came into his mind, "Why do you put things into your body that separate us?" Wow…

As I attempted to climb out of my second home, Joe warned me to be careful as my sense of balance would likely be affected. He was right. I'd just spent a week on a constantly moving, fluid platform, and all of a sudden it had become granite-hard, rigid, and unyielding. My muscles tried to compensate as my legs turned to jelly, and even trying to stand upright became an unfamiliar, almost comical act. Thankfully, my embarrassment was spared when a thoughtful person brought a golf buggy to my aid and drove me the short distance up the ramp to greet the rest of my family and friends. There was only passenger room for one, so Cara reached over, gave me another kiss on the cheek, and whispered in my ear, "Babes, you've lost so much weight!" But as my brain continued to register new references for this strange, new environment, I was unsure if this was a compliment, or a concern.

The inevitable interviews with all the news and media channels were next, followed by a near-endless series of photographs, before Joe made our excuses to everyone, and whisked me back to the leisure centre to complete his tests while the data were still fresh and unsullied. But first…

Cara, the love of my life, had packed clean clothes for me, and I wobbled off to grab a much-needed shower in the swimming pool complex. Although it was familiar territory for me, I still felt oddly nervous and out of place as a group of martial artists with their sensei entered the shower room after their training session. On seeing me there, they started giving me funny looks, and were clearly discussing me. Who was this drunken new guy, swaying from side to side, and invading their sacred space? No one said anything, and I tried to keep my wits about me as I stayed under the shower, noting that their clothing was right next to where I'd left mine. There was no way I could reach it without passing amongst them, so I stayed in as long as I could. But there's a limit to how long anyone can shower without attracting attention, and they still hadn't left so, as confidently as I could manage, I walked in a semi-straight line to my stuff, grabbed my towel, and started to dry myself off next to their leader. However, as I prepared to put my socks on, I lost balance and heavily sat down naked on top of his dry clothes.

Now back in the real world full of people who weren't me, naked within hard surroundings, unable to control my equilibrium, and with no weapon to hand, I got up quickly and apologised profusely for what I'd just done. To my surprise, the guy bowed to me, smiled kindly, and said that it was he who should apologise. His students had all been staring at me, and quietly talking about me, after realising that I was the guy in the raft. He'd told them that this was true budo – the way of life centring on developing the mind – and they'd stayed around hoping to meet me and wish me well!

Now clean, dressed, and feeling much more confident, I walked steadily to the room Joe had set aside for our tests and measurements, and boy, was this fascinating! Believe it or not, my muscular strength had increased, my grip was stronger, and I was able to push heavier weights. Apparently, there had been friendly wagers on how much flab I'd lose, starting with 5lbs at the conservative end of the scale, to 10lbs at the other. In fact, I'd lost a staggering 17.5lbs! No wonder Cara had been alarmed.

The biggest shock to me was that, even allowing for sweating, my urination output had been recorded as higher than my water intake – and I felt the need to convince him that I'd faithfully written down every single drop of water I'd consumed. But apparently, because I'd been predominately prone, and on a cold surface, this would have caused my body to excrete more. It wasn't until several days later that I received the results of my blood tests, revealing that my cholesterol levels had risen, due to my body consuming its own fat deposits. But with all that completed, I was finally free to go home and sleep in a proper bed designed specifically for the purpose.

And for the record, I slept for 14 hours straight. It felt wonderful!

> "As I reflect upon Wayne's unforgettable event at Portland Marina, the memories rush back with an intensity that's impossible to ignore. Wayne Ingram, a man I have had the privilege to support, emerged as a force of sheer commitment and unwavering determination, leaving an indelible mark on all those who were fortunate enough to witness his journey.
>
> Standing on the pontoons of Portland Marina, I watched as Wayne's audacious plan unfolded before my eyes. A full week in a life raft, tethered to a buoy, armed with only 24hrs' worth of food and 500ml of water – the simplicity of his approach struck me with awe. It was a plan rooted in the raw essence of survival, where catching fish, collecting rainwater, and embracing the rhythms of nature were his companions.

2015: The Challenge

As the ship-to-shore radio crackled to life, Wayne's voice resonated across the expanse of water. The daily comms checks at 09:00 and 21:00 served as a lifeline, confirming his safety, and in those moments the distance between us felt both vast and intimate. With each check-in, the resonance of Wayne's courage echoed in my heart, reminding me of the profound commitment he had undertaken.

When the time came for Wayne to disembark from the life raft, a mixture of anticipation and pride filled the air. His wobbly legs carried him off the raft, a symbol of his endurance and an embodiment of the support that encircled him. Family and friends gathered around, weaving a tapestry of solidarity that celebrated his triumph over the challenges he had faced.

There was a moment of unexpected joy that painted a smile on everyone's faces. Wayne's spirited duet of 'In the Summertime' with none other than Mungo Jerry himself echoed across the water, his voice a testament to his enthusiasm – if not his familiarity – with the lyrics. His cheerful rendition, though unconventional and missing a word here and there, was a melody of resilience, a celebration of his unbreakable connection to the elements that surrounded him.

As I pen these words, the images and emotions rush back, reminding me of the power of determination and the impact of one person's unwavering commitment. Wayne Ingram's journey at Portland Marina was not just an event – it was a testament to the human spirit's ability to overcome, adapt, and inspire. It's a story that continues to resonate within me, urging me to approach life's challenges with the same unyielding resolve that Wayne displayed during those days."

Paul Swain, Marina Manager
(Assistant manager at the time)

"Having spent many years working with explorers and forces personnel, I was not too surprised when Wayne got in touch with me to ask about the physiology of survival in a life raft, and to describe his plans to spend a week in one at sea with very limited rations. My natural inclination with such a project is to "Go for it", and this was confirmed when I met Wayne and spoke to him about what he wanted to do, why he wanted to do it, and how he was going to go about it. He was clearly serious, knowledgeable and committed.

There is a limited amount of published science on how the body switches to 'survival mode' in such situations, and the best things to do to assist this, and thereby maximise survival prospects. Much of what is known comes from around the time of WWII. What we do know is that what happens in the first week of a survival voyage can have a significant impact on survival prospects. So, Wayne's week, 800m offshore in Portland harbour was likely to provide valuable insights that would help others going forward, not only in survival situations but also via the money Wayne would raise for Great Ormond Street Hospital's Children's charity. So, myself and colleague Dr Joe Costello were happy to support Wayne.

Despite the planning and what we knew about survival and Wayne's abilities, I still remember being a little nervous as we left Wayne floating in Portland harbour on the first day – what could possibly go wrong!? However, as you can read, it turned out well and we collected some useful data, money was raised for a deserving children's charity, and awareness of pollution in our seas and general knowledge of survival skills were raised.

Speaking of knowledge and children, in retrospect a highlight of the whole project for me was the time Joe and I spent with Wayne before the challenge on one of his meetings with local schoolchildren – talking about what he was going to do and survival in extreme environments. In the end, so much is about education and knowledge, and I hope that some of those children who were so enthralled with what they heard on that day will be inspired to become scientists, explorers or defenders of our fragile planet".

Professor Mike Tipton MBE

I learned later that the 'sea creature' was probably a conger eel, one of many that live in the breakwater stones of the harbour.

Wayne

After the two weeks it took me to get my strength back, I was in London handing over a cheque for £12,842 to Great Ormond Street Hospital – the incredible, tangible result of the amazing local support I'd received. While there I learned that Baroness Tessa Blackstone had invited me for a coffee in the hospital admin building. Thankfully I was wearing a suit – yes, I'd learned – and readily agreed. My conversation with this wonderful, down-to-earth lady became a very special memory for me, as not only did we discuss my time in the raft, and how Stefan was progressing, but it also raised an opportunity for me to ask a favour of her...

Six months prior to the Life Raft Challenge I'd recommended Professor Dunaway for a UK honour, in recognition of the voluntary surgical work he performed around the world, and the help he'd been giving Stefan for the past 12 years. The Honours Committee clearly state that you won't hear anything for up to 18 months, but I wanted to add a bit of heft, so I informed Her Ladyship of the nomination and asked if was she in a position to support my request, please?

A consummate professional, she clearly couldn't agree to anything, and told me that the Honours System involves a strict vetting process through government departments which others could not access. In addition, she said, although David was an amazing man, he was just one of many deserving doctors and medical staff within the profession. She could, however, and without telling me anything, check on its status.

Postscript

In the 2016 Queen's birthday honours, Professor David J Dunaway, FDSRCS, FRCS (Plast), former Secretary General of the European Society of Craniofacial Surgery, and former President of the Plastic Surgery Section of the Royal Society of Medicine, received the Commander of the Most Excellent Order of the British Empire award for his exemplary services to facial surgery worldwide

Chapter 28

2015–2016

The Final Operation

A year after the raft event was nothing but a nascent idea, it was time for Stefan's fifth and final operation, which would complete both his nasal surgery and the journey we'd started together 13 years earlier. Thankfully, this would be a relatively minor procedure, and not life-threatening as previously.

This final operation was cosmetic, on David's recommendation. He'd opened up Stefan's nasal airway during the previous operation, and this one was to tidy up his nose after everything had settled down. I'd made a promise to see this through to the end, and it would finally put the candle on the cake. Call me obsessive if you like, but I'm one of those people who, if they start something, will always finish it – especially when the last hurdle is in sight.

Facing the World still held the £9,600 allocated to the operation, and David had again agreed to do the job at no charge. It would have felt fitting to use the familiarity of GOSH, especially after the raft event, but FTW worked predominately with The Portland Hospital, on Great Portland Street in London, so that's where the operation would take place. Being named after my hometown, however, a place I have grown to love, and the actual location of the raft event, it felt fitting to end our journey here.

I called Slava once more to confirm we could get the last ball rolling, to learn that she already had everything in place. The only difference was that Dzejna couldn't make it due to her work, but her sister Nevena could come instead. Though she wouldn't be our interpreter, Nevena would be essential company for Slava while Stefan was in hospital.

David confirmed the dates in October, scheduling his availability with those of The Portland, and FTW started arranging the visas, flights, and accommodation. Normally I'd be organising fundraising events by now, but this time they weren't needed because we'd completed the job already. It occurs to me, at this stage of any project, that finishing a task is usually the simplest and most straightforward part, after all the work you've put in. But it's the part where your mind often puts up the most resistance to taking the last few steps needed. You get so used to the obstacles that you've managed to overcome so far, that you imagine the most difficult, the most terrifying one, to be at the end – The Boss Level. The Black Fortress. The combined forces of hell massing against you – and you stop, thinking that if it's been so hard, so far, how can you possibly overcome an even bigger challenge? This psychological barrier can actually cause people to give up, after everything they've achieved, just a short distance away from their goal.

The other enemy at this point is that, once you can finally see the goal, you think that's it – and you stop and relax too soon. You put off a final detail. You're sloppy with the paperwork. You fail to complete your mission, your project, your destiny, because in your mind you're already there.

No! This is the time to give your all, to use all the experience and momentum you've gathered, and to put everything you've got left into it. So much in fact, that you cannot possibly fail, and nothing or nobody can stop you. To not slow down at the finish line but, instead, to carry on so far, in that final burst, that you take the finish line with you in your wake. Like that final chord in Gustav Holst's 'Mars', this is the definitive point at which you not only claim your victory, but rightfully and undeniably possess it forever as your own...

One thing I knew I could do at this point, because no publicity was required, was to keep everything so low-key that the media never found out. This time, this last chapter, would involve just Stefan, his family, and myself.

2015–2016: The Final Operation

The family flew into Heathrow without fanfare. FTW's administration was all-encompassing, covering every little detail and taking the pressure off everyone involved. They didn't just do this for Stefan, but for every family who travelled to this distant country for their children to have life-changing surgery. For many, including from Vietnam with which FTW has a permanent link, arriving in London can be a massive culture shock. FTW are aware of this and take care of all paperwork, tickets, translation, onward transport, and accommodation. As a result, all I had to do was turn up at the airport with a cheery smile, a chipper attitude, and two armfuls of hugs.

We stayed at the same places in Chelsea, though this time there was no match on. With the surgery being straightforward, we expected a stay of no more than two weeks. Our funds would be limited, and every penny needed to be used wisely. The upheaval and stress of the past 13 years had taken its toll on the family and, though they were extremely grateful for this miracle, we were glad that it would soon be over, and we'd see how Stefan would look once the last bandages had been removed.

Arriving at their hotel, I was treated to a well-remembered and much-welcomed Bosnian coffee. I gave them money for food and phone calls and offered to stay with them should they wish, though I was glad to hear they were expecting the local Bosnian church minister, whom they'd befriended during their last visit. Satisfied that they were okay, I returned to my flat opposite the hospital and got started on all the last-minute administration tasks for the following day – our first appointment with David.

Unlike some women I know, *ahem!* whenever I informed the family that we needed to leave at a certain time, they were always there ready and waiting for me. Not once were we ever late for an appointment! I met them next day at South Kensington Tube station, having planned the route with only one change to Regents Park, from where we'd walk to Harley Street. This would normally be an uneventful journey, except that Stefan found it highly amusing whenever we pulled in or out of Embankment. This station is world-famous for its **"Mind the Gap…"** announcement, so this time he started repeating it to himself, and then louder, eventually mimicking it perfectly on cue and sniggering each time, which of course prompted me to announce it with him, both of us laughing as we enjoyed the same language. This then infected three besuited young men in our carriage, who accompanied us in our rhythmic rendition for the rest of the trip. How to enrich an otherwise monotonous and self-absorbed journey!

A fascinating human story attached to this is that Embankment is the only station on the London Underground that still uses this particular voice. All the others use a variety of new voices after the system went digital in 2012 – which included Embankment. But soon after, a lady approached the staff there to ask them where 'the voice' had gone. They explained to her that the announcement was made just as regularly, but the voice had simply been updated to a new one.

"But...," the distraught lady told them, "That was my husband..."

It turned out that her husband, a theatre actor who'd died five years earlier, had voiced the original analogue recording back in the 70's, and the lady would take comfort in listening to it as she sat at the station. But when the system was upgraded, new voices of better recording quality had replaced it.

Long story short, Transport for London not only made and gave her a CD of the original recording, but then went out of their way to get it reinstated it at the station. So, hats off to them, because this lady won't be the only traveller who remembers that iconic voice, and their kind actions.

Arriving at our destination well ahead of time, as I always prefer, we stopped for a coffee, and I watched Slava and Nevena get through several cigarettes before making the short walk to David's private clinic. There, we met our new interpreter for the first time – a lovely lady who'd offered her services after being asked by the local Bosnian church. Though a little more strict and straight-laced than I was used to, and also a bit embarrassing as she kept on thanking me for what I'd done, she was extremely helpful and efficient each and every time we needed clear and precise communication. This was especially useful as David conducted his examination of Stefan's nose, informing us of how it had healed, and why the pins from his first operation had started to protrude from under his skin. Stefan had been just 4 years old then, and his facial bones had continued to grow. Now he was 17, it was time for remedial work. As if discussing the weekly shopping list, he explained what he'd planned to do and how he'd go about it.

Our questions this time were few. We were all aware that, without his intervention, Stefan would not have made it this far – and we all trusted him totally. He ended by confirming the operation tomorrow, and would they please accompany his nurse for the medical assessment?

As I stood to leave with the family, David gently tapped my arm and asked if I'd stay for a moment. When the others had left, and the door closed behind them, he looked at me wryly and asked if I'd been the one behind his recent award from the Queen. Well, I said that I might have had something to do with it, but I really had no way of knowing. All I'd done was talk with a few people, and recommended him for the kindness he'd shown to people over the course of his career, many of whom would otherwise be dead. He was the one who'd earned it. 'He went on to tell me of the wonderful time he'd had, taking his family to Buckingham Palace for the investiture. But to me, David is the wonderful one, and easily worth this recognition'.

I caught up with the family, and we arranged to meet again the following morning at Portland Hospital. I then made a swift getaway because I knew what was coming next – Slava would ask me if I wanted to join them in looking around the different shops!

I only enter a shop to buy something which I know I need, otherwise I wouldn't be there. Very occasionally, if I had time to kill while my wife was shopping elsewhere, I'd go into a hardware store to scan and commit everything they had to memory, in case I ever needed one in future.

And before anyone complains, I'm not just singling out shops. There are other domesticities that I also can't stand – like sweet potatoes. Why would you want a spud that's sweet? That's like sprinkling sugar on crisps... And while I'm at it, rhubarb and gooseberries, which are even worse than survival rations! Just what is the appeal of stringy and hairy fruit? If Matt Tebbutt from Saturday Morning Kitchen is reading this, I would be over the moon to come on your show with rhubarb and gooseberries as my food hell!

I now realise that she was inviting me as a special guest into a select social group reserved exclusively for women. She was trying to bond with me emotionally in a neutral environment – make me part of her family – and I should have been honoured. Instead, I spent the afternoon checking our funds and finding out where the hospital was, and which entrances and routes we needed to take tomorrow. As we learned in the armed forces, an effective recce is seldom wasted, and one of us now knew exactly where we needed to go, be, and by when.

The following morning, the day of the operation, we were all sitting in the coffee shop across from the hospital. After buying coffee and cake for two homeless guys, with the promise of more later if they'd disposed of the leftover rubbish responsibly, I returned to join Slava. Through our interpreter she asked me if I knew what day it was? I thought I'd organised everything *'what the hell have I missed?'* Now under pressure, and frantically trying to remember birthdays, I did my best impression of Rodin's 'Thinker', desperately trying to buy time and save face, before finally coming up with a bland but honest, "Er, no..."

Slava smiled, and said that today was the 13th of October, then paused for it to set in... *Come on! What happened then?* ...exactly 13 years ago today when Stefan had had his teeth removed! *What the hell...?* I was gobsmacked, and absolutely shocked by this revelation. I'd totally forgotten this – *how the hell had I totally forgotten this?* as I realised that I hadn't planned, pre-arranged, nor manipulated this in any way to link these two appointments together over a 13-year slice of time. How this date wasn't stamped in boilerplate on my memory was beyond me, as it was one of the scariest days of my life. However, it was patently one of those occasions when the universe sends you a notification *It's okay, my friend. I've got your back...*

It was the first thing I told David, when he came into the hospital room to see Stefan prior to surgery. Showing no surprise whatsoever, he just said, "Fantastic. Well, let's continue to do our very best, shall we?" as he started his examination and questioning. Once he'd finished, he said that he'd see us in a few hours, and left the anaesthetist and another doctor to ask their own questions. Then that was it. Stefan was taken away to theatre for his final operation. This would be the last time that Slava, her sister, and I would sit, smoke (actively and passively), and worry as to how our son, nephew, and godson respectively would look, while waiting in anticipation for the call to confirm that he was now in Recovery.

We didn't move far from the hospital to start with, after finding a Turkish coffee bar just outside, right next to my two new friends sleeping rough in the doorway behind Great Portland Street underground station. A quick check told me that they'd stuck to their word and conveyed all their rubbish to the bin across the road. True to my word, I bought them another coffee and cake each, and sat with them for half an hour learning more about their lives – especially as one was wearing dirty Soldier 95 combats, complete with bergen. Both appeared to be in their mid to late 40's but, in truth, with the hardship of living hand to mouth on the streets, they could have been much younger. Combat Guy told me that he'd been in the Parachute Regiment for several years, having seen service in the Falklands and Northern Ireland which had given him PTSD – which set another alarm bell ringing. The first had been when I asked him what his regimental number was, and he said he couldn't remember as his trauma had blocked it. This was utter rubbish, because your number is so ingrained in your memory that you carry it with you to your grave.

Secondly, there was no way he could have been older than ten in 1982, when the Falklands war erupted. Saying nothing for now, I turned to the second guy, dressed in tatty clothing, who told me that he'd been caught in bed at home with his wife's best friend, and kicked out of the house. Rather than risk a minor atrocity, he'd not returned since, and six months later he was still trying to get his life together. There was no crap with this one – just an honest story of how the grass is rarely greener on the other side of the fence, especially if your wife's friend lives there. When it comes to emotional betrayal, the term 'Hell has no fury like a woman scorned' is a gross understatement. It means that if you do all your critical thinking ruled by your sex drive, you'll end up in a far deeper hole than you could have ever imagined.

I was about to leave these two to their day but couldn't resist picking at a few more stitches in our war hero's story. When I asked him what he remembered about the Falklands, he responded with the classic "Sorry, mate. Can't say anything 'cos I was working behind enemy lines, and I'm still stuck to the Secrets Act..."

Trying to calm my anger, I kept a poker face and asked him about his time in the Province, and where he'd served. He replied with "You know... the usual places – Londonderry, and bandit country in Belfast..."

I couldn't take any more, because he'd gone too far. Everyone who was really there knew that 'bandit country' was in South Armagh, where a far dirtier and dishonourable war was fought. No one could possibly forget this – it'd be like forgetting where you'd lost your legs, or your friends – and it was clear that he'd never served in any army. He was an armchair warrior, a 'Walt,' short for Walter Mitty, and I told him to get the fuck out of here for disgracing the uniform, and using the plight of real soldiers to deceive genuinely sympathetic civilians. Quick as a flash he was up and started to leave, beckoning his mate to come with him. But by now his former ally had cottoned on. He stood his ground, shook his head, and told him, "Don't think so, pal..."

In hindsight, I reckon the guy who'd been caught 'sleeping with the enemy' had probably experienced more close quarter combat when dealing with his wife afterwards!

I returned to Slava, who straight away asked if I'd heard anything? Shaking my head, I suggested that we take a walk in Regents Park, where the squirrels were familiarised with humans. On the way I bought a large pack of unroasted nuts from a local shop, and we spent a pleasant couple of hours walking around the park to the boating lake. The squirrels didn't let us down, and happily scrambled all over us to eat nuts from our hands, while surreptitiously searching for the main pack in our pockets!

The call finally came, and we made our way back to see Stefan. We'd just taken off our coats in his room when he was wheeled in. Although still drowsy from the anaesthetic, and typical of this strong-minded boy I'd grown to love, as soon as his mother said his name, he opened his eyes, smiled at her, then gave me a thumbs up before drifting back to sleep.

David came in soon after, informing us that the operation had gone better than expected, and he was really pleased with the results. He answered all our questions, and said that he'd see us all tomorrow.

I left soon after him, aware from previous visits that this was their family time, but I made sure to go via the coffee shop to get the remaining homeless guy another coffee and cake.

Two days later Stefan was discharged from hospital, complete with a plastic nose support, and strict instructions not to remove any bandages until his discharge appointment with David, the following week. I escorted them back to their hotel and gave them new phone cards and cash for food and transport, before heading back to Portland to be with my wife, my girls, and my boys. I'd been away for over a week, and needed to get in a few ambulance shifts again. I'd always felt guilty, leaving them stuck in London while I returned to the emotional safety of my own home, but by now they'd built a strong bond with fellow Bosnians living in the city so, as soon as I'd left, they were able to conduct a fairly normal existence in their own language. This became especially evident when I called to invite them down to Dorset for a few days, so that everyone here who'd followed Stefan's progress could see him after his final operation.

Calvin had sold his taxi business, but Galaxy Cars, the agency who drove me to and from the airport when I was working in Africa, had kindly agreed to take up the slack whenever the Savic family were involved, and would collect them from their hotel in London and bring them straight to us. I'd also booked one of the upper rooms in a local hotel so that they'd have superb views of the sea. So, I was a bit upset when Slava asked if it was okay for them to stay in London, as Stefan had already made several friends there!

Of course, I agreed, but felt quite hurt that I'd let down wonderful people like Calvin, and everyone else here in Dorset who'd supported my cause, but now wouldn't be able to see Stefan on what would probably be his last visit to the UK. It was only while I was muttering to myself while cleaning out my man-shed (which I usually do when something's weighing on my mind) that Cara came in and put it into perspective for me.

1. Why on earth would a 17-year-old teenager want to visit Portland when he could be exploring London with his pals?

2. Hadn't I already reached my goal – achieving a normal life for Stefan? (See Point 1)
3. Wouldn't this be a good time for us all to move on? (See Point 2)

This is just one of the many qualities I love about my wife, and why I'd be lost without her.

This task, this mission I'd taken on, had consumed my life over the past 13 years, and much had happened since 2003. I'd been medically and expediently discharged from the Army, throwing my life into turmoil. I'd started a new career as a paramedic, during which I had a baby die in my arms, and I'd delivered another. I'd remarried, and fathered two beautiful girls.

I'd become a part of The Circuit, working in Iraq as a CP paramedic – what the hell was I thinking? I'd started a new, albeit ill-advised career in an industrial gold mine, which had led me to being arrested and detained in a third-world Islamic country.

Despite being responsible for everyone's lives out there, I lost my younger brother over here to a drugs overdose (did I not mention that? No, I don't think I told anyone else either…), I'd moved home – twice – and had helped to further science by wild-camping out at sea.

But over the whole of this time, I'd dedicated myself to fulfilling a promise I'd made to a 4-year-old Bosnian boy I'd met in my past – a promise that I'd see through to the end. What I had not done, however, was to define when that end would be, and how I'd recognise it when it happened. Cara had just done that for me, and all I needed to do now, to complete my 13-year-long mission, was to simply get them home safely, back to their own lives.

It all felt like a lifetime ago, and now here I was, on my way to London again to accompany the family at their meeting with David for Stefan's final assessment. Would he, after all this, become the handsome and mature young man that all mothers wish their sons to be when they grow up?

I didn't arrive until evening, and by the time I'd reached the hotel it was too late to do anything other than arrange our journey to Harley

Street next day. That night, although tired from travelling, I couldn't sleep. At far-too-early o'clock I got up and walked to a 24hr off-licence to buy a few cans of beer, and by 6am I was sinking cups of tea while waiting to see the family in three hours' time.

This particular Tube trip was uneventful, and no number of 'Mind the Gap's could lighten the atmosphere around us. A 13-year journey of hope was about to end in a single moment, and with just a few words.

Okay, it may not have been as dramatic as this, because everyone was just so extremely grateful it had happened at all, but I just wanted this last episode in the series to be as well-written as possible, and have a happy and memorable ending.

Once we'd checked in at the clinic, Stefan was taken away to have his dressings removed by the practice nurse, while we sat with David discussing the path we'd all taken together. After what felt like hours the nurse reappeared and informed him that the nose splint was ready to be removed, so we followed them into the treatment room where Stefan lay still on the bed, eyes closed, his face illuminated by a single lamp. David rolled up his sleeves, washed his hands, then set to work, gently wriggling the splint from side to side. At this point I took a step back to give Slava and Nevena a closer view, as I wanted them to be the first to see it. Slava, however, took my hand and pulled me forward to join them, wordlessly saying, 'We started this together. We'll be together at the end, too', and making me feel even more a part of this wonderful family than ever before.

One more wiggle to the left, and the right, and the splint was off... and with that single motion all our fears and worries departed. Stefan looked, well, just perfect, and as I turned to look at Slava, and the tears forming in her eyes, I saw her happier than I'd ever seen her before. She moved forward and kissed Stefan on his forehead, then gripped David's arm with both hands in gratitude. She then turned and flung her arms around me, holding me tightly as she kissed me on the cheek and said, "Thank you, my brother..."

The only one who couldn't see the result was Stefan, whose eyes were already welling up with tears from the sheer emotion in the room.

But then he was handed a mirror to see his completed face, which blossomed into a big, happy smile for everyone. There was just a little more cleaning up to do so, while the family stayed in the treatment room with Stefan, David and I returned to his office.

"Well, I think that went rather well..." said the calmest and most collected man I'd ever known. Me, I was just lost for words and, as I looked down at the picture of him on his desk, standing proudly with his family, holding his CBE, all I could do was shake his hand and say, "Thank you, for everything that you've done for us."

He then thanked me (!) for allowing him to complete the surgery, for raising all the necessary funds, and for joining us on this remarkable journey. Finally, to call him if I ever needed any more help. Then that was it. I rejoined the Savic family as we left Harley Street to return to the hotel.

I don't know what more I was expecting. If this had been a movie there'd have been a soaring orchestral score at this point, but we left in silence, there was no media van waiting outside, and I didn't speak a single word throughout the entire return trip. Thinking back, I reckon I was mentally and emotionally drained and exhausted now that it was finally over, like with the life raft challenge *go away...* – except that I'd been carrying the responsibility for nearly 700 times longer *no, not now...*

We arrived back at their hotel *I need to leave...* and when they invited me in to join them, I couldn't refuse. I sat down while Slava made a coffee for me, and looked at these incredible people whom I'd come to care for and love over a decade, and would never have met had it not been for their beautiful little 4-year-old boy. And that did it. I couldn't hold back the tears any longer. I tried to turn away and look through the window, but Slava had already seen right through me. She came over, sat down next to me, and hugged me, and at that point I couldn't stop myself crying, onto her shoulder and into her hair. She just held onto me until I'd finished, sharing a long, drawn-out moment usually reserved for other women. I couldn't say anything, I had no words, and this was the only way I could express myself – the way most men would avoid like the plague.

I felt highly embarrassed, not having learned a thing from the experience, I once again took the coward's way out and apologised *you...* for not being able to accompany them to the airport *heartless...* next day because I had to be *bastard...* back in Dorset. The truth was that it would have broken my heart to watch them depart from my life. I told them what time the taxi would collect them, and that their flights and visas had been arranged. Neither Slava nor Nevena needed an interpreter for what I couldn't say and, allowing me to save face, said it was okay. I turned to Stefan for a man-hug and a kiss on the cheek, and then left them to get back to my family who'd supported me on the longest emotional expedition I'd ever been on.

But I'd finally done it. I'd completed my mission – a promise I'd made to a little boy and his family an eternity ago. And, like any good British Tommy, had resolutely stuck to his guns.

Chapter 29

2016-18
Consequences

With that chapter behind me, this young boy from South London, who was never going to make anything of himself, and who'd learned experientially that every action has an unforeseen and often unpleasant repercussion, could finally move on. Fate, however, as the universe's bookkeeper, has a habit of not letting up until the paperwork's been done.

In July 2016 I was made a Freeman of the City of London, and in May 2018 I received the Wessex FM 'Local Hero' for Emergency Services Award.

But the shock, awe, and honour of these was nothing compared to when, in early 2017, I received a long-distance call from Belgrade saying that I'd been nominated and accepted for the Serbian Humanitarian award. Gobsmacked, after having established that this wasn't a hoax by my mates at the station, I realised that this required Cara and I to fly to the capital of Serbia to attend a televised red-carpet event with dinner afterwards. We touched down at Nikola Tesla airport on 6th Feb, the evening before the ceremony, and were met by an excited female reporter with a chauffeur who drove us to our hotel in the city centre. The journey took an hour and, though it was cold, wet and getting dark, they enthusiastically pointed out historic buildings, and anything related to the former conflict, to their celebrity guests along the way.

I remembered the hotel and, just before we entered, I apologised to Cara, saying that it would be extremely basic with an original 1920's

Russian décor. However, the place had changed considerably since I'd last been here and, as an international recipient in a national award ceremony, we learned that our overnight lodgings had been upgraded to a modern en-suite!

We said our goodbyes, quickly dumped our bags, and went off to find some food before everywhere closed for the night. After walking around for ages trying to find the recommended restaurant, we ended up a considerable distance away from the hotel, following a sign which led us down a flight of steps. At the bottom was a door which, as soon as it was opened, exhaled a heavy cloud of cigarette smoke. Oh well, here we go again!

It turned out to be an excellent bar/eatery with only a few people dining. The waiter spoke perfect English with a cockney twang to it, and on talking with him we discovered that he'd never ever been to London, but had learned the language and dialect solely from watching 'Only Fools and Horses'! As we were laughing, the manager and waitress came out to talk with us, saying that they'd seen my face in the newspapers and on the local news, and wanted to celebrate by sharing drinks on the house with me. Out came the slivovitz, and my mind instantly flew back to consuming a litre of the stuff with Mick, and that poor pig in Sipovo. But I couldn't let them down by refusing, so I told Cara a white lie saying that it was traditional with a couple that the wife drank first. And this is how we got away with just three small shots, each followed by "Salute!" before finally making our excuses and escape.

The following day we gave newspaper interviews and appeared on the Serbian equivalent of GMTV, before arriving early (as always...) at the City Hall. I originally thought it was going to be a low-key affair, but I couldn't have been more wrong. It was a huge, national ceremony in magnificent surroundings and, as we entered, we were immediately swamped by reporters from other newspapers and TV stations.

Eventually, just before noon, Cara and I were seated amongst several VIP's, including the deputy president of Serbia, several Serbian film stars, and the British military attaché, who was there not just on behalf of the British ambassador, but because I'd first met Stefan when I was a British soldier stationed in Bosnia.

At midday precisely, a traditional fanfare heralded the start of the ceremony, which would honour twelve people in recognition of their unique achievements. These were displayed on a large screen to the audience, prior to two attractive ladies escorting them along the red-carpeted centre aisle, past the TV cameras, and up to the stage to receive their award. It felt incredible to be there, and when I stood up after the video of Stefan and I covering thirteen years, the entire audience also rose in a standing ovation, clapping and cheering me, and I was given a mighty man-hug by a Serbian general next to me with tears in his eyes. He wasn't the only one.

The Serbs are a proud, hardened people, and rightly so as they've witnessed so much death and horror. I honestly didn't feel I'd deserved this special attention that they were bestowing upon me, but when I learned that I was the only British citizen to have ever been nominated, let alone receive this award, I realised that they were accepting me as one of their own.

To this day I keep in touch with Slava via text. Stefan is now a musician, playing keyboard in a local band who have not only appeared on TV, but also secured a recording contract. He is happily married to his beautiful wife Milijana, and also works in a local warehouse to help support his wife and parents. Each time he sends me a picture or video, he looks even more grown-up and good-looking.

Today, the Serbian Humanitarian award, one of my most treasured possessions, sits humbly on my side unit at home – a reminder of the responsibilities of being born human.

Chapter 30

2017–2019

Time Management

An honour is not without profit, except... well, you know the rest. I still needed to earn a crust and, back in the UK, without a new employment contract on the horizon, I immersed myself in bank paramedic work with my local ambulance trust. Bank work is good, allowing flexibility in when you want to work. The downside is that rather than the jobs and shifts coming to you automatically, you have to go looking for them.

With constant staff shortages, regular ambulance shifts were manned by the full-timers, with response car vacancies available for part-timers who preferred to choose their own shifts. This suited me well, moving between my three local stations – Weymouth, Dorchester and Bridport – which, I knew, always had spare slots.

As I said earlier, if you're good enough at your job, then you'll never be short of work, and you can use the breaks in between to catch up with all the little things in life which, like leaves in a gutter, clump together to clog up your mind. Before long I received an email from Dorset Healthcare, inviting me to apply for the position of HM Prison Healthcare Manager for the HMP Young Offender Institution of Portland.

Wow! This had to be worth it for the experience alone, so I called and talked with the area manager, confirming my interest and availability. I did stress that I'd never worked in a prison before, nor even been inside one. Technically, this was true, as my incarceration in Mauritania had been at an immigration detainment centre – and definitely not a prison. Honest!

She assured me that, based upon my managerial experience, I shouldn't have any problems, as one healthcare management job was pretty much the same as another. This, as I was to discover, was a critical underestimation of what the job entailed if you want to do it 'hands on', and not from the safety of a secluded office.

How I got through the interview is beyond me, as I had very little knowledge of how HMP healthcare targets and outcomes were reported and recorded. Maybe they were desperate, because by the end of the interview I was being formally offered the role, subject to their standard security. This took several months and vast amounts of paperwork, while they conducted extensive, in-depth background checks on me. Obviously, I can't go into the details, but suffice it to say that an enhanced DBS check for working with children would have been a breeze by comparison. The sheer depth of information I had to provide was equivalent to knowing my old headmaster's full name, date of birth, and National Insurance number!

'Twas on a Monday morning that the replacement prison healthcare manager arrived at work, to find that the outgoing manager had already left, leaving no handover information whatsoever. This wasn't a good start, and over the following weeks I had to learn on my own how things got done here, and get to know the prison staff and inmates. As the new guy, the long nights I spent trying to put things right, while learning the intricacies of how the department ran, were bloody difficult and intensely unenjoyable.

Before I continue, I want to say that this chapter is deliberately written to be unsensational. My job – my passion – is to save lives. If you've watched any TV prison series – the BBC's 'Time' with Sean Bean is a typical one – you'll have an idea of the layout of a British prison and how it works. What you'll rarely see is what happens to the poor sod who's just been shivved, shanked, or beaten up, and the prison officers (PO's) lead him off-camera for treatment. This is where healthcare, and my role, came in.

Employee turnaround here was akin to the Inland Revenue (sorry – HMRC), with only a few vocational staff staying beyond two years.

Most of the PO's were young, there weren't enough of them to go around, and I learned to respect them considerably for the job they had to do – because they did not run the prison. The prisoners did that. Every inmate knew the rules, and their rights. It was the first thing they learned from the experienced ones, and they all knew how to game the system and make it work for them. More on this later.

Several of the med team were NHS-trained nurses who'd left to work in prisons, and so we learned from each other. Because I'd moved around a lot, I could demonstrate a variety of new and different skills – not only in emergency medicine, but in primary health assessment, medicine, and wound care. The latter was important because, sadly, bladed cuts made up most of our daily cases – and the majority were self-inflicted.

Even worse, this was the case at every prison that I subsequently attended. The clinic – our prison hospital – received regular cases of self-harm, most of which had to be sutured. The problem was that, other than the onsite doctor – who was kept constantly busy prescribing medicines to inmates – nobody else was qualified to do this. So, whenever this happened, the patient needed to be escorted by two of our PO's to Dorset County Hospital, 16 miles away, tying up valuable members of staff just to drive, sit, and wait with them in A&E.

Prisons can be compared to fragile ecosystems – like a dry, arid savanna where one small spark can cause a conflagration. From this point of view, PO's are like professional firefighters, tamping out sparks and putting out small fires before further harm is done. But with a critically small workforce, available staff had to be taken off the wings – which necessitated their immediate closure. The knock-on effect would be instant. Inmates who'd normally be outside their cells had to be locked up. Telephone calls home were stopped. Everyone – inmates and staff – became increasingly frustrated and angry with each disruption as it developed, and the combined effect created a seething, smouldering volcano just waiting to erupt.

Each and every prisoner knew this…

The doctor I referred to earlier fought a constant battle with the inmates, who claimed that they either had pain for various ailments, or problems with sleeping, hoping he'd prescribe painkillers or sleeping tablets – both of which were bargaining currency for smokes or spice. If he prescribed medication to be taken daily, a PO would then have to watch them take it, and check that they'd not 'tongued' it in their mouth, ready to remove for bartering once the officer had left. The PO's got the worst of the aggression from these disruptions, and the only time I ever saw threats of physical violence or verbal aggression towards healthcare staff was during the dispensing of meds. Medications were delivered daily, to be dispensed in the morning and late afternoon from two secured locations – the clinic, and the Raleigh wing, which was a nexus point for two other wings.

Those inmates who could be trusted were allowed their meds in weekly or 2-weekly amounts. Others, who had threatened to take their lives, had sold or were caught trying to sell their meds could only collect them daily. Occasionally some meds would be delayed, which prompted threats to the dispensing chemist. Sometimes they were spat at, so plastic screens covering most of the dispensing hatch had to be installed.

At Channings Wood there was a difficult prisoner in solitary who received daily meds for his conditions. One morning, one of his meds was missing, and the nursing staff were reluctant to inform him, so I said that I'd do it. A PO from segregation opened his cell and, standing several feet away from him, I politely informed him of the situation. But it quickly became clear that he wasn't listening to anything I said, and that his rising anger was being directed towards the officer. Without warning he launched himself at the officer, but instinctively I blocked his way, took him to the ground, and pinned him there as the PO summoned assistance on his radio. Whenever this occurs all available officers rush to the assistance of a colleague, though I remember their look of shock, and then amusement, to see a PO and a paramedic already restraining the prisoner. Later that day, when his meds arrived and I gave them to the inmate, we both had a good laugh about it – because he certainly hadn't expected a healthcare worker to get involved.

Inmates were allowed razor blades to maintain personal hygiene, and although prison-issue blades were designed to be thinner than normal, with care they could still slice deeply, inflicting a long and nasty wound. A common trick to force an off-premises hospital visit was to wrap a blade in toilet tissue, and swallow the package whole. They'd then inform the wing officer, who'd have to report it to the healthcare team.

Every prison uses one of two emergency radio calls to summon a medic. 'Code Blue' is for drug overdoses, cardiac arrests, hangings, etc. 'Code Red' is for severe bleeding incidents, so when I first got one, I grabbed my bag and ran straight to the wing – receiving rather surprised looks from the PO's and the inmate when I got there, as though this was a highly unusual occurrence. That I'd got there so quickly told them that I was new, and the way I was limping told them that my ankle was shot. There was a large amount of blood on the floor, and a PO holding the victim's arm, wrapped in a towel, high above his head. The officer in charge briefed me on what had happened, and showed me the razor blade, which I dropped into my yellow 'sharps' box. Thankfully, the deep 5" long wound on his outer right arm hadn't penetrated his muscle tissue. I informed the Custodial Manager – the senior officer – that it'd require stitching, so as usual he got on the phone to find out who was free to accompany the inmate to the clinic, and then onward to Dorset County hospital. However, after several time-wasting minutes it was clear that no one was available, and we'd just have to wait. Which is why I offered to accompany the CM to the clinic, and stitch the inmate myself.

I soon found out that, by streamlining the process, I'd also stitched myself up good and proper. The floodgates opened, and I ended up being called in from home, days and nights, to attend every cut and self-inflicted injury, to avoid a build-up of aggro for the staff and prisoners. They say that no good deed goes unpunished – well, on the positive side, my suturing skills improved tremendously! The wounds I encountered varied in size and location on each individual's body. Outer arms and legs were the main recipients of the slash, although chests, abdomens, and the inside of thighs were also popular. I genuinely cannot imagine the mindset of anyone doing this to themselves. I once sutured the inside of an inmate's arm, only for him to return to his cell, reopen the wound, and smear excrement into it to compound the problem. This became an excessively difficult case, not only because I was now dealing with a new and probably infected wound which required deep cleaning and antibiotics, but also the related mental health issues involved.

You'd think that, in a prison, every inmate would be under so much observation that this just couldn't happen. The truth is that, with the limited staff we had, preventing it was practically impossible.

You'd also think that, in a prison, there'd be a rigorous sleeping and waking regime. This wasn't the case, as we were dealing with mainly young offenders who slept and got out of bed whenever they wanted – and the PO's allowed this because a sleeping prisoner created far less trouble.

Knowing the rules, and that it would niggle the warders, the inmates asserted their rights constantly by complaining about everything – even though they had their own TV, newspapers, books, three full meals a day, free prescriptions, and immediate face to face consultations with a doctor, dentist, or mental healthcare professional.

Considering that, for those on the right side of the law, doctors no longer make house calls, appointments are scheduled for weeks or even months ahead, getting an NHS dentist is nigh on impossible, and that prescriptions now cost nearly £10 a time, is it surprising that some pensioners and veterans deliberately get caught shoplifting in order to get 'rehoused'?

Not only that, but if a prescription was ever delivered late, an inmate felt that they had every right to kick off, and would happily smash a sink and flood their cell just to create a fuss. What could the PO's do, other than get them a new cell? It's not as if they could arrest them, or threaten them with prison. The simple fact is that prisons are not an effective deterrent to crime. It may be a useful way of taking criminals out of society, but it's also a place where they make new contacts, and learn new trades and tricks, enabling them to offend more efficiently once they get out.

While treating one young guy, he asked me if he should complain about the menu, and even get compensation, because they didn't offer enough variety at the serving hatch. When I learned that the day's menu included chips, mash, and curry sauce, I advised him that if it was me, I'd shut the f*ck up, because it was better than anything he'd get on an operational tour in the Army.

They could even get hold of drugs, which didn't make our jobs any easier. The once-legal 'Spice', a synthetic cannabis, was rife in every prison. It came in sprayed onto inmates' letters, which were then cut into strips and sold for a fiver each. The majority of 'Code Blue' calls were to overdoses of this drug, where most of those who'd smoked it became zombified to the point of it suppressing their ability to breathe. One such call was on the 3rd floor of Raleigh wing. Once on the scene, I gave the okay to the PO to leave and look after the other inmates. The patient was unresponsive and in respiratory arrest – and it didn't help that his airway was clogged with vomit. After clearing it with suction I rolled him onto his back, and started getting his breathing going again with a bag-valve mask until he could breathe for himself. Unfortunately, this prompted more vomiting, so I rolled him onto his side again to use suction, before getting an oxygen mask onto him. This alternating between suction and vomiting continued for over forty minutes until he eventually returned to some version of normality, and gingerly got himself up. Then, after refusing any further medical help, and ignoring his mates watching, he wobbled off into the distance. He'd almost died, yet the guy was so smashed that he was totally unaware. The PO on this wing was busy controlling the inmates elsewhere, so I shrugged and thought that was the end of it – until I started to pack my kit away and something wasn't right. I started to feel terrible. No – horrible... The term 'light-headed' is usually a precursor of what's to come. My vision had narrowed, my breathing rate had increased, and my pulse rate had gone up. Now the wing started to spin, and part of my brain told me that I was suffering from secondary inhalation from the patient's tracksuit top. As I staggered around trying to use my radio, before collapsing to the floor, I knew I was fucked...

Someone was shouting. Two men joined him. All wearing civvies. They picked me up, supported me steadily under my arms, and carefully carried me down and along three flights of stairs and corridors until we reached the main security office, where they knew someone could help me. I suffered with heart palpitations for months afterwards, and had to go for regular, 48-hour cardiac monitoring checks at Dorset Hospital. Other than this, thankfully, I've been okay, but the incident firmly cemented my belief that 'recreational' drugs are an absolute no-go area for anyone who values their brain.

When I eventually returned to duty, two officers told me that they'd never seen inmates care for anyone like this before. I made sure to find those three Samaritans, and thank them from the bottom of my heart. I also recommended them for enhancements – rewards for doing things well – only to learn that the officers in charge on that day had already done this.

I spent just over two years working in every prison on the south coast of England, including the infamous Dartmoor, implementing sturdy paramedic practice into the nation's healthcare system, before taking on a better-paying, less stressful role as an offshore paramedic on the oil rigs of Norway. But this isn't important. Because what happened next is a perfect example of what happens when, despite all your goals and plans, Life steps in and knocks you off-course, giving you a whole new challenge to deal with, and learn from.

> "The prison officer's role is a difficult one, and no amount of training can prepare you for the daily situations you are presented with. The levels of aggression, drug use, and self-harm within the prison walls, at times become overwhelming.
>
> I became friends with Wayne during his time working at HMP/YOI Portland, and I would frequently call on him and his team's medical assistant on a regular basis. Wayne had a natural ability to break down barriers with prisoners, enabling him to treat them within the establishment, and reducing pressure on prison staffing as hospital escorts were not needed.
>
> As staff members, we relied and depended on his skills, trusting his judgment in difficult and sometimes

life-threatening situations. Wayne's calm demeanour and professionalism enhanced his reputation across the establishment. I learned a lot from him. *Top Bloke"*

Mark Russell, Prison Officer, HMP/YOI Portland

"As an officer working on the landings, the job is tough. A lot of the time you are just firefighting, because there are not enough staff, nor do you have the time to make a difference or rehabilitate.

I remember this guy starting in healthcare, and people talking about him being a paramedic. This guy that I now know as Wayne was a big presence within the healthcare department, and made a difference from the start.

I remember, after a self-harm incident, where the prisoner had harmed and informed me that he would need to go to hospital. Wayne attended, stitched the wound, and the prisoner was told he would not be going out. I remember, in the days following this, the word soon got around, and the talk on the wing was that if you self-harmed, then someone would stitch you up and there would be no trip to hospital. I felt like this made a massive difference, as it took the pressure off stripping the staff from the landing to escort prisoners to hospital."

Mel Jess, ex PO, HMP/YOI Portland

Chapter 31

2019-20

Scoliosis - and that bloody virus!

Monday 10th June. This Monday morning was like any other school day – effectively organised chaos. My daughters were both sitting at the breakfast bar with their cereal of choice, Cara was at the other end of the kitchen hastily making their packed lunches, and I was carefully relieving the dishwasher of its previous night's work, trying not to break anything.

As I made my way to the kettle to make the first cuppa of the day, I noticed 12 year-old Freya sitting slumped over to the right, leaning on her right elbow, and almost parallel with the bar. Playfully, I asked her to sit up or she'd strain her back – but as she did, something didn't look right. Her white school shirt hung differently on her developing frame. Again, I asked her to sit up, but when she complained that she already was – alarm bells went off in my mind.

Cara heard the fluster in my voice, and came over to stand beside me as I asked Freya to raise the back of her shirt. Before she'd even got halfway, Cara told her to stop and take it off completely, so we could get a better idea of what the hell was going on here. The sight before us was a textbook image of scoliosis – an abnormal lateral curvature of the spine, and most commonly during early adolescence, during the period of rapid growth as the child becomes more adult. I knew the definition, and I'd seen it in pensioners, but this was our young older daughter!

Not wanting to accept it, I took a photo and phoned Pete, my close friend and local GP, to check with him. After a few words he confirmed my worse fears, and asked me to book Freya into the surgery to start the procedure for treatment. Then he asked for how long she'd had it, and if it was getting worse. I didn't know what to say. The awful fact was that this was the first time Cara or I had ever seen, or even known about it. Still holding the phone, we asked Freya how long she'd had this, and to our surprise she'd also had no idea that something was wrong. There was no pain and it wasn't causing her any problems. Naturally, there'd be no need for us, as her parents, to be with her while she was bathing or dressing, so neither of us knew a bloody thing. As a medical professional I felt a complete idiot for not knowing, and questioned my skills both as a paramedic and a father. *How the hell could I have missed this in my own child?!*

Several weeks passed, during which we learned two things: That her deformity measured at 74 degrees – the angle from the perpendicular at which her spine bent over to the right. And that, at this point, surgery was the *only* course of action for her to live a normal life, otherwise her spine would not only continue to curve, but to twist, further increasing her deformity, and putting unnatural pressure on her internal organs. We also learned *(far too bloody late!)* that from the onset of scoliosis the doctors would normally monitor the spine to see where it was going. Once it reached a certain degree, then a plastic body brace could be prescribed to hold it steady – but if it continued to deform, then the surgeons would need to take over. This was the stage that Freya had already reached.

As a parent, your entire world falls apart the moment you realise your child is seriously ill. You go through a complete paradigm shift as to what's important to you and realise that you've got it all wrong. Everything you've worked towards, for your family – the house, the car, all the little niceties – you want to smash the lot, because they aren't important any more. You wish to hell and back that you'd taken more care. Been more aware of the lives around you, and for whom you're responsible. Been there when they needed you. Take the pain away from them, and the illness upon yourself.

Too late. We'd missed all the clues, and our options. The only one left was surgery, and the only one on the operating table would be our child. Not only that, but the surgery would be in a critical area, all the way alongside the spinal column, where a minor drilling error, the slightest slip of the scalpel, or the smallest lapse of concentration could cause irrevocable paralysis – because once the spinal cord inside is damaged, there's no way to repair it. Only then, after all these years, with my own child's life in my hands, came the crushing realisation that this was how Slava and Milos must have felt.

We had to wait six months before the operation could go ahead, during which time the curvature of her spine, now an S-shape, had deformed to 96 degrees. It had already begun to twist, taking her entire rib cage with it – so her breathing had become more laboured as her lungs struggled for space, and she was in pain when tasked with simple functions – like standing, walking, and sleeping. This caused her to miss a lot of school, though we received much-needed support from the staff of All Saints Church of England Academy, and especially the headmaster, Mr. Cornish. They told us that several children they knew, who'd been through similar experiences, had still succeeded in going on to university. We were exceedingly grateful for this, and for all the other offers of support we received.

Through friends and contacts, the cost of the operation was covered by the Masonic Charitable Foundation, and would be conducted at the Spire Hospital in Southampton, Hampshire. We met the incredibly gifted Evan Davies, Freya's trauma and orthopaedic consultant. At first sight, I thought he'd make bloody good front row rugby player, but I quickly learned that his medical, communication, and empathetic skills were nothing short of sublime.

For half a year, even though neither of us wanted to talk about it, the operation was the primary topic of conversation for Cara and me, as we awaited the day to finally arrive. Just like Stefan, so many years earlier, Freya was stoic in her approach to the impending surgery – showing little in the way of fear, and even laughing with Lili as the four of us made the journey to Southampton. Their parents, however, were petrified, because they knew what was coming.

As we understood it, an 18" long incision would be made down her back from her shoulder line to her waistline, exposing both sides of her spine. All of her facet bones – the ones that hold each vertebra in place – would be removed, allowing direct access to the deformed length of spine. Each vertebra along this path would then be drilled on each side to accept 6mm diameter screws. Along one side of her spine, into a U-shaped, threaded hollow atop each screw, would be inserted a continuous metal rod to hold the vertebrae in place, and replacing the facet joints.

The engineering didn't stop here. This cobalt-chrome rod would then need to be secured in place by threaded bolts, and then bent manually by the surgeons to straighten the spine as far as they dared. Once they were satisfied, an identical, secondary rod would be bent to a similar shape, then inserted and secured on the opposite side of the spine, reinforcing its partner and preventing the spine from flexing and deforming again. To complete the job, her now-redundant facet bones would be ground up and mixed with synthetic bone tissue, to be applied along the repair so that her body would recognise and graft onto it as the healing process began.

All the while, they'd told us, she'd be hooked up to a medical 'circuit tester' which, after each stage of the operation, sent a signal along her spinal cord to check that, even under anaesthetic, all her basic motor functions were still working.

So, yes – petrified…

Only one parent could stay in the single room, and that choice fell on Cara. In truth, it was the natural decision, as Freya ended up needing the physical and emotional support only a mother could provide. In the meantime, I'd travel daily from Portland with lots of snacks, and collect, do, and deliver laundry and anything else needed.

While waiting during the 4–5-hour operation, I don't have the words to describe how we felt. However, we were finally informed that it had been a complete success, and Freya was even able to stand and walk a few paces the next day. Her scar seemed to extend the entire length of her torso, but her back was now straight, with only the slightest sign of a curve, and we were confident that she'd go on to live a reasonably normal life. She wouldn't be able to flex her back again, and could only bend at the waist, so sit-ups were off the agenda! Also, the line along which the incision had been made would be uncomfortable to the touch for several years to come, after having had the nerve endings cut. But despite these relative inconveniences, I have nothing but undying praise, admiration, and gratitude for the surgeons, their team, and the nurses who'd bequeathed upon Freya a full adult life.

A week of observation followed, with Cara on a makeshift bed for support whenever she was needed, and me making the daily drive to visit and provide for them both. The nurses encouraged Freya to increase the number of steps she took along the hospital corridor each day, until she was deemed physically and mentally strong enough to come home. I remember arriving at the ward that day, just as she'd walked the entire length of the corridor, before turning around and seeing me watching her. With a huge and happy smile on her face, she walked slowly but determinedly towards me while pushing a drip stand – which was still supplying essential fluids – ahead of her. I felt so immensely proud of her that day and, once she'd received her discharge papers and the drugs she'd need for recuperation at home, she was given the all-clear to travel. As we were sat on her bed, with Cara busily tidying and packing, I promised Freya that next year I'd stage a fundraising event to not only repay the financial and moral debt which had funded her operation – and for which we cannot thank the Masonic Foundation enough – but also to raise awareness of how sudden, unexpected, and terrible this condition is.

As we made plans, we were totally unaware of how much our lives would change next, courtesy of a tiny acellular particle measuring no more across than 140 millionths of a millimetre. Born in obscurity, with not long to live, it was about to embark upon a world tour. It didn't need a passport, nor even a ticket – though if it did, its identity would be shown as:

Name: SARS-CoV-2
Nationality: Chinese
DoB: 2019
Place of birth: Wuhan
Sex: Viral replicant

With so many people, and so little time, it would need to create countless copies of itself and travel by air. But it was also prepared to slum it, biding its time in body fluids until it could hitch-hike a lift. It had no way of knowing that its libertine spree would cause the deaths of 7 million human beings, while disrupting the life of every single person on the planet for years to come. As I talked with my beloved daughter, I had no way of knowing that I'd soon be drawn inescapably into helping those it affected, afflicted, and killed in its wake.

When we got back home it was obvious that both Freya and Cara were totally exhausted but, following the consultant's advice, we accompanied Freya as she walked slowly upstairs, and helped her into our bed on the top floor. In addition to regular walking, her rehabilitation included using stairs, so for the first few days she was to walk the short distance to the bathroom and back, and pretty soon she'd need to be descending and climbing two full flights of stairs.

She was in a lot of pain to start with, and every three hours our alarm would remind us to dispense various pain relievers to help with her healing. Cara had already been doing this since the operation, so for the first few days I took over to let her rest. Gradually the pain diminished, and the doses reduced, along with – thankfully – the need for any of us to get up during the night. True to her inimitable ability to quickly grasp any task she's given, Freya made such astounding progress with her recovery that she was able to return to school, starting with half-day sessions on 2nd March, and full days two weeks later.

There's a saying that 'When one door closes, another one opens…' Well, it must have been bloody draughty where we lived, because one after another had been slamming shut on us. Just a week after Freya returned to full-time schooling, the UK went into total lockdown. We all saw this coming, but no-one wanted to believe it would happen. Even working bank shifts, we were seeing more and more cases of Covid-19, and before long we'd all ditched our standard face mask, goggles, gloves and apron. Instead, we each wore a full, head-to-toe, protective white biohazard suit, with its own respiratory system that pumped micro-filtered air into our sealed head units.

During this time, I got a call from an offshore company asking if I'd work for them on their Covid helicopter flying from Aberdeen. Cases were being reported on their offshore rigs in the UK sector, and they needed a designated heli with a medical response team to fly out to the rigs and bring their people back for proper hospital care. An oil rig is a very closed environment, and the only way to keep it running in a pandemic is to isolate and remove infected staff as quickly as possible.

This was a breath of fresh air for me, flying several times a day to different rigs throughout the North Sea, and bringing sick people back to be conveyed to the main hospital in Aberdeen. The company housed me in a self-contained flat close to work, which made life a whole lot easier but, like the rest of the UK, we were also in full lockdown. A real nuisance was that all commercial flights were suspended two days after I arrived, so at the end of my shift, every third week, I had to drive three-quarters the length of the UK to get back home. The only perk was that, with just a few heavy-goods vehicles and a collection of audiobooks for company, I was usually the only car on the motorway. The downsides were that it took me 11 hours for each one-way trip, and I always arrived shattered. This was my life for several months, driving over 600 miles a time between home and work, and doing the occasional bank shift on the local ambulance. Freya had continued to improve and, several months after her operation, you'd hardly know that she'd been under the knife – other than the long, impressive scar running down the length of her back, of course – but thanks to the surgeons' superb closing skills, and Cara's insistence on rubbing in bio-oil afterwards, it had begun to blend smoothly with the rest of her skin.

Life changed for all of us once Covid arrived, as I'm sure it did for everyone. It's still not been the same since and, to be honest, I don't think it ever will. Despite all my medical awareness and protection, I still caught it – and it knocked me for six.

Towards the end of summer in 2020 the number of recovery flights had reduced significantly, so instead I got bounced around doing various ad-hoc medical jobs away from home. It was around this time that my mate Mick Cowles, my former troop sergeant, and I started to brainstorm an idea we'd had for several years – how we could use our bushcraft skills and knowledge of the backwoods to help veterans and soldiers suffering from PTSD. During our discussion he asked about my experience in dealing with the pandemic. I was brutally honest in telling him what I'd seen personally, but that it was nothing in comparison to what our doctors, nurses, and ambulance staff saw on a daily basis. I was able to dip in and out of work when I chose, but the professionals had no choice but to witness it all, first-hand, every bloody day.

One of the many stories I told him was about an intensive-care nurse who was at the pinnacle of her career. Usually, she'd have just one seriously-ill individual to look after, and the nature of her job meant that the intensive one-to-one support and care she provided was always to an exceptionally high and exemplary standard. The day I talked with her she was exhausted, both mentally and physically, and had been for far too long. She'd been pushing her hours way beyond what a normal nurse should do and, in truth, far beyond what was safe. Not only was she working in an environment where a relatively unknown virus, on which there was too little data, was killing the patients in her care, but she now had several patients a day, coming in repeatedly one after the other. To top this all off, she had to do her job wearing full, restrictive PPE, knowing the psychological effect this would have on her patients, but never knowing when she'd contract the sickness from one of them, whether or not she'd take it home to her family, and if she'd become another statistic in intensive care herself. When this happens, who's left to care for the carers?

Mick kept silent during my passionate tirade, and just sat, deep in thought, staring at his pint. When I'd finished, he simply asked me, "Bro, the military know where they can get help, but what's there for the NHS frontline?" Sadly, I said that there was very little support, because this is what everyone now demanded of them. And like a regularly beaten child, this was their normality which they'd learned to expect each day.

That conversation was how the 'Surviving Minds Foundation' got started.

Chapter 32

2021

Mental Health

With the idea firmly planted in our grey matter, we needed a natural location for our wellbeing experience. I contacted an old friend, Richard Frampton-Hobbs, a retired colonel, and explained our plans and reasons for these wellbeing sessions, including the potential clientele. Richard not only owned a large estate in Dorset, but was also incredibly supportive of the local community, and asked us to leave it with him to think of a suitable location. This was a great start because we knew that, without his support, our project would stall at the first hurdle.

A few days later, and redolent of a top-secret military operation, Richard provided us with a time to meet and a set of map coordinates. We really shouldn't have expected anything less of him, so Mick and I did our homework and ensured that we were both there in the right place at the right time to meet him. Well, what happened next left us both gobsmacked. Far from the small, out-of-the-way copse of trees that we expected, we were astonished to be introduced to Marl Pits Wood, 25 acres of ancient woodland with access from the main road, which would be ours to use for as long as we wanted – on the sole proviso that we respected the land. The three of us took our time as we walked through the wood, viewing scene after scene of outstanding natural beauty. The woodland had been allowed to overgrow, but over several days and nights Mick and I stayed there, camping in the belly of a Roman clay pit, and transforming it so that our guests could share the area with the local wildlife.

We cleared a suitable patch, and cut back the overhanging willow trees – thus allowing other trees to grow, and the willows to grow straight again. We used the branches to make windbreaks around the central campfire and kept the wands for our woodcraft projects later. But while these are practical, bushcraft skills, we wanted to go deeper to help our guests get an idea of the bigger picture around us all. I just wish that I'd started my research sooner.

I learned from Mick, who'd learned it from a Herefordshire woodsman, that the holly tree shares its kingship of the forest with the oak, alternating responsibility with each solstice. Even its name means 'holy'. The Romans deliberately planted them to stop evil spirits from entering their properties, and in medieval times their branches were used to ward off witches and demons. Holly wreaths would be hung on doors, before burning them in their gardens later on to let the smoke surround the house – again, to repel evil spirits. Holly trees were also planted for protection against lightning strikes, and we now know that the spines of holly leaves act as miniature lightning conductors, thus taking the brunt of one of Nature's most destructive forces upon itself to preserve not only the tree, but also the lives of all those nearby creatures who depended on its protection. Not surprisingly, in the face of such majesty, traditional woodlore is that you always request permission from the fairies who live in holly trees before cutting one down, or doing any kind of work on them – even if it's remedial. When Mick and I started tidying the wood, I never asked such permission of a holly tree to prune it with a machete. Well – and I still don't know how it happened – I lost focus for an instant, the handle slipped in my grip, and the blade sliced straight into my left thumb midway between the joints, severing the tendon, and resulting in a hasty drive to the hospital, followed by an urgent and thoroughly unplanned operation.

Our ancestors two thousand years ago didn't have the science we do now. Instead, they had very different skillsets, based on the experiences, customs, and understandings of their day. For the life of me, I wish I'd paid heed to them.

Anyway, we persevered with our goal, the hard work paid off, and soon we had a safe, enclosed location with a parachute awning, an eco-friendly composting toilet, and tree stumps positioned for seating, all staged around a communal area underneath the protective canopy of the 'chute.

We put the word out to our friends in the media industry, explaining that our course was based around Shinrin-yoku – the Japanese way of forest bathing – and learning practical, ancient woodland skills which, unless you're into scouting or soldiering, have all but died out. Within a year the Surviving Minds Foundation had become a complete success, helping over a thousand people – including many NHS staff – to reconnect with Nature.

If you ever start a conversation on the topic of 'Physical Health', it'll be upbeat, everyone will join in, and either listen or have something to say. Start a talk on 'Mental Health', however, and watch how quickly everyone shuts up, and then down. That's how bad things are, yet no one wants to talk about it. But 3,000 centuries of human evolution haven't eliminated our primal need to gather together in the evening under shelter around a communal campfire, telling stories, and unwinding after a difficult day.

It became incredibly gratifying to see physically and mentally exhausted NHS staff joining in the program and, throughout the day, seeing them relaxed and laughing, along with the overwhelming gratitude they gave us at the end of the session. My thumb became a constant source of amusement, quite literally sticking out from its sling like the proverbial. It was the perfect ice-breaker for our new healthcare clients, allowing me to explain what had happened, why it had occurred, and why I was such a bloody hypocrite!

Just one day in the woods is enough to undo what a month of stress has done to you, and we emphasised this in the podcasts we created and the magazine interviews we gave. We still run courses in our small patch of natural heaven, so if you ever want to learn about the magic of ancient woodlands, the benefits of phytoncides, or backwoods cooking over a log campfire, then feel free to join in.

> "That small patch of natural heaven was just what we needed. Working in a staff wellbeing service for social care and health staff in the pandemic gave me a deep

insight into these workers' lives: the added stress of the pandemic, relentless demand, and a feeling of helplessness as they could not give their best care due to restrictions of time, personnel, and infection-control practises. Stress is heightened when faced with the unknown, when so much is beyond our control – and we tend to catastrophise and lose perspective. These workers' dedication to their residents in care homes, and to their patients or clients, meant that they prioritised their care over their own wellbeing. I knew that these workers tend to go above and beyond caring for others, including their own family and friends, but this just magnified it.

SMF gave us an opportunity to offer some time to teams or individual workers to find space for themselves, to reflect away from the demands of their lives, to recuperate – either together or as a team – to connect and strengthen mutual support, and to generate ideas to ease their stress when they left the woods. Wayne and Mick reconnected us to the wonders of nature, instilling a sense of calm and hope, giving back perspective, and teaching us to appreciate the simple, available, and often overlooked ways of de-stressing. Best of all, these experiences are sustainable, and can be easily replicated beyond our work."

Laila Jamil BA MA MSc CPsychol.
Co-chair Division of Clinical Psychology.
SW of the British Psychological Society.
Senior Clinical Psychologist (in the former Staff Wellbeing Hub funded by NHS England).

"My background is 15 years in the fitness industry as a personal trainer, with many qualifications around it such as Level 4 Mental Health, GP Referral, Pilates, Yoga and many more. But before this time, it was office-based secretarial work and finance so, post-lockdown, whilst the fitness industry was still struggling to get back on its feet, I went to work part-time for my local GP surgery as a receptionist, and assisted with the administration of Covid clinics.

Following this and, together with my background, I got offered the position of Health and Wellbeing Coach for Dorset District Healthcare, and my first placement was being sent to the forest to assist Wayne and Mick to basically introduce the service that I was working for, such as access to Counselling, Physiotherapy and Psychotherapy – a service that was solely for NHS staff and Council staff. This was my dream job! I met with people from all over Dorset, all of whom had so many different experiences of lockdown – whether that be working in nursing, on emergency wards, or IT departments. Some people were so stressed from working endless hours on the wards, and others had been isolated for so long, that their mental health was really suffering, but then… the forest was there!

I was there to signpost them, and Wayne and Mick were there, the most admirable souls, having come from a military background with issues of their own, which they happily shared with the groups. People cried, laughed, hugged, made fires, relaxed in hammocks, toasted marshmallows, talked to others, and opened up about their mental health… and the best experience, I feel, was breathing the forest, touching the trees, listening to the wind and, if they were lucky enough, spotting an occasional deer!

I will never forget my experience in the forest with Wayne and Mick – and for the record, the injury that Wayne endured was merely a paper cut!!!"

Deborah Jones

Chapter 33

2022

The Walk

In 2019 I made a promise to Freya – to stage a fundraising event to help raise awareness of scoliosis. During that time Covid got in the way, like it did with everything else, but I always keep my promises. With several charity campaigns already under my belt, I was aware that for any chance of raising money, this campaign needed to be different, and physically connected with the spine and back.

So, again sat drinking a pint with Mick *we're not always in the pub!* I told him my plan – to walk from Portland, where Freya was diagnosed, to Southampton, where she had her operation. Effectively from Dorset to Hampshire. His immediate response was a derogatory reference to my buggered-up ankle, which I chose to ignore. I already knew it'd be difficult and didn't need him reminding me. I continued unabated, and told him that I'd be making the entire journey walking backwards. Mick promptly choked into his pint and then almost pissed himself laughing, before saying that he'd be joining me just to keep a note of how many times I fell over for the Guinness Book of Records! In my condition, did I actually understand the sheer impossibility of what I was suggesting? In all honesty, I probably didn't, but even I knew that I'd need someone walking alongside me, correcting my course, and pointing out the hazards en route. The moment I accepted his kind offer, he went straight into training mode, telling me which of my leg and back muscles would be affected, the training programme I'd need to do, and how fit I'd need to be before starting, to have even a hope in hell's chance of finishing.

It must be said, at this point, that I was then in my early fifties, over two decades past my prime, and registered 'Disabled' – a label I hate with a vengeance. Armed with my medical data, any health professional would conclude that this campaign was not only woefully ill-advised, and would be extremely painful to the point of serious injury, but it bore the severe possibility of long-term catastrophic effects on my future mobility. As such, nobody could sanction the campaign as they did with the Life Raft Challenge, and if anything broke, or suffered permanent damage, then I was on my own. Well, I have just one thing to say about that – this is just a small sample of what it's like for children with scoliosis, and their parents.

Mick was fully aware of this, and all those who served under him will remember his training schedules as a series of beasting sessions, one on top of the other. One time in Bosnia, we had one of his training sessions at the troop house, inside a disused and battered basketball court. Nine soldiers being pushed to their absolute physical limits brought out the locals to watch and, at the end, one of them dared to ask him what they'd done to deserve such punishment. Mick gave him a look, and told him, "Nothing! These are British soldiers, this is how we train, and my job's to make sure they stay fit..."

Officially titled 'Let's Reverse This Together', the campaign was planned to run for five days, covering around 15 miles a day from Monday to Friday, 11-15 April. We'd walk throughout the day, predominantly on A and B roads, with footpaths where we could, and stopping at pre-planned pubs and hotels along the way at night – all generously donated in advance by their proprietors. The route, according to the map, measured 70.6 miles, though the actual distance we covered became 77 miles due to necessary detours, and sometimes going off-route while chatting with people.

As things turned out, Mick had been spot-on from the onset – it was far more bloody difficult than I'd imagined. I couldn't even complete the training course he'd insisted on, because as soon as I started my knackered ankle began to play up, with the usual swelling and crunching sounds that went with the injury. I didn't mind, because the entire intention of the exercise was to make it as painful as possible for me. What I hadn't expected was just how easily, quickly, and intensely this could be achieved.

Unwilling to renege on a promise, and remembering the pain and bravery shown by Freya and all the other children on her ward, on Monday 11 April 2022 Mick and I set off on our eastward journey. I soon learned that he was absolutely crucial to the entire event, and without him I wouldn't have been able to go on. To understand why, try walking backwards over any distance and see what happens.

The human body was designed, and evolved, to walk forwards – in the same direction as everything else on your body points. Normally, the direction of momentum of your body mass works in harmony with your muscles and tendons to create the fluid motion known as 'walking'. Do this backwards, however, and with every step you're fighting your own weight. Muscles you didn't know you had start to hurt. Your walking stance changes out of necessity, to the extent that, by the end of the campaign, the new pair of boots I'd bought had worn out at the toes!

My doctor prescribes codeine phosphate for my ankle, and I'd brought loads. But pretty soon I was having to buy more paracetamol and ibuprofen to replace the quantity I'd packed, because I was already getting through the maximum amount allowable within any given time period. But even with this chemical diet, with every step I took my ankle felt as if a red-hot blade had been embedded in the joint. Even worse, although the human mind is capable of coping with excruciating amounts of pain, it's there for a reason – usually to tell you to 'Please stop that!' or 'I need help!' in order to protect the body's self-healing mechanics – so you can't avoid thinking how much permanent and irrevocable damage you're doing.

But let's keep it positive. This was nothing to the pain experienced by the children who'd had their spines cut open and drilled in the scoliosis ward. What kept me going was the thought that, for each searing step I took, I'd be helping a child who'd be going through far, far worse.

As with everyone who finds their life irretrievably changed, your brain, body, and cognitive abilities adapt to the task in hand, and you find new ways of doing things. It's always difficult to start with and, until it becomes third nature, all you can do is keep putting one foot in front of the other. Well, over those five days, my sole focus was to keeping putting one behind the other. You feel it in the lower thighs first, as your body adapts to a new means of perambulation whereby your toes replace your heels to propel yourself backwards. You then wish that, like your wife, you had eyes in the back of your head, and that your ears could swivel 180°. Next, you start to establish a cadence, and you learn to trust your companion. You actually develop an uncanny awareness sense of what's coming next, without seeing it. Mick and I quickly became attuned to each other and, very soon, little in the way of communication was needed between us to know what lay behind me.

Ironically, once I'd got started properly the pain began to lessen, though the moment I stopped, the swelling and pain would return – and I'm putting this down to my body being in 'survival mode'. Mick noticed that, under the uncommon walking conditions, my fused right ankle was actually forcing my toes downwards into the toecap of my boot, which explained why it was getting steadily more worn at the front than the left one!

Numerous memories were created along our journey, including the guy living on the streets putting his last £1.56 into our pot, and the lady who called me over to her blue van as we sat resting on a main road through Bournemouth, to ask what I was doing. As often happened throughout the journey, I walked backwards across to her to explain the incongruity of what she was witnessing. Amazed at what we were doing, she said that she wanted to give us some money, and started a crazed search throughout every pocket she had. Just as she was going through the last one, she apologised, remembering that she'd put it in her sock. Reaching down, she pulled out a banknote which had clearly been folded and unfolded many times before. It was as she opened the last fold, I noticed the white powder within, which prompted her to ask if I'd like a little 'C' to help me along my way? Laughing, I told her, "Thanks, but no thanks, sweetheart." She just shrugged, poured the drugs into another piece of paper then, wishing us luck, handed me the well-used banknote. Well, that tenner is probably still in circulation with 'C' residue on it...You never know what Class A substances you could be carrying in your pocket!

One thing we did learn on the walk was the large number of people who approached us to say that they either had, or knew of someone who'd been affected by, this supposedly little-known condition. Research at the time indicated that scoliosis affected four out of every thousand children in the UK. But from the sheer number of those who shared their stories with us, Mick and I are certain that this figure should be a lot higher.

It was sheer joy to have my wife and daughters join us for the last 10-mile stretch, and to take us home afterwards. In total we raised over £10,400 which was split between the two scoliosis charities. In answer to media questions:

Was it hard? Yes. It was meant to be...

Did it hurt? Absolutely. I lost the toenails adjacent to the inner and outermost toes on each foot, mirrored on both feet. My right ankle swelled up black and blue each night, and for several days after the event – during which times I needed to keep it raised, and stay on the painkillers.

Did you fall over? Yes, but only once, as we approached the finish line at the hospital *bloody typical!*

How was returning to normal walking? Shocking. The worst pain I've ever experienced.

What was the verdict on your ankle afterwards? I didn't get it checked professionally. I know I should have done, but I was too scared to find out. Remember, this was a simulation of what a scoliosis victim goes through.

Was it worth it? Yes, it was – and I'd bloody well do it again.

Postscript

In 2023 Freya passed her GCSE exams, achieving all the grades she needed to attend a college where she is studying Biology, Physics and Chemistry, the stepping stone to her dream career as a marine biologist.

As stated at the front of this book, all royalties from its sale will go to good causes around the world, including Scoliosis Support & Research, to discover what causes the deformity, how to prevent it, and avoid others from going through what we did
https:/ www.ssr.org.uk

Chapter 34

1993–2023

Mental Injury

A broken ankle is not an illness.
Neither is a bullet wound, nor a concussive blow to the head.
These are all injuries.

Though if not treated soon enough, an illness will follow – and often for the rest of your life.

So, when the British Army states that no soldier has ever left the service with a mental illness, they are absolutely correct
Because it comes later…

The year is 2024, and I'm adding my final notes to this book for my editor. Most of it was fun, and it was wonderful to hear from so many people across the world after reconnecting with them for their recollections. Wherever possible I've used their full and correct names, but where I couldn't gain permission due to a failure in communication, or the person said no for their own good reasons, I've had to improvise to fill the gaps. Thankfully these are few, as most of my former contacts were more than happy to be associated with this literary fundraising campaign.

Before we discuss the dreaded subject of PTSD, I need to say that I sat for several weeks, my mind and notebook blank, trying to pluck up courage to write the next few pages. This chapter has been, by far, the most difficult for me to recall, let alone write.

My PTSD, my personal traumatic stress demon, has always been the one thing of which I was repeatedly ashamed. Now, in putting myself on the line as never before, and having read it over and over again, I can honestly say that a huge weight has been lifted from my shoulders by doing so. If honest, I never knew why I suffered the symptoms, and have always been embarrassed to admit that war affected me in this way at all. I still watch, with pride, admiration, and respect, documentaries of our forefathers retelling how they stormed off a landing craft in June 1944 to retake Europe from the enemy's grasp, knowing that, the very second the armoured landing ramp was lowered, a fiery stream of red-hot lead would attempt to stop them from reaching the shore at all costs.

Then there's the imagery of our Tommies going over their trench walls during the Great War, knowing that most of them would be dead or fatally wounded within seconds of leaving safety, their lives taken by concealed enemy fire – but if just a few could get through, then the tide of that war could be changed. The term 'Great War' does not mean that WWI was wonderful, nor that one should look back at it with fondness – not by any means imaginable. As with 'The Great Flood' the word simply signifies the sheer scale of the bloody conflict, death count, and misery inflicted worldwide.

No, there is nothing whatsoever 'great' about war itself – just the opposite, in fact – and as I advance in age then so does my conviction of this. But at the same time, I can understand the convictions of the day – the selfless willingness of countless individuals to make the world a better place – and know that had I been in their place, at any point in history, I'd have done exactly the same thing.

I'd always thought I was strong in both mind and body. I've never turned away from danger, from when something needed to be done, nor from a fight. I've even instigated the latter, to my eternal shame. But I've learned that there's no rhyme nor reason as to why some people experience PTSD, while others can see the same things and be okay. I've also learned, from talking with many seasoned professionals, that it has nothing at all to do with being cowardly, afraid, or weak-willed, and have since come to understand that each person's brain is wired as individually as their finger and tongue prints, ear shape, body scent, and DNA.

My own PTSD has been officially attributed to my traumas as a soldier, with the trigger point being the bomb in Belfast, 21 Sept 1993 – a full fifteen years before it was officially diagnosed. Because I didn't realise there was a problem at the time, I never dealt with it, nor had it treated. Since then, some of the things I've seen as a paramedic have added their own ingredients to the roiling brew, and the internal blockage had caused the pressure to keep building. But we'll come to that later, because first I need to explain how it all links together.

Let's start with basic military training – the process of converting a civilian into a soldier. When I joined, back in 1986, this was different from the basic training of today's military. The world changes, people change, and I can guarantee that my training was very different from when my grandfathers enlisted!

I was an immature 17-year-old boy – and there was no way I could have classed myself as a man. There was nothing on my chin worth shaving, and by law I wasn't even allowed to enter a pub, let alone get a drink. Although I was never mollycoddled at home, and always had plenty of freedom, it was still the first time I'd ever been away from my family.

I thoroughly enjoyed basic training as I'd always wanted to join the Army, and although I never witnessed any bullying per se, we were still shouted and sworn at every single day. This was called 'character building' and was used by the military to turn raw recruits into warriors capable of going to war, fighting, and killing when necessary. This is why constant aggression was used in our training. Aggression which, we were taught, could be quickly turned on or off by either a rapid culmination of events, or a single word.

The inevitable always happens, and there comes a time in every soldier's life when he must experience violent and lethal conflict. My first war was in Northern Ireland, and this is where I know the problems started.

The military doesn't wake up one morning and decide to send a regiment to war that day. There are the occasional extreme circumstances where a deployment may be extremely rapid but, for most of the time, sending a force to a conflict zone will have been planned for many months or even years before. Before any British soldier lays a foot on foreign soil, months of training will be spent covering a range of different scenarios prior to the forthcoming tour. Physical exercise would increase, to ensure that each soldier is as fit as possible. There'll be increased firing on the ranges, and one technical exercise after another to ensure that each and every basic and advanced skill is honed to give the greatest chance of collective mission success.

There'll be countless presentations on what could happen while out there, and these were often presented by experienced officers from the unit we'd be replacing, to give us the lie of the land, and know what to expect. These would always cover worst-case scenarios, like the results of an exploding culvert bomb, or the devastating use of .50 calibre sniper rifles – to randomly pick off British troops undetected.

Then there was Tin City, a purpose-built training village in Sennelager, Germany that had been constructed to represent different areas of Northern Ireland. The squadron being deployed would spend a week living in these makeshift suburbs carrying out daily foot or mobile patrols, and in 99% of them there'd be a shoot against your patrol, an IED would go off, or you'd encounter violent crowd trouble. It was your job to deal with each different scenario, with a debriefing afterwards.

The final day would always involve you in a riot, with another regiment providing the rowdy element, or civilian population (CivPop). This was always supposed to be monitored by Tin City staff, who also threw petrol bombs at your feet to get you used to the heat and flames on the other side of your shield. *NOTE: In reality, nobody ever throws them at your feet. They're thrown to come over your shield, so that you're showered and spattered with fiery fuel. Which is why our 'shield-and-baton' riot control troops always had guys backing us up with fire extinguishers.*

As you can imagine, with no live-fire allowed, these simulated battles became free-for-alls, creating a perfect environment for you to settle personal scores – and for others to settle them with you – so real kicks and punches would land, and plastic bricks would be thrown to inflict as much real-world damage as possible. *NOTE: Plastic bricks do not inflict anywhere near the same flat, corner, and edge damage as real bricks, and you really don't want to be in the path of one thrown in anger.* But it wasn't just bricks. The reality is that everything was used against us. If it wasn't bolted down, then it'd be thrown at us. The worst of all are broken roof slates because, regardless of size or shape, they fly like frisbees, they have an exceedingly low profile, and – especially at night – you can't see them incoming at your face.

With your aggression already simmering as your tour of duty approached, you'd be fed with daily intelligence briefs pertaining to what had occurred in your intended battle zone, and the whole of Northern Ireland, over the previous 48 hours. Some poor sod – soldier or civvy – had been killed or injured in an attack, a bomb had exploded underneath a vehicle causing so much ground-level damage, and numerous other examples of violent hatred – as already covered in the earlier chapters of this book – will have been inflicted on others.

So, prepared for the worst, but with eternal optimism, you'd be sent to War, knowing that as soon as you arrived in-country you were a target. With your adrenaline already surging like a petrol pump, you'd deploy immediately to your given location to spend six months awaiting your turn for the bullet or bomb to get you. You've already read my story, and I was no-one special. Now multiply that by every serviceman and woman – because you'll know by now that women were not spared – and that was the feedback you'd get every single day. And whether it happened or not, you're always expecting it any... second... now... and it becomes totally impossible to switch off...

By definition, it simply isn't possible to relax in a war zone, and each new day – if you've survived it – immense stress is imposed upon your mental health. When you think about it, if humans evolved – or were designed – for war, then we wouldn't have skin as supremely sensitive to the touch as we do now. We'd have armoured carapaces like beetles, and our minds wouldn't be as finely attuned to love, beauty, art, music, culture, and each other. There'd be none of that. Pure survival would be programmed into our every sense, reflex, and action, and passed on through our DNA to the next generation. It wouldn't be much of a life, and it sounds like everything that most of us have been trying to move away from for hundreds of millennia. Our human sensibilities are simply not equipped for the kind of horror you experience in war and, although you could try going to the gym to bash the weights, military bases house the only gymnasia in the world where your body armour, helmet, and rifle need to be constantly within arm's reach – because you're always mentally alert for an assault on your camp by either a force majeure, or an inbound rocket/mortar attack.

As part of the UK, Northern Ireland is an unusual place in which to believe that people are being killed, and want to kill you, which is why the daily Northern Ireland Report, (NI-REP) always kept us informed of the previous day's atrocities. But the streets that you patrol look exactly like the streets at home – the same high street shops carrying the same brands, the same cars which drive on the same side of the road, the same kind of people who speak the same language. It's not even as if you're a thousand miles away in a British colony – and it's this dichotomy that creates a massive sense of mis-identity and dislocation.

As I understood it from my counsellor Jinny, at the exact second that the improvised grenade went off, taking the car and my friend Jamie with it, my fight-or-flight mode went into overdrive, trying to simultaneously process thousands of pieces of sensory data to make sense of what had just occurred. This caused a massive rush of adrenaline and neurochemicals to my brain, causing an overload, and the event to lodge inextricably in my amygdala without having been fully processed and understood.

A neural image – a sensory snapshot – of the event would be created as a memory, so that it wouldn't be forgotten, and filed away for later processing, replaying it over and over in an endless loop from start to end inside the emotional side of my brain – the part disconnected from reasoning and cognitive processing. In practical terms, the lid on the cooker had now been sealed until the job was done, and anything and everything that came in afterwards would need to wait, stacking up on the pile, and adding to the head of pressure.

As when the death of a loved one presses 'Pause' on your life – though it actually feels like 'Stop' or even 'Eject'- a new, darker normal comes into existence, as you're forced to focus on the necessities of Now. I've read that bereavement time is roughly 10% of the time you spent together. Personally, I'd raise that figure substantially. It can take over a year to sort out a deceased partner's affairs. Only then can you start thinking of pressing 'Play' once more, and getting around to everything that's built up on your To Do list in the meantime

What I couldn't fathom was that, following the bomb, I was still feeling, seeing, hearing, and smelling the memory – no matter how tightly I shut my eyes and covered my ears. And then I was sent off for R&R, with a short flight taking me straight from full body armour, helmet, and rifle at the ready, scanning every open window for movement, while avoiding suspicious boxes lying in the street, to another place called 'home' where everything looked and sounded exactly the same!

It's like being in a nightmare that constitutes your entire existence, fully indistinguishable from reality until you actually wake up, and impossible to switch off manually while you're within it. No wonder I became a silent, nervous wreck, unable to discuss it with anyone. Who could possibly understand? This is why you hear of family members going off to war, and coming back a different person, with their own internal battles, and who 'never talked of it'. Because you can't, unless it's to someone who's had the same experience. That's why the Royal British Legion clubs have been around since 1921.

During one R&R period I was in my bedroom playing a computer game. My dad, who had obviously missed me, came in to stand near me, chew some gum, and just watch me play. But to my heightened senses this figure standing over my shoulder constituted a threat, and his relaxed chewing became increasingly aggressive. Before I knew what had happened, I'd turned and snapped at him, shouting at him to stop fucking chewing so fucking loudly, and to get the fucking hell out of my fucking room!!!

It didn't stop there. I transformed into a full-time, hyper-aggressive, belligerent arsehole, spoiling for a fight with anyone who dared look at me wrongly or answer back. The only way I got any kind of comfort was in the dark and bawdy humour of the barrack-room, back with my mates in NI, many of whom *I realise now* were going through the same thing. My mind had become like my ankle, a cracked and broken state of new normal, and *I didn't realise then* I was going to stay like this until I finally received help.

Unfortunately, at the time, it was never offered, because its need wasn't yet recognised. If you'd told anyone then that you might have a 'mental health' problem, you'd have been reported as unreliable, your weapon confiscated in case you were a danger to others, and RTU'd until you were deemed fit enough to carry it again.

Although our tour in Ireland had ended in January 1994, I had to reluctantly return to Belfast Crown Court in 1995. One of our guys was being tried for the attempted murder of a known IRA operative, at the wake of one of the terrorists who'd killed nine civilians (including two children) blast at Frizzell's fish shop on Shankill Road, but had also died when his device exploded prematurely. I wasn't in the Doyne at the time of the shooting, but the vehicle commander told me later on what had happened.

They'd passed a gathering outside the house of the dead terrorist and, unbeknown to him, the trooper on top cover was exchanging confrontational words with the guy. The Snatch Land Rover went around the block and, once more, pulled up near the house, where the trooper and the guy continued to exchange harsh words. But this time, the trooper effectively told him "If you don't shut the fuck up, I'll fucking shoot you…"

Again, the Snatch went around the block, the local guy started gobbing off again and, true to his word, the trooper drew his SA80 and, on full auto, emptied a mag of 5.56mm rounds at him, hitting him several times. The commander at the time said that he immediately called in a contact report, before realising that he wasn't on the receiving end of the fire. At the back of the vehicle, he found the trooper in the act of reloading his rifle. The commander promptly asked him to relinquish his weapon, which he did without question, and they returned to camp where the trooper was put under arrest.

The night this took place, Dom and I were on guard duty together. A trooper on the front gate came to the guardroom window and informed us that there were several guys outside with a present for the trooper. Dom and I went to speak with them, and learned that they were Protestants and members of the UFF – the Ulster Freedom Fighters. They gave us a bunch of flowers, and a card which had been signed by all the Protestant inmates incarcerated within the Maze prison. We told them that we'd pass it onto the relevant people, closed the gate, then dropped it off with the int department.

Trooper AC was found guilty of the shooting and sentenced to ten years. As a member of the same regiment, I could go down to the cells and have a quick chat with him. He was very calm about his sentence. We chatted about nothing for several minutes, before he told me he was going to ask to stay in the Maze, since he already knew he'd be treated like a hero. We said our goodbyes, he gave me his regimental tie, and we parted ways. That was the last I heard of him, and I don't know if he completed his full sentence, or was released as part of the Good Friday Agreement.

This was the reality back then, and no soldier in his right mind (ha!) wanted it to happen to them. Nowadays, if you go into any hospital reception, you'll see posters advising that, if you're a veteran of the armed forces, then you're eligible for mental health and well-being checks and support – even if you'd only served for a day! Back then, as a soldier, you just shut up about it, because that would have been an admission of weakness and incompetence in front of your mates and superior officers. This is why I shall be eternally grateful to little Stefan, who bravely showed me a new, unknown, and very welcome side of myself that I'd not even known existed.

Every traumatic event I witnessed in the military became another ingredient in the pot. And then came the ambulance service. It's pretty much a given, being a paramedic, that you'll encounter death at some point. Some are lucky, and rarely see anything really bad, whereas others seem to be shit magnets. Earlier, I said that I'd acquired the nickname 'Shipman' due to the sheer number of people who ended up dead on my watch. This wasn't normal, and maybe it was the bike that connected me to these critical callouts. All I know is that I went through a spate of really horrible assignments – and here's an example:

At around 2pm I received news of a road traffic collision, on a fast stretch of road where a dual-carriageway merged into a single lane. The torrential rain was 'accident weather', and I was manning a response vehicle. Back then, paramedics usually arrived before the police, and I was greeted by an older design of car embedded in the front of a lorry. It had crossed the carriageway and hit the lorry head-on at speed, resulting in the car's engine being rammed backwards into the driver's compartment. I couldn't find the lower half of the body, which had been replaced by everything from under the bonnet. There was no carotid pulse and, combined with the massive lower-body trauma, it was clear that the driver had died quickly. I turned to walk away, and see if anyone else needed help, when I noticed on the back seat the bottom part of a child's seat, into which the main part would slot. Without knowing why, I looked away from the accident and further along the road, behind the lorry. Initially I couldn't comprehend what I was seeing, but it slowly dawned on me that what looked like a rubbish bag lying in the road, about 75 metres away, was a small child still strapped into her seat. The impact had jettisoned her head-first, straight through the shattered windscreen, past the lorry, to bounce and skitter along the road way ahead of the car, before finally coming to rest on the carriageway (the road was empty as the traffic had been forced to stop). I'd never in my life sprinted as fast as I did to this little bundle, but another ambulance had just arrived, and together we carefully lifted her, still in her safety seat, into the back where we started medical treatment. The child was in cardiac arrest, but we couldn't risk removing her from her seat in case of neck injury, so we started CPR from any position we could. I don't think I'd ever been so focused on giving emergency treatment before, putting my heart, body, and soul into bringing this little girl back to life until we'd finally got ROSC (return of spontaneous circulation), a steady pulse, her breathing stable with a bag & mask, and an I/O needle into her leg for handing her over to the air ambulance. As it lifted off for

Dorchester Hospital, all I wanted now was to be alone, get back to my truck, and cry. I've never made a secret of finding children's illness and death difficult, and can only put this down to being a father.

I'd just walked past the collision point, where the lorry driver was being treated for shock, when a female police officer informed me of another child who'd been hurt from the same car, and presented me with the slightly older brother of the girl I'd just treated. How the hell he'd escaped with just one small scratch on his neck is beyond me, but I gave him a cheerful smile and applied a single plaster – and at that instant he reached out and threw his arms around me. An expert in the field of fatherly hugs, I knew from the vice-like grip he exerted he had absolutely no intention of letting go anytime soon. The boy was about six, and just wanted to feel safe after the emotional trauma he'd just experienced, with the *worst still to come...* so I found myself sitting on his stretcher in the back of the ambulance, while the police followed in my vehicle, cuddling this little stranger as the crew drove us back to hospital. I sang nursery rhymes with him, trying to make him feel safe, and direct his mind from what had just happened – while inwardly wishing he could go off with someone else, so I could just get the hell away from it all myself. I stayed with him in the children's ward until around 8pm several hours after my shift was up, simply because he refused to leave my side. He let go only when his mother arrived – still holding the teddy bear that she'd brought for her daughter – and bearing the news that they'd just switched off her life support. The look of sheer devastation on her face, and the way she clung onto the only surviving member of her family, told me that their lives had been changed forever – so I crept away, broken-hearted, to let them grieve. I managed to keep it together until I was alone inside my response car, before pouring out all the pent-up emotion of the previous six hours.

This was just one of many traumatic deaths I witnessed in the ambulance service, and each one added to the emotional pile-up. Bear in mind that I'd not come into the job with a clean slate, but from the military – pre-loaded, pre-cocked, and with the pressure increasing on the trigger. Which is why, in the early hours of that morning, I woke up in the dark with severe chest pains.

Soldier of Conscience: From Fighting the IRA to Battling PTSD

For me, PTSD has not fully gone away. I still have the odd wobbly moments, but these are thankfully getting fewer and farther between. Cara knows intuitively when things are getting difficult, and is always there for me – but even though I'm still off and on the antidepressants, I'm now writing things I've never spoken of before.

The one thing which still hurts, to this day, was the final event at Bovington on my discharge. Being billed for my PT kit was a kick in the balls for starters, but the last strand of dignity I held onto was severed by a lad who was still in nappies when I arrived at Catterick to start my basic training. There was no senior officer present, representing Her Majesty. No thanks for a life of service to my country. No appreciation for a job well done. There was no gravitas whatsoever. No sense of awareness nor understanding of what the word 'honour' actually means to a soldier. All you get, in the end, is the equivalent of a cheap, unsigned 'Thank you for your service' gift card. Even worse, there's not even a name on the card. Just a serial number. So, is it really of any surprise that our veterans, of every war that's ever been fought, feel dishonoured, let down, and neglected? And that, to those who have served, this ignominious act – this single cut – can feel like castration of the heart?

In the Scouts Association, senior volunteers receive 40, 50, 60, and even 70-year service awards at annual presentations, to honour their lifetime (so far) in public service – and it always feels wonderful to attend one of these, to see such outstanding and exemplary individuals still giving their all.

Surrounded by sensory devastation #24794746 can still see his friend #******** lying on his back in a Belfast street, and will forever try to stem the eternal bleeding from his horrific leg wound. He will never staunch the internal bleeding of his own soul, inflicted by the hatred of those who stand watching, as he still tries to save them all. He'll be constantly shot at on the Crumlin Road. He'll continue to watch, count, and smell the never-ending bodies being exhumed from the mass graves of Bosnia. To combat all this, he'll spend his memories in nights of drunken indulgence, laughing and joking with his brothers in arms and heart, whose collective job it is to clean up every squalid mess in the world, and try to prevent it from ever happening again.

Would he do it all again? Yes, because he firmly believes that the Army is an amazing place for young men and women, where they'll meet the best friends of their lives and have no end of adventures. Would he do things differently? Of course, but everybody says that about everything, and how else would you learn or improve anything without experience? But to senior officers, please do not treat your soldiers – your staff – as they were treated in the past, because the past is rarely a good example for the future. If you do that then you'll destroy them and, though you may know them only as a number, they're numbers who have served their monarch, their country, and you – with diligence, dignity, and devotion to duty.

And not just those in the military. The NHS is currently haemorrhaging money because their staff are leaving in droves due to stress and burnout. The average job expectancy of a trained paramedic is just five years, the point at which they simply cannot take any more. This is why staffing agencies and 'bank workers' – contractors like myself – are being used as substitutes. But this is a reactive and not a reparative process, liken to an unsustainable consumerist society where you throw something away it when it breaks, or a newer model comes out, instead of looking after and fixing what you have. It's a terrible business model, and assumes a constant influx of human beings willing to become more cannon-fodder for the industrial machine.

To all those who employ passionate, enthusiastic, dedicated, and self-sacrificing workers, whether in the field of health care, youth care, community or pastoral care. Those whom, if looked after properly, would willingly give the best years of their lives for your cause. Please care for them, too, because they're the life blood, the acolytes, and the future teachers of your organisation. They should not be like the disposable vapes you see on the streets nowadays – discarded, burnt out, and empty.

When you think about it this way, you'll realise that it's a no-brainer, win-win-win situation, for your management, your staff, and your clients. Like putting your litter into a bin, instead of dropping it onto the floor, it takes a little more effort – but the cumulative result is better for everyone.

Chapter 35

2021

Respect, Reparation, and Recognition

They have lived lives of service
They have lost lives in service
They have left their loved ones to serve
They have been left unloved, fragile, and broken
They have upheld justice
They have secured freedom
They have maintained peace
They did not receive justice
They have lost their freedom
They will never feel peace
They have been fêted and honoured
They have been hated and profaned
We owe them everything we have
They ask for nothing but respect
They are not forgotten
They are forever remembered

Anon.

A Prayer of Remembrance

Heavenly Lord defend us from evil.
Vanquish all the devils.
We pray for peace and Mercy, Lord we call your name.
Repent our sins and set us free.
Lord help us. Lord graciously hear us.

Give thanks to those who made a sacrifice to our country.
Remember, Remember the 11th of November.
O' Lord we beg for your protection and defend those who served in honour.
Your peace and loyalty has got us to remember.
Lord help us. Lord graciously hear us.

Poppies grow to show the sacrifices that were made on the 11th hour of the 11th day of the 11th month.
Graciously we show our eternal thanks.
The soldiers layed their body for us.
Lord help us. Lord graciously hear us.
Lord help us. Lord graciously hear us.

Defend them day by day with your heavenly powers.
To protect the armed forces.
Your Justice and faith has got us to hear.
Bring peace again.
Lord help us. Lord graciously hear us. Amen

Lili Ingram: Age 11

Chapter 36

2021

Postscript

◇◇

In the 2021 Queen's birthday honours, Wayne Edward Ingram received the Member of the Most Excellent Order of the British Empire award for his notable services to charity worldwide

His only regret is that his headmaster wasn't there to witness it...

Dedication

2023

Not the end. Nowhere Near, in fact...

Before I end this book, I would like to say to all those people I have hurt, in any way, shape, or form, that I am extremely sorry – especially to my own family, friends and all the guys I served with, I realise now it must have been like being with a walking, talking minefield, never knowing where or when I'd explode. I am truly sorry.

To those who have stuck by me, I am eternally grateful – my parents Glenn and Brenda, my sister Karen, my wife Cara, my sons Harry and Toby, my daughters Freya and Lili, my ex-wife Tracy, my ever-supportive bro Mick, my Irish wolfhound Jonathon Brosnan, my friends Mark Vine, Andy Randell, Calvin Stone, and Steve Osborn – and my in-laws Doug and Babs, and sister in law Lois, for trusting this broken soldier with their sister.

I'd like to say a huge thank you to David Dunaway CBE for his phenomenal surgical skills, uncommon generosity, and enduring support. To Slava, Milos, Nada, and Dzejna for their unwavering trust in me, and embracing me into their family. To Stefan for being the toddler, boy, adolescent, and man who changed my life forever, and of course his wonderful wife Milijana.

And to Michael Stout for his incredible friendship and outstanding literary skills. Thanks must also be extended to Tara Moran and Harriet Fielding at Pen & Sword Books for allowing mine to be published. Thank you, Tara, for believing in me, and your constant encouragement while the book was in its early stages. Also, to Margaret Moran for not using any red pen!

I want to dedicate this book to my younger brother Tony (aka Tucker), who was sadly taken from us on 22 Sept 2009. Bro, I love you, and you are missed by us all every single day. Also, to my friends who have passed during the course of writing this book: Bob MacDonald, Aleric Harrison, Phil Marson, Neil Murray, Nick Wilby, Darren (Daz) Langston, and James Rickett – who were all taken from us far too early. All served their country, Queen, and King with excellence and unquestionable dedication. We'll see you, someday, on the great parade ground in the sky, for that eternal smoker. Stand easy, brothers!

To Damien Lewis for his friendship, support and direction in the world of publishing. To Chris Lawlor of Lawlor Marketing for his brilliant computing skills in making my website and social media look awesome. To Roger Barnes, our family's surrogate father, grandfather, and dog walker all rolled into one – and the most knowledgeable Portlander there is! And a massive thanks to Cara – my rock, my best mate, mum to our girls, and stepmum to the boys. The constant and loving support you've given me during the dark days will forever be remembered. xx YOU xx

Finally, my eternal gratitude goes out to the veterans of history who made the ultimate sacrifice – to shelter and protect us from the conflicts of war with their own bodies and minds.

Now here's where I'd customarily say – The End
                    But it isn't. Not by a long chalk…

As you'll know by now, after leaving the Army I struggled to find an alternative life path that, as a civilian, provided the same sense of fulfilment. The closest I ever came was on the response bike during ambulance service and, to a lesser extent, in the fire service. Even doing close-protection work as a medic in Iraq didn't quite cut it, although we all found it bloody funny watching the civvy contractors running around like headless chickens every time we received incoming fire, especially when we were sat nonchalantly eating in the cookhouse, or sunning ourselves on top of our mortar-hardened shelter!

Of course, I've changed and matured since then – but old habits still die hard. I recently received a proposition which ticks all the right boxes for me – and, I'm hoping, for others too. In Mato Grosso do Sul, Brazil, near the border of Paraguay, is the Pantanal – one of the most verdant and luxuriant wetlands in the world, and home to a panoply of exotic wildlife. Here is a privately-owned area of land with a 2.25 mile perimeter, its own valley, a natural stream-creating spring, and 35 acres of untouched ancient hardwood forest. It has a 3-phase electrical supply, and a submerged pump drawing pure, volcanically-filtered mineral water from 120m underground, which irrigates its 250m x 100m organic orchard adjacent to the main road. Moreover, much of the plant life here has been validated by a professional local botanist as being supportive of naturopathic healing. There's plenty of room for expansion, too, including buying surrounding land for planting trees. The owners don't want to sell it, because they know that nobody there buys land just to keep it as it is – and that creating a 'cattle run', between one piece of grazing land and another, means clearing a path a hundred metres wide! This is why they'd prefer to donate it to create a children's centre and ecological project, including an orphanage for unwanted children. This would be affiliated with the Scouts Association for their local and national activities, and to connect with the orphans of all age groups, from Squirrels, Beavers and Cubs, to Scouts, Explorers and Network Scouts – ensuring that these girls and boys are constantly supported throughout their growth to adulthood.

The greatest danger in this natural paradise comes, not from the four, six, eight, or multi-legged wildlife here, but from the two-legged predators who believe that any land that's not being cultivated, or stripped bare for cattle farming, is up for grabs by any squatter who comes across it and claims it as their own – often by violence, or at the point of a gun, against the legal owner who dares to challenge them. Hence the need to develop it on altruistic and ecological grounds, while highlighting the plight of the nation's homeless children. Working with local experts and international volunteers, I strongly believe that this template has the possibility of being replicated in countless developing countries worldwide.

So, if any production company wants to follow me here, exploring the territory and its potential, and learning from the local community – especially in the field of medical skills from Nature, then feel free to contact me via my website. Alternatively, to champion or explore any worthy cause for them – especially if it's for children – anywhere in the world.

Wayne

Bonus Page

2024

Afterthoughts

Well, that's it. Are you still here? Well, well done! If you've made it this far, then I sincerely thank you, and hope that you've enjoyed the ride. If you're looking for some bonus features, here are a few thoughts before we part ways for now.

You don't spend as much time as I have, staring at myself in a campfire, gazing up at an awe-inspiring night sky, seeing so many people in their worst state possible, and having so many others die in your arms, without drawing a few conclusions.

Regardless of the state of the world when you're born into it, and how it is now, your job is to make it better. Every time you help someone, if it's with the right motivation, then you make yourself a better person, especially when you make a habit of it.

Simply being kind to someone qualifies as helping them. It may be the only time they've experienced it all day – and it may save a life.

Please don't complain if a member of the emergency services uses 'inappropriate language or humour', because it's appropriate for them. This is their coping mechanism, in having to deal with this shit every single day of their lives.

We know that each of our brains is wired differently. That everybody is different. Everyone. Not only that, but every single person ever born –without any prior knowledge of the world around them – thinks differently too. And based upon their environment, their upbringing, what they've learned from others, and what their subjective and limited senses tell them, everybody views things differently – even you. Once you truly accept that, then life becomes a lot easier to understand, and that fact alone has got to be worth what you paid for this book! It also means that each of us has our own, unique 'particular set of skills', to make a positive and appreciable difference in the world – in a way that no one else can...

This chapter we call Life is far too short and, just as we're getting the hang of it, we die. So, what if it's really an Introduction, to prepare ourselves for the main story to follow? If so, are we happy for the adventure to continue, using the main character we've created – or do we need to develop it further?

This makes sense to me, and it's the way I now choose to live – no matter how difficult it gets – because that's who I want to be, despite the bad habits I picked up along the way and am still working to correct.

But feel free to disagree. I'm just an ordinary ex-soldier trying to help as many people as I can while I'm still here.

To end, I'd like to leave you with one final thought, for everything you do in life...

The bit you've been waiting for...

Are you ready?

Here it comes…

GO! GO! GO!